Time and History i
Deleuze and Serre

Bloomsbury Studies in Continental Philosophy
Series Editor: James Fieser, University of Tennessee at Martin, USA

Bloomsbury Studies in Continental Philosophy is a major monograph series from Bloomsbury. The series features first-class scholarly research monographs across the field of Continental philosophy. Each work makes a major contribution to the field of philosophical research.

Time and History in Deleuze and Serres

Edited by
Bernd Herzogenrath

Bloomsbury Studies in Continental Philosophy

B L O O M S B U R Y

LONDON · NEW DELHI · NEW YORK · SYDNEY

Bloomsbury Academic
An imprint of Bloomsbury Publishing Plc

50 Bedford Square   1385 Broadway
London   New York
WC1B 3DP   NY 10018
UK   USA

www.bloomsbury.com

First published by Continuum International Publishing Group 2012
Paperback edition first published 2013

British Library Cataloguing-in-Publication Data
A catalogue record for this book is available from the British Library.

ISBN: HB: 978-1-4411-6386-8
PB: 978-1-4725-0506-4

Library of Congress Cataloging-in-Publication Data
A catalog record for this book is available from the Library of Congress.

Herzogenrath, Bernd, 1964–
Time and history in Deleuze and Serres/Bernd Herzogenrath.
p. cm. – (Continuum studies in Continental philosophy)
ISBN 978-1-4411-6386-8 – ISBN 978-1-4411-4274-0 – ISBN 978-1-4411-8570-9
1. Deleuze, Gilles, 1925–1995. 2. Serres, Michel. 3. Time. 4. History–Philosophy.
I. Title. II. Series.
B2430.D454H47 2011
115.092′2–dc23

2011028612

Typeset by Deanta Global Publishing Services, Chennai, India
Printed and bound in Great Britain

Contents

Acknowledgements

I would like to thank Continuum (in particular, Tom Crick) for giving me and us the opportunity to publish this book, and all those wonderful people who contributed to this volume – it has been a pleasure! A special thanks! goes to Benjamin Betka and Sebastian Scherer.

While working on this book, two important and life-changing things happened to me – in the summer, our little daughter Janna was born … she's our cute little *clinamen*, the tiny little thing that makes life swerve into unforeseen directions. And in the early morning hours of Christmas Eve, my beloved little brother Frank died, after more than 4 years of living under the shadow of an incurable, malign brain tumour. I can only now, in retrospect, see how brave he had been all those years. Frank now has gone farther than the farthest place, and my only hope is that this turns out to be the closest place as well. It is to Janna, and to the loving memory of Frank Herzogenrath that I dedicate this book.

List of Contributors

Maria L. Assad was born in Holland and has lived in the United States since 1961. She is Professor emeritus of French Literature and Language, State University College at Buffalo, New York. She authored *La fiction et la mort dans l'oeuvre de Stéphane Mallarmé* (New York: Peter Lang Publishing Inc., 1987); a translation into English of Raymund Schwager's *Brauchen wir einen Sündenbock?*, entitled *Must There Be Scapegoats?* (San Francisco: Harper & Row, 1987); *Reading with Michel Serres: An Encounter with Time* (Albany, NY: State University of New York Press, 1999); and articles as well as book chapters on 19ᵗʰ Century French authors and on the writings of Michel Serres. Her research interests focus on interdisciplinary studies of science and literature, nonlinear dynamics and the nature of metaphors, and time and historical representation. She is a member of the International Society for the Study of Time (ISST).

Jane Bennett is Professor of Political Science at Johns Hopkins University, and is the author of *Vibrant Matter: A Political Ecology of Things* (Duke University Press, 2010); *The Enchantment of Modern Life* (Princeton University Press, 2001); *Thoreau's Nature* (Rowman and Littlefield, 1994); and *Unthinking Faith and Enlightenment* (New York University Press, 1987). She is currently trying to learn things about materiality from critical geography, archaeology, performance studies, (post)medievalists, and architecture.

Hanjo Berressem teaches American Literature and Culture at the University of Cologne. He has published books on Thomas Pynchon (*Pynchon's Poetics: Interfacing Theory and Text*. University of Illinois Press, 1992), and on Witold Gombrowicz (*Lines of Desire: Reading Gombrowicz's Fiction with Lacan*. Northwestern University Press, 1998). He has edited, with B. Herzogenrath: *Near Encounters: Festschrift for Richard Martin* (Peter Lang, 1995), with D. Buchwald und H. Volkening, *Grenzüberschreibungen: Feminismus und Cultural Studies* (Aisthesis, 2001), with D. Buchwald, *Chaos-Control/Complexity:'*

Chaos Theory and the Human Sciences. (Special Issue: American Studies, 1.2000) and with L. Haferkamp, *site-specific: from aachen to zwölfkinder - pynchon\germany* (Special Issue: *Pynchon Notes*, 2008) as well as *Deleuzian Events: Writing | History* (LIT, 2009). His articles are situated in the fields of French theory, contemporary American fiction, media studies and the interfaces of art and science. At the moment, he is completing a book on Gilles Deleuze: *"Crystal Philosophy:" Radical Constructivism and the Deleuzian Event.*

Kelvin Clayton has recently completed a PhD Student at Staffordshire University (researching the application of the work of Michel Serres to social theory) where he has also been employed at a part-time lecturer. He entered higher education as a mature student after having spent seventeen years working as a firefighter. His first degree was in Literary Studies, and his MA was in Modern Continental Philosophy. Since his first degree he has also trained to become a qualified careers adviser, and has worked within the government's 'social inclusion' agenda. His recent research has been a merging of these two streams, one theoretical, the other practical, and has been motivated by his experience of their lack of 'communication.'

William E. Connolly is Krieger-Eisenhower Professor at Johns Hopkins University where he teaches political theory. His most recent book is *A World of Becoming*, published with Duke in 2011. It examines relations between heterogeneous human and nonhuman systems. Recent publications include *Neuropolitics: Thinking, Culture, Speed; Why I Am Not A Secularist; Pluralism;* and *Capitalism and Christianity, American Style.* He is currently working on capitalism, ecology and cosmic force fields.

Claire Colebrook is Edwin Erle Sparks Professor of Literature at Penn State University. She has written books on literary theory, feminist theory and continental philosophy. Her most recent book is *Deleuze and the Meaning of Life* (Continuum 2009).

Elizabeth Grosz teaches in the Women's and Gender Studies Department at Rutgers University, New Jersey. She has worked on the writings of Deleuze and Guattari for many years and is the author of *Chaos, Territory, Art. Deleuze and the Framing of the Earth* (Columbia, 2008).

Bernd Herzogenrath teaches American Literature and Culture at the University of Frankfurt, Germany. His fields of interest are 19th and 20th

Century American Literature, Critical Theory, and Cultural|Media Studies. He is the author of *An Art of Desire: Reading Paul Auster* (Rodopi 1999) and *An American Body|Politic: A Deleuzian Approach* (Dartmouth College Press, 2010), and the editor of *From Virgin Land to Disney World: Nature and Its Discontents in the USA of Yesterday and Today* (Rodopi 2001), *The Films of Tod Browning* (Black Dog 2006), *The Cinema of Tod Browning: Essays of the Macabre and Grotesque* (McFarland 2008), *Edgar G. Ulmer: Essays on the King of the Bs* (McFarland 2009), *Deleuze|Guattari & Ecology* (Palgrave 2009), *The Films of Edgar G. Ulmer* (Scarecrow 2009), *An [Un]Likely Alliance: Thinking Environment[s] with Deleuze|Guattari* (Cambridge Scholars 2009). Further publications include *The Farthest Place: The Music of John Luther Adams* (Northeastern UP, in print), and *Travels in Intermedia[lity]: ReBlurring the Boundaries* (Dartmouth College Press, forthcoming 2011). He is currently working on a project called *cinapses: thinking|film*, bringing together film studies, neurosciences, and (media) philosophy.

Eugene W. Holland is the author of *Baudelaire and Schizoanalysis: the Socio-poetics of Modernism* (Cambridge, 1993) and *Deleuze & Guattari's Anti-Oedipus: Introduction to Schizoanalysis* (Routledge 1999), and co-editor with Charles Stivale and Dan Smith of *Gilles Deleuze: Image and Text* (Continuum, 2009).

Recent essays include *"Jazz Improvisation: Music of the People-to-Come,"* in *Deleuze, Guattari, and the Production of the New*, Simon O'Sullivan & Stephen Zepke, eds. (London: Continuum, 2008); *"Schizoanalysis, Nomadology, Fascism,"* in *Deleuze and Politics*, Nick Thoburn & Ian Buchanan, eds. (Edinborough: University of Edinborough Press, 2008); *"Nonlinear Historical Materialism and Postmodern Marxism," Culture, Theory, Critique* 47:2 (2006): *"Nomad Citizenship and Global Democracy,"* in *Gilles Deleuze and the Social: Toward a New Social Analytic,* *"Representation and Misrepresentation in Postcolonial Literature and Theory," Research in African Literatures* (2003); and *"Infinite Subjective Representation and the Perversion of Death," Angelaki: Journal of the Theoretical Humanities* (2000).

He has just finished a book entitled *Nomad Citizenship and Global Democracy* which constructs a new concept of post-state citizenship based on the principles of schizoanalysis and affirmative nomadology, forthcoming from the University of Minnesota Press in 2011.

Dr. Holland is Professor and Chair of Comparative Studies at the Ohio State University.

Paul Patton is Professor of Philosophy at The University of New South Wales in Sydney, Australia. He is the author of *Deleuze and the Political* (Routledge,

2000) and *Deleuzian Concepts: Philosophy, Colonization, Politics* (Stanford, 2010). He is editor of *Deleuze: A Critical Reader* (Blackwell 1996), (with Duncan Ivison and Will Sanders) *Political Theory and the Rights of Indigenous Peoples* (Cambridge, 2000), (with John Protevi) of *Between Deleuze and Derrida*, (Continuum, 2003) and (with Simone Bignall) *Deleuze and the Postcolonial* (Edinburgh 2010). He has translated work by Deleuze, Foucault, Nancy and Baudrillard. His publications deal with aspects of French poststructuralist philosophy, Nietzsche and a variety of topics in contemporary political philosophy.

David Webb is Senior Lecturer in Philosophy at Staffordshire University. His interests are mainly in recent and contemporary continental philosophy, and above all in the work of Michel Foucault and Michel Serres. He is the author of *Heidegger, Ethics and the Practice of Ontology* (Continuum, 2009). He has also published 'Gianni Vattimo: Hermeneutics as a Practice of Freedom', in Silvia Benso and Brian Schroeder (eds) *Between Nihilism and Politics: The Hermeneutics of Gianni Vattimo* (SUNY Press, 2010); 'Praxis and the Time of Ethical Life in Aristotle', in *Époche*, spring 2010; 'Penser le multiple sans le concept: vers un intellect démocratique' in *Michel Serres* (Éditions de l'Herne, 2010); 'Michel Serres on Lucretius: atomism, science and ethics', in *Angelaki* (Vol. 11, No. 2, 2006); 'Cavaillès and the Historical a priori in Foucault' in *Virtual Mathematics: the Logic of Difference,* ed. Simon Duffy (Clinamen Press, 2005); 'Cavaillès, Husserl and the Historicity of Science, in *Angelaki* (Vol 8. No. 3, 2004). He is currently completing a book on Michel Foucault's *The Archaeology of Knowledge*, to be published by Edinburgh University Press.

Nathan Widder is a Reader in Political Theory in the Department of Politics and International Relations at Royal Holloway, University of London. His research focuses on ontological issues related to identity, difference and time and how they bear upon questions of political and ethical pluralism, and he has developed this work through engagement with both major and marginal figures in the history of Western philosophy and contemporary Continental thought. He is author of *Genealogies of Difference* (University of Illinois Press, 2002) and *Reflections on Time and Politics* (Penn State University Press, 2008) and he has recently completed *Political Theory after Deleuze* (Continuum, 2012).

Introduction*

In 1969, Michel Foucault called for the 'introduction, into the very roots of thought, of notions of chance, discontinuity and materiality' (Foucault, 1972, pp. 215–37; p. 231). In a move that already showed that his project will not be solely concerned with the effects of discourse on bodies, he shifts from the merely discursive practices to materiality, to an underlying operative force-field combining discursive and extra-discursive effects. Foucault is not refer-ring to simple randomness here, but to the notion of complexity, as developed for example by Michel Serres, who was a colleague of Foucault at Clermont-Ferrand and the University of Paris VIII at Vincennes (Serres et al., 1995, p. 37), by Gilles Deleuze and by Ilya Prigogine and Isabelle Stengers, whose groundbreaking work has inspired both Serres and Deleuze and whose find-ings and "applications" Prigogine and Stengers, in return, acknowledge.

Foucault stresses the event-character of power and of history, and he wants to substitute dynamic complex processes for notions of continuity and tele-ology. Here, the interface of science and history is in particular fruitful, since there has been a mutual "fertilization" in the last few years – a tendency that for the context of American History reaches back at least to Henry Adams's attempt to read history in terms of physics. As Prigogine|Stengers state,

> [w]e have seen new aspects of time being progressively incorporated into physics, while the ambitions of omniscience inherent in classical science were progressively rejected ... Indeed, history began by concentrating mainly on human societies, after which attention was given to the tempo-ral dimensions of life and geology. The incorporation of time into physics thus appears as the last stage of a progressive reinsertion of history into the natural and social sciences (Prigogine et al., 1985, p. 208).

Thus, if we study an open physical system – such as a human being, or a community or society – 'we need to know its history to understand its current dynamical state' (De Landa, 1997, p. 11). Likewise, as 'much as

---

* Parts of this introduction are reprinted from my book *An American Body|Politic. A Deleuzian Approach*, Hanover: Dartmouth College Press, 2010: 49–52; 97, with kind permission.

history has infiltrated physics, we must now allow physics to infiltrate history' (De Landa, 1997, p. 15).

This volume situates itself within a larger project of a Deleuzian and Serresian Historiography. The last major encounter between the historical sciences and post-structuralist theory dates back to the year 1973, when Hayden White's *Metahistory* (White, 1973) confronted the historical sciences' claim to objectivity with the post-structuralist idea of the linguistic construct-edness of reality. In a seminal article on 'The Historical Text as Literary Arti-fact', White asked the crucial question – 'What authority can historical accounts claim as contributions to a secured knowledge of reality in general and to the human sciences in particular' (White, 1974, p. 277)? White put the focus on the graphein in historiography and by that pointed the finger at the dilemma of the discipline of history, which saw itself as a science and not as belonging to the field of literature and fabulation. However, as interpreta-tions of the past, White claims, historical texts are exactly that – narratives, 'verbal fictions, the contents of which are as much invented as found and the forms of which have more in common with their counterparts in literature than they have with those in the sciences' (White, 1974, p. 278). Hayden stresses the fact that the historian, as a historiographer, fabulates history by sorting, interpreting and contextualizing it, by creating structures and causal relations, and thus constructs history in the first place.

> If we recognize that there is a fictive element in all historical narrative, we would find in the theory of language and narrative itself the basis for a more subtle presentation of what historiography consists of than that which simply tells the student to go and 'find out the facts' and write them up in such a way as to tell 'what really happened' (White, 1974, p. 302).

Repudiating Leopold von Ranke's claim that the historian should – and is actually able to – reconstruct the past 'as it actually was', White imports the concepts of deconstruction and cultural|linguistic constructivism into the historical sciences, the concepts closely connected to the theories of Derrida and Foucault, according to which realities – life, and history as well – are always already regulated and constituted discursively – reality is an effect of the logic of the signifier. Thus, if the historian aims at recon-structing a reality that is not found in the text, but beyond the text, if, however, this beyond [the textual unconscious] is always already discur-sive (a Lacanian unconscious) – then the historical sciences become a 'talking (or better, writing) cure' in which "history" finds "itself": the historical is 'a prose discourse that purports to be a model, or icon, of past structures and processes in the interest of explaining what they were by representing them' (White, 1973, p. 2).

If, in general, the awareness of the vicissitudes of representation is a good thing in that it questions the existence of an "objective Truth" (or "objective data") and of "universal laws" and teleologies (and thus, ideologies), the result is – again – the disregard of the material constitution of history. As within the larger framework of Cultural Studies in general, historiography – or *Metahistory* – concentrates mainly on representation, on the cultural|linguistic constructedness of reality, in order to ban essentialism. And again, the Deleuzian conception of a 'machinic nature|reality' operating on complex and non-linear logics bypasses the twin spectres of essentialism and determinism – the concept of production connects nature and culture, materiality and history. History is a complex and non-linear system, which means that between micro- and macro-history, regional and world history, part and whole, there are feedback loops, couplings and interferences. In contrast to linear systems, non-linear systems do not react "proportionally" to disturbances|turbulences – this is what the proverbial butterfly-effect signifies, according to which a flap of a butterfly's wing can trigger off a tornado (or not): the system's sensitivity to initial conditions.

Deleuze "thinks history" according to a completely different set of parameters and according to completely different concepts of time, event and materiality. For Deleuze|Guattari, history is 'a dynamic and open social reality, in a state of functional disequilibrium ... comprising not only institutionalized conflicts but conflicts that generate changes, revolts, ruptures, and scissions' (Deleuze and Guattari, 1998, pp. 150–51). Chance (the uncontrollability|indeterminacy of the event) plays a crucial role as well – history is '[f]irst of all ... the history of contingencies, and not of necessity. Ruptures and limits, and not continuity ... great accidents ... and amazing encounters that could have happened elsewhere, or before, or might never have happened' (Deleuze and Guattari, 1998, p. 140). Likewise, for Serres, molar history poses as a sum of stabilities, 'stupid, heavy ... statues, [like] sandbags on the ground' (Serres, 1995, p. 120), whereas in fact it is '... a turbination which, by advancing, always seeks and loses equilibrium. Here, precisely delineated, is the vertical solution: it is rigorously isomorphic to natural genesis beginning from chaos. History is indeed a physics, quod erat demonstrandum' (Serres, 2000, p. 179).

Thomas Carlyle, the nineteenth century historian and contemporary to Leopold von Ranke, was already aware of the important factor of "chance" in the "construction" of history, as this remarkable passage from his lecture 'On History' shows:

The most gifted man can observe, still more can record, only the series of his own impressions; his observation, therefore … must be successive, while the things done were often simultaneous; the things done were not a series, but a group. It is not in acted, as it is in written History: actual events are nowise so simply related to each other as parent and offspring are; every single event is the offspring not of one, but of all other events, prior or contemporaneous, and will in its turn combine with all others to give birth to new: it is an ever-living, ever-working Chaos of Being, wherein shape after shape bodies itself forth from innumerable elements (Carlyle, 1970, p. 95).[1]

Chance (the unpredictable complexity of material self-organization) is a determinant factor in the overall system's production of a new macro-state. Observable phase states (historical phases|epochs) that have remained stable over a period of time can perform a relatively fast and turbulent transition into another phase state – the phase state thus always is only a semi-stable system, a complex dynamic aggregate and not a stable unity|entity, the more so since in one phase state, other states are "virtually" present. In such a non-linear conception of phase transitions, all phase states exist at the same time in a continuous process of change and becoming (with different temporalities of their own). Because of the simultaneous activity of the "parts", the "whole" of such a dynamic feedback-system shows properties significantly different from that of the parts. As Deleuze|Guattari observe, '[a]ll history does is to translate a coexistence of becomings into a succession' (Deleuze and Guattari, 1993, p. 430), to translate non-linearity into linearity. Such a "reductive analysis" loses sight of those self-organizing emergences that in particular non-linear systems reveal – a (non-linear) history has to precisely concentrate on those modalities of becoming, on the becoming of the event itself.[2]

The historical sciences break down the continuum of time – the continuum of history – into cuts, into data|dates and into historical events. These dates|events are then put into linear causal relations (this is where Hayden's critique comes in). For Deleuze|Guattari, however, historiography is always a history of making cuts, of creating differences and hence of a perceiving consciousness, whereas 'what we make history with is the matter of a becoming, not the subject matter of a story' (Deleuze and Guattari, 1993, p. 347). The Deleuzian event is precisely not the "historical event", the date that the historical sciences are so obsessed with. It is neither the big historical event on the stage of World History, nor is it the culturally produced|represented "fact|date". For Deleuze, events take place on all levels of life (and history), on the level of the molecule as well as on the level of narration, on the level of the human and of consciousness (individual and|or institutional decisions) as much as on the level of the non-human, unconscious and "non-historical" (materiality, chance). The historical sciences run the risk of losing sight of the fact that the fact is a factum, that it is made on an infinite number of levels at the same time and that it produces|is produced auto-poietically – this fact is then reduced and condensed (in physical sense) to a date, or a datum [a given], before it is condensed again (this time in the poetical sense) and inserted into causal chains: in between the cuts and in between the perceivable (historical) dates of historical science, there is the non-historical becoming, the complex dynamics of multiplicities. A Deleuzian historiography has to put the focus on these multiplicities, these becomings. The consciously perceived and discursively represented date is only the tip of the iceberg, comparable, according to Deleuze, 'to a mist rising over the prairie, ... precisely at the frontier, at the juncture of things and propositions' (Deleuze, 1990, p. 24). With his focus on the becoming of the event, however, Deleuze is more concerned with a different kind of mist, what Nietzsche calls the 'mist of the unhistorical' (Nietzsche, 1980, p. 11), with the differentiation (and ultimately combination) of historical fact|date and unhistorical becoming – 'What History grasps of the event is its effectuation in states of affairs or in lived experience, but the event in its becoming ... escapes History' (Deleuze and Guattari, 1994, p. 110). The 'event in its becoming' is precisely the level of the historical fact|date that the (discursive) measuring devices of the historical sciences do not grasp. The becoming of the event 'has neither beginning nor end but only a milieu. It is thus more geographical than historical' (Deleuze and Guattari, 1994, p. 110) – geographical|physical insofar as its operations follow a dynamic and non-linear logic. Here, history is seen as a history of intensities, where historical dates do not so much signify "objective facts", but force-fields, like 'in physics, where proper names designate such effects within fields of potentials: the Joule effect, the Seebeck effect, the Kelvin effect. History is like physics: a Joan of Arc effect, a Heliogabalus effect ...' (Deleuze and Guattari, 1998, p. 86).[3]

For Deleuze, becoming is closely connected to geography – '[b]ecomings belong to geography, they are orientations, directions, entries and exits' (Deleuze and Guattari, 1987, p. 2). Deleuze's concept of 'history as becoming' thus reveals a close proximity to the "geohistory" (Deleuze and Guattari, 1994, p. 95) of Fernand Braudel – '[g]eography wrests history from the cult of necessity in order to stress the irreducibility of contingency' (Deleuze and Guattari, 1994, p. 96). With the concept of longue durée, Braudel commented on the "geographic aspects" of (historical) time itself.

According to Braudel, '[h]istory exists at different levels, I would even go so far as to say three levels but that would be … simplifying things too much. There are ten, a hundred levels to be examined, ten, a hundred different time spans' (Braudel, 1982, p. 74). History – thus Braudel, thus Deleuze – happens at ten, at a hundred levels and time spans [at thousand plateaus] simultaneously. This coexistent and dynamic becoming is to the static succession of being what locus is to datum, space is to time, and in analogy regards 'geography as opposed to history, … the rhizome as opposed to arborescence' (Deleuze and Guattari, 1993, p. 296). History is a rhizome that historiography aims at translating into an arborescent order, with the rhizome standing for the complex interplay of necessity and chance, human and non-human, culture and materiality, intention and self-organization.

Deleuze's and Serres' concepts of time as 'out of joint' (Deleuze) or as 'a crumpled handkerchief' (Serres) explicitly refer to the non-linear dynamics of Chaos and Complexity Theory and the New Sciences, and thus have the potential to re-write traditional (essentialist) theories of time and history. A 'historiography according to' both Deleuze|Guattari and Serres elevates the differences and multiplicity immanent to the event over the concepts of unity and reconciliation, and focuses on the role of materiality and its self-organizing properties. If there is a unity, it is not uniformity, but an exploration of multiplicity, an experiment in diversity. History/historical events are not islands, isolated and with fixed boundaries, but actualizations of a virtual field, not predicted and predictable interactions of particular (discrete and "compartmentalized") identities, but machinic aggregations – experiments.

In his essay 'What is Revolutionary in Deleuze and Guattari's Philosophy of History?', Eugene Holland analyzes what is "revolutionary" in D&G's philosophy of history in two senses of the term "revolutionary" – a casual sense and a literal sense. He first examines what is philosophically innovative about Deleuze's philosophy of time and then concludes with what is revolutionary in the properly political sense of the term. Both the philosophy of time and the philosophy of history based on it are extremely complicated – and doing justice to the relationship between these two complexities is one of the great virtues of Jay Lampert's recent book, entitled *Deleuze and Guattari's Philosophy of History* – which now constitutes the necessary starting point for any discussion of the topic. The book's first virtue, however, is recognizing and insisting that Deleuze and Guattari indeed have a philosophy of history in the first place. The book's second virtue is that it thereby lays the groundwork for what Holland wants to do here, which is to explain the potential for revolution in history, when capitalism makes history universal by intensifying its potential for becoming, thereby altering the ratio of merely "performing" history to actually changing history, in favor of the latter. But one first needs to consider what is revolutionary about D&G's philosophy of history in the casual sense of the term, by doing something that Lampert's book unfortunately does not do – which is to consider the resources Deleuze finds in Leibniz and Bergson, the relations of his philosophies of time and history to science and above all to non-linear science and complexity theory. Holland navigates implicitly, then, between the Scylla and Charybdis of Lampert's overly a-scientific and Manuel De Landa's overly a-political takes on Deleuze and Guattari's philosophy of history. The end result is a twofold clarification of the nature of political struggle. For one thing, Deleuze and Guattari insist that struggles with capital and the State (often referred to as "reformist") are legitimate and necessary. But at the same time, struggle should lead past, outside of, or away from capital and the State – and here, Holland's essay argues for the 'slow-motion general strike' as a revolutionary strategy.

The work of Michel Serres can appear as an enigma, not technically difficult, but hard to hold onto; while the work of Gilles Deleuze can be technically difficult and just as hard to hold onto. Juxtaposing their writing on time and history, primarily in *Genesis* and in *Difference and Repetition*, reveals a remarkably similar ontology expressed through a radically different methodology. Kevin Clayton's 'Time folded and crumpled: Time, history, self-organisation and the methodology of Michel Serres' first of all offers an exposition of this ontology, describing time as a multiplicity, as a phenomenon (or, more accurately, phenomena) that is (are) emergent from what Serres terms the background noise – from the void or sea of nothingness. Clayton describes this "time" as a process with degrees of actuality resulting from a number of syntheses, and describes history as a practice of codification that attempts to slow down and control this process. He suggest that, at this level, the only important difference between the two approaches is one of focus, with Serres' focus being on the background noise and Deleuze's being on the resultant syntheses. Clayton goes on to argue that while both the writers are attempting to 'think the multiple as such', Deleuze's methodology comes into direct conflict with such an attempt, while Serres' attempts to actively demonstrate the process. This demonstration is revealed through an appreciation of his comparative method; a methodology that demonstrates a deep self-organizing and creative principle in nature, and one that opens the door onto a fresh perspective of history, of 'time folded and crumpled'. Clayton suggests that a comparison can be made of both the works with that already produced by Claude Lévi-Strauss and Georges Dumézil and with that being produced by a growing number of scientists; work that reveals a creative self-organizing process founded on the repetition of a limited number of evolving "forms", forms that through their repetition give a fresh perspective to the traditional linear concept of history.

In 'Michel Serres: From the History of Mathematics to Critical History', David Webb identifies two key elements in Serres' conception of history and traces their development. The elements in question are mathematics and atomism. Webb's account begins with Serres' early enthusiasm for structuralism, and his expectation that it could transform the human sciences into a new kind of critical discourse. He not only outlines the reasons for this enthusiasm, but also notes a determination on Serres' part that the model by virtue of which a given field has meaning should be found within the field itself and not imposed on it. For this to occur, the relation between form and what is determined by form needs to be re-conceived. The first important step towards achieving this is found in mathematics, its epistemology and work done on the historical character of mathematical formalism. Serres himself devotes a significant portion of *Hermès I* to this question, but Webb illustrates it here by referring to Jean Cavaillès, whose work seems to precisely lead in the direction that Serres was looking. However, there is a second step, accomplished by the incorporation of atomist philosophy. Serres' reading of Lucretius in *The Birth of Physics* leads to a conception of form as a rule describing emergent regularities within an open and ultimately aleatory system. His reflections on history in *The Birth of Physics* then reveal a mode of thought that accounts for both the emphasis on the emergence of meaning in local contexts and the recurrence of similar models across history. In his conclusion, Webb outlines how this conception of history can be understood as what Serres was looking for when he first looked forward to a new form of historical critique.

In *What is Philosophy?* and other texts, Deleuze presents his own analyses of "becoming" (devenir) as in full accord with Foucault's method of diagnosing the present. He argues that Foucault writes from the perspective of the actual (actuel), by which he does not mean the ordinary French sense of this word that refers to that which is current or present. Rather, he points to a passage in The Archaeology of Knowledge in which Foucault draws a distinction between the present (notre actualité) and 'the border of time that surrounds our present, overhangs it and indicates it in its otherness', in order to suggest that Foucault writes from this border between present and future (Foucault, 1972, p. 130). According to Paul Patton's essay 'Deleuze, Foucault, and History', even though Foucault's text does not describe it in this way, this border region is what Deleuze means by the actuel. *What is*

Philosophy? affirms the proximity of Deleuze's "becoming", Nietzsche's untimely (l'inactuel or l'intempestif) and Foucault's actuel in suggesting that all three terms refer to 'that which is in the process of coming about': not what we presently are or recently were, but rather to 'what we are in the process of becoming – that is to say, the Other, our becoming-other' (Deleuze and Guattari, 1994, p. 112). However, while Deleuze regularly compares Nietzsche's untimely and Foucault's actuel with the realm of becoming and pure events that is the object of his own philosophy, he nowhere undertakes the same kind of genealogical interpretation that we find in Foucault. The difference between them emerges, for example, in Deleuze's analysis of the society of control that is supposed to have replaced disciplinary societies in the West. According to Deleuze's account of Foucault's method in '*What is Philosophy?*', he should have been concerned with what we are in the process of becoming, that is the society of control. In fact, Foucault devoted Discipline *and Punish* to the analysis of the kind of disciplinary society that, on his own account, is already beginning to disappear. There is therefore an important discrepancy between the kind of history of the present undertaken by Foucault and Deleuze's account of Foucault's method. Patton's essay further explores the tensions between Deleuze and Foucault's conception of history.

Michel Serres' 'philosophy of circumstances', which describes his work, from the *Hermès* texts to *Le Tiers-Instruit*, evolves in *Atlas* into a discourse on space and time, dissolving the dialectical understanding of history into a dynamical history of open-ended questions. The virtual folds, lines and mappings in this text end in an accounting of Serres' own writings including *Atlas* itself. For Maria Assad, this feedback loop invites a new look at those prior texts that offer a coherent outline of a non-linear view of time and its implications for a new knowledge ('le nouveau savoir'). In her essay 'Ulyssean Trajectories: A (New) Look at Michel Serres' Topology of Time', two key elements crystallize out of this reading: the excluded middle ('le tiers exclu'), which evolves into an instructed-middle ('le tiers-instruit'), and the notion of immortality that is void of any transcendent attributes. Emblematic of Serres' early critique of dualistic, static thinking, the excluded middle becomes more concretely the parasitic operator in *Le Parasite* whose intruding and contentious actions grow linearly into violence and combat, marking human relations. In search of an alternative to this 'history of death', Serres develops the notion of a qualitative "multiple" in a series of texts where time is the dynamical element that allows for creative and inventive action. Expressed in terms of immortality in *Détachement*, the multiple becomes the life force for the education of the instructed-middle in

Le Tiers-Instruit. In the light of these writings, the more recent *Hominescence* is the unfinished story of the instructed-middle growing into adulthood, the hominescent whose inventive drive tends towards all "possibles", an infinitude of contingencies and immanent self-created immortality. Exhuming the "why" of global pollution, *Le Mal propre* is the dire account of failing the responsibilities of this "omnipotency", under the pressures of globalization.

In her essay on 'Posthuman Humanities', Claire Colebrook looks at the ways in which concepts of the human, and specifically the modern logic of "man", underpin both the standard defenses of the humanities and supposed "post-human" notions of inter-disciplinary study. All these seeming corrections or overcomings of humanism are, Colebrook argues, forms of ultra-humanism. By contrast, Serres' concepts of pollution and parasitism, along with Deleuze and Guattari's distinction between concepts and affects/percepts, allow for radical incommensurable and productive directions of disciplinary distinctions. These are inhuman, rather than post-human, in their futural and creative dimension. For Serres, humanity is a meteorological concept, required by shifts in systemic disturbance. For Deleuze and Guattari, the 'still-missing people' is also created in disciplinary incoherence, in maximizing differentials among systems, not communicative recognition. Their approaches to distinctions among disciplines are not only futural in their attention to what has not already taken place. For both, history, once removed from the humanist logics of narrative comprehension or perfectibility, becomes non-linear and productively destructive.

One of the remarkable aspects of Deleuze's early essay and monograph on Bergson is that these works consider and defend two of Bergson's texts that are generally considered his weakest: *Duration and Simultaneity*, often seen as a regression of Bergson's thought and one based on severe misunderstandings of the special theory of relativity; and *The Two Sources of Morality and Religion*, frequently dismissed as the work of an aging Bergson turning to mysticism and transcendence. With respect to the first, Deleuze argues that Bergson does not return to a weak psychologism but instead offers to modern physics the metaphysics needed to underpin it. And with respect to the second, Deleuze maintains that Bergson's account of duration as difference actualizing itself (the process of *élan vital*) provides the underpinnings of moral and social development. Both defenses accord with Deleuze's more general thesis that Bergson's theory of time expresses a conception of internal difference, which Deleuze deploys explicitly against a Hegelian conception of internal difference as contradiction. Nevertheless, Deleuze never returns to either text in a serious way in his later work, and despite

Bergson's presence throughout Deleuze's work and against the many scholars who see Bergson as Deleuze's principal inspiration, Bergson ultimately plays only a limited role in Deleuze's philosophy of time, being relegated on several occasions to a middle position in the development of Deleuze's thought.

Nathan Widder's essay 'Deleuze on Bergsonian Duration and Nietzsche's Eternal Return' examines Deleuze's development of this ontology of time through Bergson and then Nietzsche, arguing that whereas Bergson sought through his ontology of duration to ground the chronological passage of time, Deleuze's ultimate break with Bergson is precisely in favor of an ontology that ungrounds time's chronological passage. The key in this respect is Bergson's privileging of quality over quantity, and his failure, as Deleuze will argue, to consider the possibility of an intensive quantity that Deleuze finds in Nietzsche. While Bergson promises that duration both escapes the linear time of mechanical causality and explains time's novelty, Deleuze maintains that it does not and that the source of Bergson's transcendence lies precisely in duration's privileging of the pure past. By contrast, Deleuze contends that an ontology of the event, understood as eternal return, maintains an absolute independence of the present from the past, establishes time as a true generator of creativity and completes the contemporary philosophical project of immanence. In contrast to many interpreters who align Deleuze with Bergson, Widder shows how, through his shift to Nietzsche, Deleuze develops an ontology of time that accounts for the contingency and complexity of history without reducing it to mere randomness or accident.

Deleuze's move to Nietzsche has profound consequences for the relationship between the event and history, as the event can no longer be assigned to a pure past that delineates some sense of historical "truth". In an obscure passage in *Difference and Repetition*, Deleuze criticizes conceptions of the event that tie it to reminiscence such that, even where the event has not occurred in historical time, it nevertheless serves as the ground for history. Consequently, Deleuze maintains that in the end the eternal return is concerned solely with the future, never with the past or present. In his conclusion, Widder briefly examines this claim by relating the eternal return not only to Bergson's notion of the pure past but also to Lacan's notion of reminiscence (the Lacanian traumatic event not necessarily being a historical event but nevertheless delineating the truth of the patient's history), arguing that while both Bergson and Lacan criticize Platonic reminiscence, from a Deleuzean perspective both remained trapped in a Platonist search for foundations.

Elizabeth Grosz's 'Time Out of Joint' is a brief analysis of the movement of time and futurity that haunts the work of Deleuze, figured through his brief elaboration of the peculiar broken temporality of Hamlet, and the ways in which Hamlet's haunting problematizes the temporal clarity of Kantian concepts of time. Time is not the neutral and passive medium, whether psychical or material, within which acts are placed: time inheres in action, it is immanent within action and contains both the forces of actual dispersion (the opening up of the indeterminate future) and virtual accumulation (the past as the evergrowing size of the past the present carries with it). Grosz explores how the dislocated temporality of Hamlet anticipates and leads to the fractured temporality of cinema.

Today, a significant minority of political theorists, philosophers, anthropologists and historiographers affirm a cosmology of "becoming". Drawing variously upon Nietzsche, Bergson, Whitehead, Deleuze and Guattari, Serres and others, they define the cosmos as an interacting set of temporal systems punctuated by an ontological ruckus. This cosmos goes through periods of creative flow or generative process. Such references sometimes give short shrift to the tendency of specific things and relations to congeal, persist and even perdure against disruptive pressures, particularly when political life is discussed. In this essay, we acknowledge the uncanny fact that individuated entities emerge, collaborate and manage to withstand the hustle and flow of a world of becoming.

In their joint essay 'The Crumpled Handkerchief', Jane Bennett and William Connolly deal with the following questions: How do shapes manage to distinguish themselves from the onto-field? What initiates congealing into objects? Once a congealing occurs, what kinds of pressures help to destabilize it? The goal is to attend to both the fragile, contingent quality of any process of self-ordering and the strange systematicity proper to a mobile and protean world. They use Serres' figures of ontological "noise" and "crumpled" time and Deleuze's notion of the 'powers of the false' to both reflect critically upon the tendency to privilege process over product within ontologies of becoming and begin to refine our understanding of the complex oscillations between becoming and persistence. At the end of their essay, Bennett and Connolly draw out some implications of these notions for the practice of historical analysis.

This study ends with a "double feature" on the Deleuze|Serres connections and the American historian Henry Adams. Bernd Herzogenrath's essay 'A Physical Theory of Heredity|Heresy: The Education of Henry Adams' focuses on the writings and ideas of Henry Adams, grandson and great-grandson to American Presidents, a member of one of the most important and influential political dynasties in American history. Situated at the cusp between two centuries, which also saw the rise of new technologies and sciences (Equilibrium Thermodynamics was about to be replaced by the "new sciences" of Quantum Physics and Relativity, orthodox Darwinism by Genetics and the advent of Molecular Biology), Henry Adams – historian, man of letters, novelist and political journalist – shows both the nostalgic yearning for a "virginal past" and a unifying principle, and the intellectual curiosity for multiplicity and chaos he displays in his book *The Education of Henry Adams*, a book that is as much an autobiography as a biography of America, its intellectual and political climate. In the 'Education', the seeming opposition of concepts such as "unity" and "multiplicity", "order" and "chaos" are brought into a (chiastic) complication|complexification and related to both a political theory and scientific analysis – Adams is said to be '[t]he first American author who attempted to integrate the findings of thermodynamics into the humanities'. However, Herzogenrath claims that Adams tried to go beyond Thermodynamics in order to come up with a new 'science of the Body|Politic'. If Thermodynamics and Darwinism presented the 'scientific status quo' at the end of the nineteenth century, for Adams they failed as heuristic models. Thus, while Adams today is generally regarded as a brilliant but erratic figure in American Thought, Adams's interest in the interrelations of chaos and order, multiplicity and complexity, and his highly idiosyncratic way to think this interplay, at least points into the direction of Complexity Theory. Herzogenrath reads Adams's discontent with Darwinism on the background of Deleuze and Serres and further relates it to recent developments in Complexity Theory and Biology, disciplines that in turn reflect Adams's idea of the self-organization of the democratic Body|Politic at the beginning of the twentieth century.

Hanjo Berressem's 'Crystal History – You Pick up the Pieces. You Connect the Dots' draws the resonances of the theories of history developed by Gilles Deleuze, Michel Serres and Adams even tighter. Berressem argues that in dealing with the problematics of history, one needs to resist two complementary temptations: to dissolve history in historiography and to dissolve historiography in history. To maintain that these two levels should be kept as categorically separate registers shifts the historical problematics to the notion of their 'reciprocal presupposition' (Deleuze, 1989, p. 69). How to relate history to historiography and historiography to history, or, how to think, historically, a 'transcendental empiricism' (Deleuze, 1994, p. 56)? How to reciprocally attribute the 'concrete machine' and the 'abstract machine' (Deleuze, 1999, p. 34)? Through a terminological differentiation into actual and virtual history, Berressem's essay develops the concept of a 'crystal history' in the sense that crystal images are points of 'the indiscernibility of the actual and the virtual' (ibid., 87).

Berressem shows that Deleuze, Serres and Adams negotiate questions that have always reverberated through historical studies. The fundamental conceptual given of all three theories is that both actual and virtual history emerge from within an originary multiplicity. This is why the closest relation between their respective theories of history is that all three aim at retaining, in all of its implications, this multiplicity. In this context, their most fundamental realization is that even the a prioris of time and space are inherently multiplicitous. It is from under the shadow of this fundamental realization that Adams, Deleuze and Serres develop their respective "historical studies", and it is this realization that is responsible for their conceptual resonances.

From this realization follow a number of implications: 1. Evolution and history are defined by a fundamental drift. 2. As everything is historical, historical studies need to become radically site-specific, which means that they need to work from within a tangle of local spaces and times; from within specific local milieus and local circumstances. 3. These analyses should encompass the activities of non-human agents. 4. Historical studies need to include the condition of contingency in its conceptualizations. 5. The probably most crucial implication of maintaining that history emerges from an originary multiplicity concerns the fact that the historian him|herself is immersed in the field and as such in a constant energetic exchange with the universe of forces. S|he is him|herself energetically enmeshed in the milieu, although s|he is, simultaneously, cognitively separated from it. S|he is both virtual observer and actual assemblage.

Notes

1 Carlyle also is already anticipating the claim that White was to make almost 150 years later: 'For as all Action is, by its nature, to be figured as extended in breath and in depth, as well as in length … so all Narrative is, by its nature, of only one dimension; only travels towards one, or towards successive points: Narrative is linear, Action is solid. Alas for our "chains", or chainlets, of "causes and effects", which we so assiduously track through certain hand-breadths of years and square miles, when the whole is a broad, deep Immensity, and each atom is "chained" and complected with all!' (95).

2 See e.g., Manuel De Landa's *A Thousand Years of Nonlinear History* for such a project inspired by Deleuze|Guattari and Complexity Theory. See also Ludolf Herbst's *Komplexität und Chaos. Grundzüge einer Theorie der Geschichte* and his 'Entkoppelte Gewalt – Zur chaostheoretischen Interpretation des NS-Herrschaftssystems' in *Tel*

Aviver Jahrbuch für deutsche Geschichte, also see George Reisch's 'Chaos, History, and Narrative' in *History and Theory*.
[3] This is precisely how the dates that provide the titles to the various chapters of Deleuze|Guattari's *A Thousand Plateaus: Capitalism and Schizophrenia* function – as proper names for force-fields.

Bibliography

Adams, H. (1995), *The Education of Henry Adams*. Ed. with an introduction by J. Gooder. London: Penguin.

Braudel, F. (1982), 'History and Sociology', in *On History*. Translated by S. Matthews. Chicago: University of Chicago Press, pp. 64–82.

Carlyle, T. (1970), 'On History', in F. R. Stern (ed.), *The Varieties of History. From Voltaire to the Present*. London: Palgrave Macmillan, pp. 91–101.

De Landa, M. (1997), *A Thousand Years of Nonlinear History*. New York: Zone Books, p. 333.

Deleuze, G. (1990), *The Logic of Sense*, in C. V. Boundas (ed.). Translated by M. Lester, with C. Stivale. New York: Columbia University Press.

— (1991), *Bergsonism*. Translated by H. Tomlinson and B. Habberjam. New York: Zone.

—(1994), *Difference and Repetition*. Translated by P. Patton. New York: Columbia University Press.

Deleuze, G. and Guattari, F. (1986), *Kafka: Toward a Minor Literature*. Translated by D. Polan. Minneapolis: University of Minnesota Press.

—(1993), *A Thousand Plateaus: Capitalism and Schizophrenia*. Translated by B. Massumi. Minneapolis: University of Minnesota Press.

—(1994), *What Is Philosophy?* Translated by H. Tomlinson and G. Burchell. New York: Columbia University Press.

—(1998 [1972]), *Anti-Oedipus. Capitalism and Schizophrenia I*. Translated by R. Hurley, M. Seem, and H. R. Lane. Minneapolis: University of Minnesota Press.

Deleuze, G. and Parnet, C. (1987), *Dialogues*. New York: Columbia University Press.

Foucault, M. (1972), 'The Discourse on Language' in *The Archeology of Knowledge*. Translated by A. M. Sheridan Smith. New York: Harper Torchbooks, pp. 215–37.

Freese, P. (1997), 'Henry Adams: The History of Degradation and the Degradation of History', in *From Apocalypse to Entropy and Beyond. The Second Law of Thermodynamics and Post-War American Fiction*. Essen: Die Blaue Eule, pp. 164–71.

Herbst, L. (1999), 'Entkoppelte Gewalt – Zur chaostheoretischen Interpretation des NS-Herrschaftssystems'. *Tel Aviver Jahrbuch für deutsche Geschichte*, 28, pp. 117–58.

—(2004), *Komplexität und Chaos. Grundzüge einer Theorie der Geschichte*. München: H. C. Beck.

Lampert, J. (2006), *Deleuze and Guattari's Philosophy of History*. London: Continuum.

Nietzsche, F. (1980), *On the Advantage and Disadvantage of History For Life*. Indianapolis: Hackett Publishing Co.

Prigogine, I. and Stengers, I. (1985), *Order Out Of Chaos: Man's New Dialogue With Nature*. London: Flamingo Books.

Reisch, G. (1991), 'Chaos, History, and Narrative'. *History and Theory* (30 February), pp. 1–20.

Serres, M. (1982), *Hermes: Literature, Science, Philosophy*, in J. V. Harari and D. F. Bell (eds). Baltimore: Johns Hopkins University Press.

—(1995), *Genesis*. Ann Arbor: The University of Michigan Press.

—(2000), *The Birth of Physics*. Manchester: Clinamen Press.

Serres, M. and Latour, B. (1995), *Conversations on Science, Culture, and Time*. Ann Arbor: University of Michigan Press.

White, H. (1973). *Metahistory. The Historical Imagination in Nineteenth-Century Europe*. Baltimore and London: The Johns Hopkins University Press.

—(1974), 'The Historical Text as Literary Artifact'. *Clio* 3:3, pp. 277–303.

Chapter 1

Non-Linear Historical Materialism; Or, What is Revolutionary in Deleuze and Guattari's Philosophy of History?

Eugene Holland

My aim today is to lay out the main features and some of the potential political implications of Deleuze and Guattari's philosophy of history, which is the best formulation of a non-linear historical materialism that I know of. My points of departure are the two books that cleared ground for the view developed here: one is Manuel De Landa's *A Thousand Year of Non-Linear History*, and the other is Jay Lampert's *Deleuze and Guattari's Philosophy of History*. The two books have reciprocal strengths and weaknesses: De Landa's book is strong on science, but almost willfully incompetent on question of politics; Lampert's book provides significant insight into politics, but is practically silent about science. I hope to remedy the shortcomings of both in what follows. Since I have already published a long review essay on De Landa in *Culture, Theory, Critique*, I will briefly mention here only two things, and develop them later only parenthetically, as it were (Holland, 2006, pp. 181–96). First of all, it is symptomatic of De Landa's approach that, in summing up the five systems comprising the version of non-linear historical materialism he wants to derive from Deleuze and Guattari, starting with the solar system and including the biosphere and language, De Landa completely leaves out the sixth system: capital – which is, of course, a vital topic of concern for Deleuze and Guattari from their very first work of collaboration through to the very last (De Landa, 1997, pp. 261–62). It is impossible, in other words, to do justice to the politics of Deleuze and Guattari's non-linear historical materialism without taking capital, and hence Marx, into account – as we shall see. The other thing to be said about De Landa, though, is that he is not really interested in politics in the first place and that he therefore refuses (or fails) to distinguish between science and politics, as Deleuze and Guattari do with great care.

About Lampert, I will have more to say, although I have also published a review of his book: Lampert's study of Deleuze's theory of time as it bears on Deleuze and Guattari's philosophy of history, difficult though it is, merits closer examination and provides much of the framework for what follows (Holland, 2008, pp. 156–59). Yet, illustrations of contemporary science and complexity theory drawn from De Landa (as well as others) will be required to supplement Lampert's account in crucial respects. In its basic outlines, this essay explores three inter-related topics: 1. emergence (as a category of non-linear complexity theory), 2. time and history (as they appear in Deleuze's solo works and in the collaborations with Guattari, respectively) and 3. revolution (which is a persistent theme in all of Deleuze and Guattari's works).

Emergence

Emergence is a key concept in non-linear mathematics, complexity theory, and contemporary science: it refers to the spontaneous self-ordering of physical as well as social systems. Order emerges from chaos, without that order being imposed from above or pre-determined from before. In Deleuze and Guattari's more philosophical idiom, order arises immanently instead of being imposed transcendently. In a very interesting, later essay in which Deleuze is referenced by name, Louis Althusser coined the term "becoming-necessary" to characterize this kind of immanent self-ordering (Althusser, 2006, pp. 163–207). Let me say in passing that, in many respects, Deleuze's debts to Marx pass through Althusser's work; yet it must also be said that Althusser, particularly in the later works, acknowledges important debts to Deleuze's work. In any case, the issue Althusser is addressing in this later essay, with help from Deleuze, is the systematicity of the capitalist system or the capitalist mode of production. It is one thing to explain how a given system works, when you take it as given; it is quite another thing to explain how it arose in the first place.

Taking this question seriously means reading *Capital* Volume 1 backwards, as it were: it entails prioritizing the emergence of capitalism through so-called "primitive accumulation" – the subject of the closing chapters of *Capital* Volume 1 – over the abstract systematicity of an already-constituted capitalism as embodied in the commodity form – the topic of the famous opening chapters. One of the outcomes of reading *Capital* this way reflects and reinforces a long-standing preoccupation in Althusser's work: the perennial problem of reproduction, the sheer difficulty of assuring the system's internal consistency and ability to perpetuate itself. So-called "primitive" accumulation, in this light, turns out not to be so "primitive" after all: it becomes a continual, if often overlooked, accompaniment and precondition of capital accumulation proper. And this will turn out to have important consequences or implications for political strategy, as we shall see.

For Althusser, like Fernand Braudel and Deleuze and Guattari in this respect, capitalism arose literally by accident. At some point, conditions were such that there happened to arise a critical mass – in the chemical or thermonuclear sense – of so-called "free" labour available for hire, and at around the same time and place, there happened to be a critical mass of the liquid wealth available for investment. A fortuitous encounter between these two critical masses created a specific reaction – commodity production by means of commodified labour-power – and the reaction eventually became self-sustaining. The "laws" of capitalist production were not necessary to begin with: they became-necessary – in Althusser's felicitous phrase – as the system consolidated itself. Crucial to this process of consolidation, as Robert Brenner has usefully pointed out, was an unusually high (that is to say, practically unheard of) degree of market dependency for both groups (Brenner, 1982, pp. 16–113). The owners of what soon would become capital could not establish or maintain their social position outside the market economy; the owners of what would soon become labour-power could not maintain their social position either – or even their bare existence – without recourse to that same market economy. Indeed, so-called primitive accumulation is in large part a misnomer, since, as Marx says, its key feature is not accumulation at all but rather a kind of "dis-accumulation" or dispossession: that is to say, a forced separation of masses of people from their means of life. In the process called primitive accumulation, the chance encounter of these two critical masses gave rise to a system or mode of production that gradually became capable of sustaining or reproducing itself.

Now, imagine in the place of these two critical masses of human agents, two masses of chemical agents, brought together at a given temperature and in the presence of a certain catalyst. The fortuitous encounter creates a reaction, which results in the formation of a new chemical compound. If the chemical reaction continually produces more of the catalyst as a by-product of producing the new compound, the reaction will become "auto-catalytic", and the new compound will spread throughout the solution, in a manner somewhat like crystallization spreading through a super-saturated solution. Now let us say that heat turns out to be another by-product of the auto-catalytic reaction: the solution may then pass a threshold beyond which it starts oscillating back and forth between two different forms of the new compound – creating what is called a chemical clock. It may happen, furthermore, that the chemical reaction produces not just an auto-catalyst but various alter-catalysts, which break down the chemical agents in the surrounding environment and make them susceptible to incorporation into the initial reaction. Then again, as this critical mass continues to develop, incorporating more agents and generating more heat, it may pass yet another temperature threshold or tipping point beyond which everything suddenly stops and there are no longer any chemical reactions whatsoever. The solution has transited a bifurcation point, or passed from one phase-space or basin of attraction to another: that one additional degree of heat has completely transformed or undone the systematicity of the system. Looked at strictly within the bounds a given phase-space, the systematicity of the system of chemical reactions appeared absolute and necessary; in fact, however, such systematicity arises out of the pre-existing conditions and parameters of an encounter: the system becomes-necessary upon entering that phase-space – and may become equally unnecessary if certain conditions are no longer met or successfully reproduced, and the system transits into a different phase-space.

This is what I am trying to get at here: the abstract systematicity captured in the opening chapters of *Capital* Volume 1 is actually a result of what Althusser wants to call a 'becoming-necessary' of the encounter evoked in the closing chapters of the same volume. The concept of becoming-necessary is meant to emphasize (among other things) the importance, the omnipresence, the contingency and the fragility of system reproduction: despite impressions generated by the opening chapters, the systematicity of a mode of production is never absolutely necessary and never guaranteed: it is always only becoming-necessary, like an asymptote approaching without ever reaching the line, or the lonely hour of a last instance that never comes. Note the essential role of market dependency as the key catalyst of capitalism: capital accumulation and wage-slavery are now seen not as the "laws" of capitalism, but as products of the material conditions (not of our own choosing) under which we live our lives and make history. The oscillation of a chemical clock, moreover, resembles the historical periodicity of capital accumulation described by Marx, or the ups and downs of the business cycle. Note, also, the role of imperialism as an indispensable alter-catalyst: so-called primitive accumulation is not only not really accumulation, but rather dispossession, it is also not really primitive, but rather always ongoing, as Rosa Luxemburg insisted in her landmark study of capital accumulation (Luxemburg, 1913, 1951). But note, finally, that the potential for widespread social change in the context of a non-linear historical materialism may reside in the slightest variation of conditions at a tipping point. Non-linear revolution, in other words, may not require the kind of massive force of resistance aimed directly against the massive power of capital prescribed by the dialectic of labour and capital located squarely within near-equilibrium capitalist phase-space, but only require some slight and apparently inconsequential shift in the balance of social relations at a far-from-equilibrium bifurcation point on (what becomes) the edge of capitalism.

In order to understand how this could be so, we need to take a closer look at both Deleuze's theory of time and the philosophy of history Deleuze and Guattari developed on the basis of it.

Time and History

Both Deleuze's theory of time and Deleuze and Guattari's philosophy of history are extremely complicated – and doing justice to the relationship between these two complexities is one of the great virtues of Lampert's book, which constitutes the necessary starting point for any discussion of the topic. The book's primary virtue, however, is recognizing and insisting that Deleuze and Guattari indeed have a philosophy of history in the first place. There could be legitimate doubts about this, inasmuch as Deleuze and Guattari consistently express a preference for what they call becoming over what is conventionally considered "history": Lampert's book lays such doubts to rest, by explicitly addressing the relationship between becoming and history. The book's second virtue is that it thereby lays the groundwork for what I want to do today, which is to explain the potential for revolution in history, when capitalism makes history universal by intensifying its potential for becoming, thereby altering the ratio of merely "performing" history to actually changing history, in favour of the latter.

We turn first to Deleuze's philosophy of time. In his magnum opus, *Difference and Repetition*, Deleuze presents a view of time in terms of what he calls three passive syntheses, those of present, past and future (Deleuze, 1994). For brevity's sake, let me say that these time-binding syntheses are considered by Deleuze to be strictly passive because of his concern to avoid the transcendental subjectivism of phenomenology: the syntheses of time are not the operations of an active self or ego managing or processing its experience, they are passive operations, which in fact give rise to all experience in the first place, including our experience of the self.

In his exposition, Lampert describes these syntheses as a 'phenomenology of the present', an 'ontology of the past' and a 'pragmatics of the future' – which is good as far as it goes. It might be said that "phenomenology" is a rather curious choice of name for the synthesis of the present, given the general antipathy to transcendental subjectivism I have just alluded to, but I think the choice is tenable in this particular sense: Deleuze's account of the temporal syntheses in *Difference and Repetition* seems to take as its point of departure the way we experience time and deduces from that the way the syntheses must operate, as we shall see.

The conventional, linear depiction of time – as old as Newton, at least, and probably far older – presents it as a straight line in which each passing moment recedes behind the present, just as each approaching moment arrives from a future stretched out in front of us along the line we are travelling. It is surprising how pervasive and apparently convincing this depiction is at first blush – given that it is simply not true to our experience of time at all. For the past exists for us as a whole, not strung out along a line: to retrieve a past moment from two weeks ago, we do not have to rewind the entire chain of events to get there: we jump immediately to the first day of March. And we can jump from there to any other past moments, without having to trace out or locate those moments on any linear timelines. The past is, if you will, omnipresent to itself. At least that's the way it seems to us.

But then the question becomes: is this true only of our experience of the past? Or is it true of the past itself? Reverting to Lampert's terms: how do you get from phenomenology and how things appear, to ontology and how things actually are? To be sure, past events co-exist in memory – we can scan the past and access this event or jump to that event, without having to replay the entire succession of moments between them. But how do we get from this psychological experience/recollection of the past to the notion that past events themselves co-exist ontologically?

This is where Deleuze draws on Bergson, Nietzsche, and Leibniz. The past for Bergson is not the repository of a linear series of passing presents, but an a-temporal bloc where each and every passed event co-exists with all the others. For Bergson, it is not just in memory that one event can be connected with any other, irrespective of their respective places on a timeline: in the Bergsonian past, past events themselves co-exist and 'undergo constant combination', as Lampert insists; and this in turn entails – and here he quotes Deleuze – '"the ever-increasing co-existence of levels of the past within passive synthesis" as time passes' (Lampert, 2006, p. 48; Deleuze, 1994, p. 83). So pastness, as Lampert puts it, 'is the logical capacity to

undergo inexhaustible transformations; it is the virtuality of the event'
(Lampert, 2006, p. 48).

Here, with the introduction of "virtuality", we need to take a detour and
a short cut. Virtual and actual are central concepts in Deleuze. For present
purposes, think of the language-system as Saussure describes it, as an illustration. It is the accretion or sedimentation of countless actual speech-acts
extended over time, but it exists as a synchronic structure completely
omnipresent to itself, to revert to the term that I used a moment ago. The
language-system as virtual structure is to speech-acts as the past as virtual
structure is to historical acts. The past as a virtual whole (or as a bloc) is the
condition for actual events to take place in the present, just as the language-system as a virtual whole (or as a structure) is the condition for
actual speech-acts to take place in the present. The Bergsonian past, then,
is a realm of virtuality.

Now to account for the actuality of the event, Deleuze draws on Nietzsche's anti-Platonic elevation of becoming over being and on Leibniz's
principle of sufficient reason. Being is merely a momentary, subsidiary and
largely illusory suspension of becoming, according to Nietzsche; becoming
is always primary and fundamental. This means not merely that each and
every thing has a history – rather, each and every thing simply is its history:
apparent being is always the temporary but actual culmination of real
becoming; it is the present actualization of antecedent conditions contained in the virtual past. But to say that any entity is "its" history is not
quite right either: each entity or state of affairs is not just its own self-
contained history, but in fact the history of the entire universe, the entire
past contracted via passive synthesis (as Deleuze puts it) from the perspective of that present thing or monad. This philosophical view aligns directly
with contemporary science as informed by non-linear mathematics and
complexity theory: basins or islands of linear determinacy certainly exist in
the universe, but they emerge out of non-linear dynamics of the kind illustrated a moment ago with chemical reactions. Determinate being does
emerge occasionally from becoming, but it arises always from a broader
context of non-linear indeterminacy.

However – and this is crucial – the determination of any and every actual
being by the virtual past in its entirety remains contingent for Deleuze: it
only has determinacy when read retroactively; it could always have happened otherwise. (Think of evolution as a model of this retroactivity:
rewind evolution and replay it one hundred times, as Stephen Jay Gould
once put it, and you could end up with one hundred different results.)
Couched in terms of the Deleuzo–Guattarian opposition between Royal or

State science and nomad science or philosophy, we can say that State science tries to narrow down any thing's antecedent conditions to the point where virtual becomings succumb to actual being and the thing appears to obey the eternal "laws of nature"; nomad philosophy, by contrast, retains the complexity and non-linearity of antecedent conditions, so that a thing's present being is understood as a more or less temporary and unstable, contingent contraction of its becomings (Deleuze and Guattari, 1987; Holland, 2006, pp. 191–206).

This is the place to open a parenthesis to address one of De Landa's two failings: his refusal to distinguish clearly, as Deleuze and Guattari always do, between science and philosophy, which amounts in his case largely to neglecting politics altogether. As Deleuze and Guattari explain in *What is Philosophy?*, the relations between the virtual and the actual in science and philosophy are the inverse of one another (Deleuze and Guattari, 1994). Entities and states of affairs come into being when a set of virtual conditions gets actualized in a specific way. By controlling variables and repeating experiments, science focuses squarely on actualized being, turning its back on multiple virtuality to define singular actuality as precisely as possible. Philosophy, by contrast, moves in the reverse direction: away from a given state of affairs, philosophy turns towards the virtual conditions from which it emerged. The task of philosophy is to extract from a state of affairs a map of the virtual of which it is an actualization – for any state of affairs is but one among many potential actualizations of its virtual conditions. The virtual is always richer in potential than the actual.

To be fair to De Landa and do justice to Deleuze and Guattari, it must be said in closing this long parenthesis that the foregoing stark contrast between science and philosophy is ultimately too schematic. De Landa is right to point out that contemporary sciences, the sciences informed by non-linear mathematics and complexity theory, are able to take into account a far greater portion of processes of becoming than, say, Newtonian science ever did. This is one reason the interplay between contemporary math and science and philosophy is so fruitful in Deleuze and Guattari. What De Landa is unable to appreciate, though, is that even if they share more than ever an interest in becoming, the aims of science and philosophy are nevertheless quite different: one is to denote actual reality (including its coming-into-being) as accurately as possible, and the other is to map virtual potential as suggestively or productively as possible.

On the basis of this understanding of the past as the virtual repository of multiple potentials and the present as a single actualization of such potentials – returning now to Lampert – the third synthesis of time, the future, appears as the unforeseeable selection, from among the inexhaustible recombinant set of virtual conditions, of a sub-set that will become determinant through actualization: while 'one moment is in the past', Lampert explains, 'and the other is in the present, the relation between them is in the future, determined by neither one nor the other (neither the past nor the present), but by the possible meanings and causes they create together' (Lampert, 2006, p. 57). Lampert boldly calls this synthesis a pragmatics of the future because, along with attractors operating in the antecedent conditions themselves, desire is a force that scans the past from the perspective of the present in search of possible recombinations to actualize. Nomad philosophy is an explicit mode of such a pragmatics: it scans the virtual realm from within a problematic actual state of affairs in order to map its potential to be otherwise, in order to re-submerge inert islands of apparent being in the oceanic flux of becomings with a view to actualizing something else, something different, something better.

We are now in a position to consider what this philosophy of time contributes to Deleuze and Guattari's philosophy of history and to examine the relations between history and becoming. We can start with the distinction between merely performing history (as if according to some pre-written script or score) and actually making or changing history. By "performing history", I mean acting in accordance with and thereby reinforcing a causally determined, linear chain of events. Although Lampert says at one point that 'the theory of succession as causal determinacy is a theory we simply reject, on account of its erroneous assumption that events have power centers sufficient to determine one result rather than another' (Lampert, 2006, p. 9), I take him to mean that causal determinacy cannot by itself constitute a complete philosophy of history: for surely there are times in history when power centres do chain events into causally determined series. But there are also moments when causal explanation fails and temporal succession becomes indeterminate – these are the moments that complexity theory, as we have seen, calls 'bifurcation points', where a power centre or attractor is not strong enough to determine one result rather than another, and history is as likely to swerve off in one direction as it is to stay the course, or swerve off in another. This is consistent with what Lampert says later, that 'events still have a level of becoming even when [they are] most determinate' (Lampert, 2006, p. 139): bifurcation points occur when the force of non-linear becoming exceeds that of linear causal determination, and it becomes possible to change history, rather than merely perform it by following the chain of causal succession.

Deleuze and Guattari's philosophy of history, then, distinguishes centrally between linear historical causality – which I have called merely performing history – and non-linear becomings, which appertain to virtual events and problems, and which at certain historical moments – called bifurcation points – can change history or "make history" in the strong sense, that is by taking it in a different direction.

The encounter between labour and capital with which we started is clearly one such bifurcation point. And like Marx before them, Deleuze and Guattari assert that the advent of capitalism inaugurates universal history: even though it was a chance or contingent encounter, once it attained a critical threshold of systematicity, it became self-sustaining and transformed history into universal history. Furthermore, and again like Marx before them, Deleuze and Guattari take what Hegelian Marxism would call a dialectical approach to capitalism: its advent must be assessed in terms of both its positive and its negative contributions to history. And one of the positive contributions of capitalism, according to Deleuze and Guattari, is that it changes the proportion of non-linear becoming and linear causality in universal history – and changes it for the better.

So why does the ratio of non-linear becoming to linear causality change – and improve – so dramatically under capitalism, according to Deleuze and Guattari? Part of the answer lies in a tension that exists between capitalism and the State. 'State historical occurrences and minoritarian becomings are not two kinds of things that happen', Lampert explains; rather, any event 'has both [linear] history and becoming co-existing within it' (Lampert, 2006, p. 168). The difference between State history and the minoritarian becomings unleashed by capitalism – to quote one of Lampert's most cogent formulations – is that whereas the State 'adds developments to its past, [a minoritarian becoming] subtracts the codifications of its past, until it "has realized the immanence" of each phenomenon' (Lampert, 2006, p. 140, emphasis added). The narratives of State history and the actions informed by that history retrace and reinforce the causal chains that produced and/or consolidated State rule – this is one sense in which history is always written by the victor. Minoritarian becomings, by contrast, strip away (or de-code) the actual determinations of the past and restore its virtual potential to become-otherwise. This potentially-revolutionary de-codification of the past (which Foucault would famously call "discontinuous history") is fostered by the future as pragmatic search engine that scans the past in order to counter-actualize the present. Now the potential revealed by counter-actualization is by no means infinite: the virtual past is not pure chaos, but rather exists in the form of determinate problems and events. And indeed, a central task of political philosophy is precisely to map such events and problems, in order to ascertain where the potential immanent to them lies for propitious change, as we have seen.

Given its inherently contradictory or ambivalent makeup, capitalism itself fosters such minoritarian becomings, as we shall see, while at the same time it uses the State as a model of realization to consolidate and extend its rule. Lampert will thus assert that 'our struggle against capitalism is not a struggle against a state of affairs, but a struggle with the ontology of the virtual and its effectuation' (Lampert, 2006, p. 166). The struggle against capitalism is thus simultaneously a struggle with (or within) capitalism to turn its historically unparalleled mobilization of the virtual to better account, to realize the potential of universal history.

But if the relation between the virtual and the actual, as we have seen, is built into Deleuze's philosophy of time and underlies his philosophy of history, how can it be that capitalism transforms the salience of the virtual, making it more accessible and giving it new force as a component of universal history? The answer, in a nutshell, is this: it does so by reversing the priorities of production and exchange and effectively subordinating the former to the latter. Now money has always been an incarnation of the virtual: buying something is the moment where virtual exchange-value gets actualized in the concrete determinations of the commodity and its use-value. But until capitalism, production always preceded exchange: pre-existing concrete determinations embodied in a commodity had to be virtualized in a first transaction – that is, instantiated in the exchange-value of money (through the sale of a commodity for money: C-M in Marx's formula) – after which said exchange-value would then get re-actualized in other concrete determinations through the purchase of a different commodity with that money (M-C). For capital, however, which always starts with money in order to beget more money (and whose formula is thus M-C-M'), all concrete determinations come after an investment decision has been made on the prospect of making a profit: the exchange-value of capital is not merely money's ability to appropriate (to actualize as mine) an object that was already produced, but the ability to actualize production itself. What is crucial is not just that, unlike spiders with their webs, humans produce goods in the imagination or in "virtual reality" before producing them in actual reality; it is that, under capitalism, decisions as to if and what to produce, and as to when and how and where, are all made in the virtual realm, before a single dollar is actually invested, before the first factory actually gets built and before the first workers actually get hired; only after all that do the goods in all their post-hoc objective determinacy actually get produced for eventual sale and use. Capitalism thus for the first time in history makes the virtual realm the basis and fulcrum of most, if not all, social activity. And in the course of its self-valorization and self-expansion, capital incessantly "revolutionizes" the means of production and consumption, and along with these, constantly transforms society itself at so great a rate of speed that meaningful codification and even profitable axiomatization cannot always keep pace. So every historical event anymore, as Lampert rightly insists, has both a singular linear history and multiple non-linear becomings co-existing within it; all historical events participate simultaneously in a causal series deriving from and contributing to capital accumulation and state power, and in becomings that may escape capitalist axiomatization and state codification altogether.

Revolution

Political struggle thus necessarily involves two co-existent kinds of activity: on one hand, there is struggle within the axiomatic, for whatever ameliorations can be wrung from capital and/or the State through direct confrontation – and this is a mode of struggle that Deleuze and Guattari insist is perfectly valid and necessary (Deleuze and Guattari, 1987, p. 471). On the other hand, there is the struggle to escape axiomatization and codification altogether – the mode of struggle via de-coding and "lines-of-flight" that they in some sense prefer. What is given is always 'the coexistence and inseparability of that which the system conjugates, and that which never ceases to escape it following lines of flight that are themselves connectable', as Deleuze and Guattari put it in *A Thousand Plateaus* (Deleuze and Guattari, 1987, p. 473). And this connectability of lines-of-flight is crucial, politically. What in the first volume of *Capitalism and Schizophrenia* were called "schizophrenic" lines-of-flight are politically useless – or worse – if they do not intersect and connect up to constitute some kind of critical mass, as Deleuze and Guattari are careful to specify more clearly in the second volume. Yet even here, the conditions for such a critical mass becoming revolutionary are left somewhat vague: the slogan 'a new people on a new earth' echoes throughout their collaborative work as a kind of refrain; and they do suggest that the ultimate challenge is to 'construct revolutionary connections over and against [contre] the conjugations of the axiomatic' (Deleuze and Guattari, 1987, p. 473). But we need to try to get clearer about just which conditions are conducive to the formation of connections among lines-of-flight and about how a critical mass of revolutionary connections could overcome the conjugations of the capitalist axiomatic.

For insight into these questions, I propose that we return to the process with which we started: reading *Capital* backwards. This would mean

focusing less on the power of capital accumulation than on so-called
"primitive accumulation", which as we saw is not really primitive but
always ongoing, and not really accumulation but rather dispossession;
and it would mean, like Althusser, highlighting in our considerations the
non-linear conditions of reproduction rather than the linear causality of
production/accumulation. And I propose that we examine in this light
the key political-economic strategies of anti-capitalist struggle – and
I specify "political-economic" strategies (those of radical syndicalism, if
you will) to rule out of consideration what we might call more narrowly
political strategies – state-centric or party-electoral strategies – as insuffi-
ciently revolutionary. These political-economic strategies are the strike,
and especially the general strike. As Walter Benjamin has very clearly
noted, the general strike is distinctive in that it is non-confrontational
(although he would say non-violent, which is not quite the same thing,
and perhaps a little too optimistic) (Benjamin, 1978, pp. 277–300). In
principle, a strike does not involve one power bloc directly confronting
another, but rather one bloc withdrawing from its previous mode of
engagement (wage-slavery) vis-à-vis the other. The same is true of the
general strike, which expands the act of withdrawal to a larger scale: here
we have a critical mass of workers walking away en masse from their
engagement with capital. Yet from the perspective of reproduction and
so-called primitive accumulation – and this is key – what the masses are
walking away "from" – capital accumulation – is actually less important
than what they are able to walk "towards": rejecting capital is less important than having something sustaining and sustainable to rely on. You
will recall that the crucial catalyst entailed by primitive accumulation was
enforced dependence on capitalist markets: remove this catalyst, and
capitalism no longer "becomes necessary", to invoke Althusser once
again. More important than directly confronting capital, in other words,
is securing alternative means of life, an alternative mode of reproduction. Even more important: such alternatives already exist. One of the
great virtues of Gibson-Graham's work is to demonstrate how incomplete
capitalism actually is and how many alternative economies co-exist within
or beside it (Gibson-Graham, 1996; 2006). Community Supported Agriculture; the co-op movement; the Open-Source Software movement; Fair
Trade – all these, and many more, constitute viable, actually existing
alternatives to capitalism. And all it will take for them, in connection with
others, to become revolutionary – in the specifically non-linear sense
I am proposing – is for a critical mass of people to invest their life-activity
in them, rather than in capitalist markets. We tend to think of linear

revolutions as punctual: 1917, 1848 and so on – even though they probably were not. But the non-linear revolution I am talking about is even less punctual: it entails instead what I elsewhere call the strategy of the 'slow-motion general strike' (Holland, forthcoming). Critical masses of people in various aspects of their life-activity just walk away from capital – having secured in advance at least the rudiments of alternative means of life. This does not have to happen all at once: but as soon as sufficient numbers of people in enough areas of life do so, a tipping point will have been reached, a non-linear bifurcation threshold crossed, beyond which capitalism will not only no longer be necessary, it will actually become-unnecessary. As the slow-motion general strike reaches completion, that is to say, it is not just the State, but also capitalism itself that ends up withering away.

Bibliography

Althusser, L. (2006), 'The Underground Current of the Materialism of the Encounter', in F. Matheron and O. Corpet (eds), *Philosophy of the Encounter, Later Writings 1978–1987*. London; New York: Verso.

Benjamin, W. (1978), 'Critique of Violence', in P. Demetz (ed.), *Reflections: Essays, Aphorisms, Autobiographical Writings*. New York: Harcourt Brace Jovanovich, pp. 277–300.

Brenner, R. (1982). 'The Agrarian Roots of European Capitalism,' *Past & Present*, 97, pp. 16–113.

De Landa, M. (1997), *A Thousand Years of Nonlinear History*. New York: Zone Books.

Deleuze, G. (1994), *Difference and Repetition*. New York: Columbia University Press.

Deleuze, G. and Guattari, F. (1987), *A Thousand Plateaus*. Minneapolis: University of Minnesota Press.

—(1994), *What is Philosophy?* New York: Columbia University Press.

Gibson-Graham, J. K. (1996), *The End of Capitalism (as We Knew It)*. Oxford; Cambridge: Blackwell.

—(2006), *A Postcapitalist Politics*. Minneapolis: University of Minnesota Press.

Holland, E. W. (2006), 'Nonlinear Historical Materialism and Postmodern Marxism'. *Culture, Theory, Critique*, 47:2, pp. 181–96.

—(2006), 'Nomad Citizenship and Global Democracy', in M. Fuglsang and B. Meier Sorensen (eds), *Gilles Deleuze and the Social: Toward a New Social Analytic*. Edinburgh: Edinburgh University Press.

—(2008), 'Review of Jay Lampert's Deleuze and Guattari's Philosophy of History'. *Symposium: Canadian Journal of Continental Philosophy*, 12:2, pp. 156–59.

—(forthcoming), *Nomad Citizenship: Free-market Communism and the Slow-Motion General Strike*. Minneapolis: University of Minnesota Press.

Lampert, J. (2006), *Deleuze and Guattari's Philosophy of History*. London: Continuum.

Luxemburg, R. (1913, 1951), *The Accumulation of Capital*. London: Routledge & Kegan Paul.

Marx, K. (1967), *Capital*, Volume 1. New York: International Publishers.

Chapter 2

Time Folded and Crumpled: Time, History, Self-Organization and the Methodology of Michel Serres

Kevin Clayton

Introduction

Juxtaposing two centres of thought, two series of creative philosophical writing, particularly in the case of Michel Serres and Gilles Deleuze on time and history, is always of value. Placing the two thought streams in close proximity not only reveals more about each, in the sense that each is given a contrasting background that reveals its nuances and subtleties, but also allows a certain creative play – perhaps, to evoke Deleuze's term, calls forth the dark precursor – that allows something more to emerge from their differences. Of the two, Deleuze offers more of a theory of time in the philosophically traditional sense. He presents a more technical, perhaps an overly technical, description that explains time as an emergent phenomenon, as a process with degrees of actuality that are the result of a number of syntheses. Serres, while basically agreeing with the description of the emergent process, offers a less technical, a less abstract and a more experiential account. Engaging with the creative output of these two centres, however, is never a straightforward task.

The work of Michel Serres can appear as an enigma; not technically difficult, but hard to hold onto. It moves with speed as it journeys through the sciences, philosophy, mythology and literature such that in the space of one paragraph we can, to quote Bruno Latour, 'find ourselves with the Romans then with Jules Verne then with the Indo-Europeans then, suddenly launched in the Challenger rocket, before ending up on a bank of the Garonne River' (Serres et al., 1995, p. 43). The work of Gilles Deleuze, however, is technically difficult. Reading Deleuze, and in particular *Difference and Repetition*,[1] can be hard work and a perplexing experience, but one that richly rewards a persistent endeavour. This book, I would rather provocatively suggest, is probably one of the most important books written on ontology. However, while Deleuze's "theory" responds very effectively to many of the traditional philosophical questions regarding time – that is not the point. Other than not contradicting science, the task of philosophy is not to define (which, ironically, Deleuze says he is doing in many places) but to describe – to create concepts that challenge our presuppositions and allow us to see things in a different way, or, to follow Serres, to guide us in our explorations. And it is on this point, that, I would suggest, *Difference and Repetition* becomes the victim of its own success; it reads too much like a technical definition of time. Serres, on the other hand, presents us with a very different methodology; or perhaps a non-methodology would be a more apt description as he has commented: 'Method seeks but does not find', whereas 'I do not seek, I find' (Serres, 1997, p. 100). A comparison between *Difference and Repetition* and Serres' *Genesis*, the other work that I wish to focus on, reveals a very similar ontology and description of time; the differences between the two being really just a matter of focus. Method-ologically, however, they are very different, and it is these differences between the two approaches that I want to highlight, while eventually con-centrating on the latter. These differences, though, can only be effectively revealed following some exposition of their respective ontologies.

In the opening section of *Genesis*, Serres offers 'a new object for philoso-phy'. This new object is the multiple as such. His aim, he says, is 'to raise the brackets and parentheses ... whereby we shove multiplicities under unities'. He warns of the dangers of subsuming 'multiplicity under unity', and asks a profound and challenging question: 'Can I possibly speak of multiplicity itself without ever availing myself of the concept?' Space, all space, any space, whether it is biological, geo-physical, socio-political or epistemologi-cal, is composed of the multiple; but, Serres points out, 'we are fascinated by the unit; only a unity seems rational to us'. Even our attempt to think the multiple as such seems to require our use of conceptual unities. We only seem to attach the status of being to the groupings of the world, he says, when we subsume them beneath a unity. The problem is that when we attempt to delimit such a multiplicity, when we try and draw a line, a bound-ary around and between the fragments or crowds within such a multiplicity, we try and capture what we like to think of as a pre-existing unity, a pre-existing form or classification, a being that has up until now avoided our capture, and in so doing we miss the dynamic emergence of its form; of time itself.

Deleuze's task in *Difference and Repetition* is similar: 'Opposition, resemblance, identity and even analogy are only effects produced by ... presentations of dif-ference, rather than being conditions which subordinate difference and make something represented' (Deleuze, 1994, p. 145). Both writers argue for the rug to be pulled from under the feet of representational thinking, thinking where form and concepts are related either to Forms or to other concepts through relations of identity, similarity, opposition, or even difference when that difference is 'a difference form'. Instead, they attempt to illustrate how form emerges from nothing, not nothing as the absence or opposite of things, but a no-thing-ness that may be void of form, but is far from being a total absence; a dynamic background from which form emerges on the tide of intrinsic differences and faint repetitions; a dynamic which is time, but a dynamism which is lost when defined or explicated in terms of clear concepts or representations. Deleuze attempts to explain this process, to offer a detailed analysis through a debate with many of the canons, an attempt that he knows is not possible: 'Difference is not and cannot be thought in itself, so long as it is subject to the requirements of representation' (Deleuze, 1994, p. 262). How then can we think difference without the use of concepts? How can we tame the 'four iron collars of representation': identity in the concept; opposition in the predicate; analogy in judgement; resemblance in perception? Deleuze attempts to fight his way through, to perturbate our thinking with a plethora of technicalities perhaps in the hope that it will reorganize from within in such a way that we will become intensively aware of the process.

Serres' approach, however, is far gentler, far more poetic – though he confesses to making 'language live at the price of clarity'. Serres is strongly opposed to analysis, preferring, instead, a method of synthesis that is at the very core of his comparative methodology. He has compared these two approaches to the use of style and grammar: both explore language, but by different means. Grammar analyses and leads to debate, while style experiments and leads to exploration. The analyst, he argues, 'cuts up, makes distinctions in order to recognize the elements, [he] stops, breaks, theorizes'. The philosopher-writer, on the other hand, 'tries things out, he essays ... He experiences, experiments' – he explores; and the price we have to pay is the loss of a certain amount of clarity, but a clarity that masks the dynamic nature of things (Serres, 1997, pp. 78–9). Analysis is heavily dependent upon sequential thinking, whereas synthesis involves a different style of thinking: 'synthesis will no doubt be made more through comparitivism than by sequential linking, more through Hermes's swift travels than by deduction or solid construction' (Serres et al., 1997, p. 73). This comparative methodology, I will argue, actively demonstrates the deep self-organizing and creative principle in nature – an approach that is in accord with his deep distrust for abstract thought and his faith in quite a radical empiricism.[2]

But, as I said above, to get to such an appreciation we first need to do some exploration of the ontological terrain. Such an exploration will reveal differences of focus to otherwise very similar conceptual approaches, but differences that also reveal the bifurcation point in the above methodologies. Serres focuses on, gives emphasis to, the background, to the sea of nothingness from which form emerges, with the hope, perhaps, that if we follow suit, and hold fast to the realization that everything is, quite literally, multiple, our thinking will be prevented from solidifying, that it will remain dynamic and creative, and that it will, in its attempt to keep thinking in terms of multiplicities, glimpse the true complexity of life. Deleuze instead focuses on the process and codification of emergence, perhaps with the hope that politically if we become aware of this process of codification, we can offer greater resistance. Both approaches, separately, offer insight, but together they are inspirational.

Noise and the In-itself of Time

Time is intrinsic to an understanding of both ontologies, and our starting point has to be the background nothingness from which it emerges or, to be more precise, they emerge. An entry point into Serres' particular understanding of time is through his use of the word "noise". He reprises it from the Old French where it meant fury, uproar and wrangling, as well as sound, as in the phrase chercher noise – to pick a quarrel with. For Serres, *noise* (italicized to differentiate it from the word meaning just sound in English) 'may well be the ground of our being'. It is the pure chaos, the pure undifferentiated, totally symmetrical fury, the pure multiplicity out of which everything emerges like Aphrodite out of the sea. 'Noise cannot be a phenomenon', he says, because 'every phenomenon is separated from it, a silhouette on a backdrop ...' (Serres, 1995a, p. 13). 'Classes', states Serres, 'are a result of fury' (Serres, 1995a, p. 82). All patterns, any notion of order – classes, genera, concepts, unities, entities – emerge out of noise; and this noise, this pure multiplicity is time – or rather time, he says, 'is a threshold between disorder and redundancy, it is the multiplicity next to chaos and prior to all spatialities. It is the first injection of redundancy into a pure multiplicity' (Serres, 1995a, p. 117).

For Serres, "redundancy" is a key term, and one that is closely synonymous to Deleuze's "repetition". Serres' use of the term, here as elsewhere in his writings, is derived from information theory where it refers to the difference in the number of bits of actual information in a transmitted message and the total number of bits that were used to make the transmission. It is the wastage, but expressed in positive terms; it is the initial repetition that allows or makes further repetitions possible; at its minimum it is the first, faintly perceived echo, that initial repetition from which everything that follows depends upon but which will no longer be perceivable as such. As Serres describes:

> A fluctuation appears, it is lost in the desert or the packed-fullness of background noise, either through lack of reference, or through excess of difference. It vanishes, it gets buried. In order to be or to make an appearance, it needs a reference, it needs an analogy. It is either set in the laminar, then, or it is distinguished through its identity in the differentiated. It thus needs an other, it needs a same, it needs an echo. The echo alone is discernable here. Either through its position or through its redundancy. In the beginning is the echo. Background noise, fluctuation, echo. Everything begins on the threshold of the echo ... The echo is the minimum of redundancy, then, sown in pure multiplicity. Time is born with the echo, the echo is from birth to make time begin (Serres, 1995a, p. 119).

A pure multiplicity, noise, while "containing" a multitude of elements or atoms (yes, we can think of Lucretius and atomism here),[3] is in a sense unthinkable, in as far as the perfect symmetry of the laminar flow prevents any differentiation, and thus any sense of either space or time. None of the atoms has any relationship with any other atom – all is chaos. For relations or emergent patterns to begin to form certain elements will start to stabilize into a quasi-stable turbulent relationships with other elements; relations formed by the repetition and redundancy of energy flows between them. From this turbulence, all things, all classes are born; born from these first relationships between certain elements, born from these first codes. As Serres says: 'Life, invention, violence ... a processual flux codes a classing' (Serres, 1995a, p. 95). Fury becomes a classifier, a giver of form.

In *Difference and Repetition*, we find the same background nothingness. Time is constituted through a series of repetitions, through a series of contractions, syntheses and differentiations experienced by the mind. Now while Deleuze makes a very strong link between time and thinking, it should be noted, perhaps, that this link is made stronger by Deleuze's focus on the later "stages" of the series of syntheses. So while time can only be thought through an active synthesis, the passive synthesis is performed by all organisms, and in effect we have a description of the emergence, first of living organisms, of lived time and rudimentary consciousness, and then self-consciousness, mind and the meaning of time. These syntheses are not carried out by a pre-existing mind, but occur in a "mind" that is being formed by the process itself. Put in its most straightforward way, and loosing some of the technicalities that only serve to obscure the process rather than reveal it, Deleuze cites three instances whose repetition and synthesis constitute time: the in-itself, the for-itself and the for-us. It is the former of these that I wish to focus on at the moment, but for purposes of orientation let me say that the in-itself is unthinkable as such, that it disappears as soon it appears, and which, I argue, equates to *noise* (as well as the notion of the void in Badiou,[4] and very obviously Sartre's nothingness); the for-itself emerges out of this nothingness through a passive synthesis (the details of which I will examine later) and forms what Bergson would term duration (and Sartre consciousness?); the for-us is grounded upon this passive synthesis but emerges through an active synthesis, which allows the emergence of reflected representation, of both memory (in the sense of actual memories) and understanding. Both the for-itself and the for-us are the results of differentiation/differenciation, the former exists virtually as a product of differentiation, while the latter has actual existence as a product of differenciation. This first instant, the in-itself of time is, for Deleuze, pure, in the sense that it is the general a priori element of all time; it is the pure past, but not in the sense of one instant or present passing only to be replaced by another:

> The past ... neither passes nor comes forth. For this reason the past, far from being a dimension of time, is the synthesis of all time of which the present and the future are only dimensions. We cannot say that it was. It no longer exists, it does not exist, but it insists, it consists, it is. It insists with the former present, it consists with the new or present present. It is the in-itself of time as the final ground of the passage of time. In this sense it forms a pure, general, a priori element of all time (Deleuze, 1994, p. 83).

It is, in other words, that pure multiplicity that Serres refers to as *noise,* where any "standing" is not on the outside, is not existent, but is internal and differential, is insistent and consistent.

Particularly in *Genesis,* Serres uses various forms of the word "clamour" to great effect to refer to the background noise: 'What are called phenomena alone are known and knowable, avatars of a secret remote process emerge from the clamorous sea' (Serres, 1995a, p. 18). Perhaps in reference to the modern belief that life on earth first emerged and then rose out of the sea, perhaps in reference to the mythology of Aphrodite, goddess of love and fertility born from the foam of the sea, perhaps even in reference to his own maritime experiences of its power, the sea, for Serres, becomes heavily symbolic of the background *noise*, from which, quite literally, everything emerges. In other words, this process of emergence from the *noise* is a single process. In similar fashion, Deleuze refers to the univocity of Being, to a "single voice" that 'raises the clamour of being' (Deleuze, 1994, pp. 35–7). This single voice, however, is not "the One"; it is not in any sense a unity, it is a pure multiplicity – pure in the sense that nothing can be distinguished or differentiated within it (in fact it does not even make sense to refer to either "within" or "it"). It is, in Badiou's terms, the void, an inconsistent multiplicity. Deleuze aims at the collapse of the traditional "one/many" distinction – a distinction that he refers to as a distorted dialectic. For him, the pure multiplicity of the in-itself, as the noise does for Serres (and arguably the void does for Badiou), replaces the one and the multiple as the true substantive (Deleuze, 1994, p.182). Organization, or distribution, occurs from within; it becomes a self-distribution, or, to equate it to one of the key features of complex systems, self-organizing; organization results from the intensive relations that emerge from within any emergent consistent multiplicity, not from some transcendent power above or some transcendental principle below. We have, to use Deleuze's phrase, a demonic rather than a divine distribution. All limit is imposed from within through the intensive process of immanent wrapping or enclosure – enveloping. 'Univocal Being is at one and the same time nomadic distribution and crowned anarchy' (Deleuze, 1994, p. 37).

The Emergence and Synthesis of Time

Serres' response to attempting to the think 'the multiple as such' is to think in a manner he terms "vectorially" – in a manner that maps the relations that form between the units or atoms within a multiplicity and which allow the emergence of form. We can, on the one hand, group those elements that, through repetition and redundancy, have formed an emergent pattern together, and view them as a unity, as a collective – as a noun or as a verb. This, Serres argues, is the traditional way we believe we make sense of our world. His methodology, however, is to abstract what it is that connects these elements together, the prepositions; the messengers, bonds, cords, links that 'comprehend, since they join or grasp or seize several things, beasts or men together' (Serres, 1995b, p. 107, original emphasis). The former method produces stasis, stable objects and "processes", linear logic, statues; the latter produces fluid and turbulent patterns – patterns, I want to argue, that can actualize into any number of different forms in different spatial and temporal locations, patterns that are relational in a topological or non-Euclidian sense rather than relational in a conventional geometrical sense, patterns that are fluid, turbulent, non-linear and very adaptable. This is what Serres means by weaving together networks into a general theory of relations. It is these relations that supply the sufficient – not necessary – conditions for all phenomena: 'Relations spawn objects, beings and acts, not vice versa' (Serres et al., 1997, p. 107). In other words, by constantly being aware of the open, dynamic and multiple nature of any existent, we may be able to experience, become aware of the process whereby the relations that allowed for the emergence of the "count-as-one" came about. Serres' focus is on the constant proximity of the background noise rather than on the process of emergence.

Deleuze, however, attempts a more detailed, a more technical account of this emergence. He first of all develops a twofold synthesis of time (passive and active), which he later develops into a threefold synthesis. Which of these do we need? Or, do we need to understand both? Does it really matter? Now in asking this last question I do not wish to sound flippant, merely to point out that, as Deleuze himself argues, in total agreement with Serres, 'categories belong to the world of representation', and that in their place he has 'continually proposed descriptive notions' (Deleuze, 1994, p. 284). As one of the key purposes of *Difference and Repetition* (again, in total agreement with that of *Genesis*) is to subvert the privileged place that essence and definition have traditionally held, a descriptive rather than a definitive account of the process is what is called for, and as such we need to avoid definitive statements as to the precise stages or categorization of it. It is this difference between description and definition that lies at the heart of the difference between Ideas and concepts that runs through the whole of this work. As Deleuze says: 'Ideas are not concepts; they are a form of eternally positive differential multiplicity, distinguished from the identity of concepts' (Deleuze, 1994, p. 288). This is Serres' challenge, to think the multiple without 'availing myself of the concept', without recourse to the safety and certainty of identity and definition. Serres achieves this, I suggest, partly through a far more descriptive and, dare I say, literary style, whereas, rather ironically, Deleuze attempts it through in many ways a more traditional technical and philosophical style where he very frequently "defines" his terms. Serres is quite opposed to this "technical" style, and in his conversations with Latour expresses his dislike of jargon, suggesting that "hypertechnicality" is not only 'useless, redundant, harmful' but also that it 'breeds fear and exclusion' (Serres et al., 1997, p. 23–4). On the other hand, I think it could be argued that in doing so, Deleuze does at least attempt a more detailed account of the emergence of time within consciousness that provides insightful and useful concepts to those of us working within the humanities and social sciences. It is with this spirit that I will describe two types of multiplicity found in *Difference and Repetition* – one virtual, intensive and implicit, formed from the passive synthesis; the other actual, extensive and explicit, formed from the active synthesis.

Both these syntheses are formed through processes of differentiation, but different types of differentiation: 'We call the determination of the virtual content of an Idea differen*t*iation; we call the actualization of that virtuality into species and distinguished parts differen*c*iation' (Deleuze, 1994, p. 207). The former of these, differen*t*iation, refers to the echoes, to the initial repetitions that emerge from the background noise or in-itself of time, to the faint rhythms that can only be distinguished from the background, and from which, through redundancy, a series of repetitions emerge. At this "stage", all difference is internal to the series, and as such it is intensive. It is intensive because it cannot be measured, because there is nothing except itself to be compared against, and measurement and extension, like tangos, require two. Deleuze also describes such multiplicities as implicit, as being formed through a process of implication. Implication, derived from the Latin word for "fold", to enfold, or in-fold, suggests a self-same relationship, a relationship formed completely internally to the series or system, a coming together or enveloping of emergent terms (to use Badiou's word) to form a series of repetitive "states" whose only relations are the internal holding or folding together of these terms. It is this passive synthesis that forms the virtual, a "state" that is real, but which has not been actualized: 'The virtual is opposed not to the real but to the actual. The virtual is fully real in so far as it is virtual' (Deleuze, 1994, p. 208). This is important because the virtual "state" of the system should carry neither any sense of the negative, nor any sense of relationship usually associated with representation – 'the negative is always derived and represented, never original or present: the process of differen*t*iation and of differen*c*iation is primary in relation to that of the negative and opposition' (Deleuze, 1994, p. 207). Even though the internal relations that form the virtual cannot be perceived, because to be perceived they would need to be actualized (the series of states that form them would need to form a relationship with another series of states), they are every bit as real – it is just that their reality is of a different order than the actual. The virtual, though, is the basis of all actual structure: 'The reality of the virtual consists of the differential elements and relations along with the singular points which correspond to them. The reality of the virtual is structure' (Deleuze, 1994, p. 209). This is why Deleuze, in terms of consciousness or mentality, describes the virtual mental states as Ideas, as opposed to their actualized concepts, as it is from them, from their virtual structure, that our everyday concepts capable of representation are derived.

Actual phenomena are emergent from an active synthesis between two or more virtual series, from their differenciation, from the establishment or communication of differences between the two series. This often invisible and imperceptible difference between two intensities that allows "thunderbolts" to explode between them Deleuze terms, rather provocatively, the dark precursor – dark because unseen, yet a precursor to all seen phenomena:

> Given two heterogeneous series, two series of differences, the precursor plays the part of the differenciator of these differences. In this manner, by virtue of its own power, it puts them into immediate relation to one another: it is the in-itself of difference or the 'differently different' – in other words, difference in the second degree, the self-different which relates different to different by itself (Deleuze, 1994, p. 119).

Once the thunderbolts start flashing, once Hermes establishes communication between two or more series of intensive differences, virtual differences are actualized and phenomena emerge. These actualized phenomena are both extensive and explicit. Differences of time can now be measured. Virtual differences, intensive differences are purely internal to the series, and as such measurement of them is nonsense; they are like unheard rhythms that only make sense when they form a relationship with another series of rhythms – a hearing subject. And, of course, the now formed actual phenomena are explicit: they are capable of being unfolded, analysed and represented.

Before moving on to discussing how both thinkers view history as a form of codification of the very complex and dynamic process that I have been outlining (and no doubt grossly oversimplifying), I would like to pause for a moment to reflect on the notion of "folding", of implication and explication, referred to by Deleuze. In his conversations with Latour, Serres also discusses these terms in relation to his comparative methodology, which I shall return to later, and particularly in relation to his use of Hermes, the messenger god, as a motif for the communication between different spaces of enquiry, between disparate systems of knowledge. In the same section, on method, he also describes time as being folded and crumpled. This has importance for what I am attempting to unfold myself, but will, I think, be best considered with the discussion on methodology, which is to follow.

History and Codification

For Serres, history is the process that divides, that classifies groups, that sorts populations into classes. History is related to representation and reason, and in *Genesis*, it is often referred to as the 'great chain of reason'. The process outlined above is complex, dynamic and turbulent, but it is precisely these qualities that give it its creativity and maximize the chances of survival of any emergent form. Representation and reason, to some extend quite necessarily, dampen the dynamics, reduce the turbulence and allow us some sense of orientation and understanding, but at the cost of a loss of creativity – a loss that, at its extreme, produces stagnation and death. The chain of reason, though, is a chain of death not only because of this reduction in creativity, but also because it creates a false understanding of the dynamic nature of things: representation is 'the great wall of appearance' that stabilizes the flow of life (Serres, 1995a, pp.76–7); the 'stable chain of the rationalists only expresses ... their desire for domination' (Serres, 1995a, p. 72). But, as I said, some degree of solidification of this dynamic process is necessary, so it is never a case of being a chained or unchained melody, but rather of degrees of codification – with sufficient codification to allow navigation of our environment, but not to the extent that the maps we use become fixed and unresponsive to changes of our environment. To this extent, Serres often talks of quasi-objects: bonds, cords or contracts that enfold or hold together terms of a multiplicity, and in *Genesis*, history is often referred to as a "soft quasi-chain" as well as of a more solid make. Coding, for Serres, 'is nothing more than showing unities in the stead of multiplicitary noise'. It is the taming of wild and turbulent multiplicities and the birth of concepts (Serres, 1995a, p.86).

In *A Thousand Plateaus*, Deleuze and Guattari offer a threefold differentiation of social structuration based on degrees of codification (Deleuze and Guattari, 2004, pp. 244–55). The middle line of the three is constituted of 'a relatively supple line of interlaced codes and territorialities', but on either side we have, first, 'a rigid line' where 'the social space implies a State apparatus', where there exists a 'generalized over-coding', and secondly, on the other side, 'one or several lines of flight', which offer resistance to state control and which are 'defined by decoding and deterritorialization. For Deleuze and Guattari, the greater the codification, the more rigid the situation and therefore the less the degree of flexibility or adaptability the social system or situation has to respond to a constantly changing and dynamic environment, going so far as to refer to the severe over-coding of state control as cancerous, a reference to Solzhenitsyn's allegorical novel *Cancer Ward* and the "cancerous" Soviet police state of the 1950s in which it is set. Coding, though, to various degrees, is the bonding or contracting that allows for repetitions: 'From chaos, Milieus and Rhythms are born ... Every milieu is vibratory ... a block of spacetime constituted by the periodic repetition of the component ... Every milieu is coded, a code being defined by the periodic repetition' (Deleuze and Guattari, 2004, p. 345).

So, whether we are talking about over-codification or de-codification, we are still talking about codification – to some degree and from some source. Without codification to some degree there would be nothing, without some taming or slowing down of the emergent flows or series of repetitions there would be nothing discernable, no phenomena standing out from the background noise. But from where do these codes originate? The answer to this question is of vital important for both writers – to both perspectives on time and history. In Serres' words: 'The flux is at all points self-coded' (Serres, 1995a, p. 99). The codes emerge naturally from the noise, they result from what, in complexity terms, is referred to as self-organization: through a process of differential selection of the many and various relationships that form between the terms of a multiplicity, those that survive and become relatively stable are those that are the most adapted and robust within their particular environment, and it is these that form phenomena. Form and structure did not pre-exist, they are, for both Serres and Deleuze, the result of the emergent rhythms stabilizing within their milieus. For Deleuze, this forms the essence of his critique of both Platonic and Aristotelian forms: forms are neither transcendent nor teleological. Such forms are the logos of the tradition that provide for a fixed and proportional distribution; they are imposed, for Deleuze, by the State, or agents of the state acting in the guise of philosophers wishing to uphold it. Such a way of understanding organization (for Deleuze in *A Thousand Plateaus*, social organization) needs overturning in favour of the nomos; a nomadic distribution or self-distribution; a demonic rather than a divine distribution. 'What is lacking', he claims, 'is a Nomadology', which is 'the opposite of a history' (Deleuze and Guattari, 2004, p. 25). This self-distribution (Deleuze), self-coding (Serres) or self-organization is the inversion of representation and the tradition, and the breaking of the chains imposed by the 'one–many' dichotomy. There is only the multiple, there are only multiplicities, and all forms are emergent and the *result* of self-organization. 'Classes are a result of fury' says Serres (my emphasis), 'Fury is a classifier' (Serres, 1995a, p. 82). Fury is the energy that drives self-organization. But it is not just the emergence of patterns, of classes, it is a certain invariance of these classes across space and time, and their repetition, which causes Serres to refer to time being folded and crumpled, a gathering together, a percolation; and not only does this gathering together best describe his methodology, but it is his methodology itself that best describes his understanding of time and history.

Self-Organization and Methodology

This emergence of patterns that exhibit a strong degree of invariance across space and time is being described by a growing number of scientists. Brian Goodwin, for example, argues for the assimilation of theories of natural selection with our emerging understanding of the intrinsic dynamics of complex systems such that evolution is understood as the evolution of generic forms (Goodwin, 2001). Goodwin describes, in a later work, what he terms 'fractal patterns in space'. Noting that mathematically 'fractals are defined as self-similar structures on all scales' he points to the self-evident self-similarity between the patterns extended in space between river systems, a lightening bolt, the root system of a plant, the branching structure of trees and the human circulatory system. 'These can all be understood', he says, 'as patterns that use minimal energy to achieve the most efficient flow through a system' (Goodwin, 2007, p. 43). Other writers, such as Philip Ball (1999) and Mark Buchanan (2003), have collected a body of scientific evidence revealing such a self-similarity of pattern formation in nature. While Serres claims that he derives his structuralist background from mathematics, the similarities of his comparative methodology to that of Claude Lévi-Strauss are nevertheless important.[5] In the same way that Goodwin argues that in biology there are only a limited number of stable forms available, Lévi-Strauss argues the same for human culture; that while each of these forms will be different according to the context, and thus unpredictable in its actuality, there lurks beneath this surface appearance of a self-similarity of (virtual) structure. But while not dismissing the links between his methodology and that of Lévi-Strauss, Serres explains that he feels closer to Georges Dumézil, who he considers 'applied an authentic structuralism to the humanities' (Serres et al., 1997, p. 36) and refers, throughout his own work, to the three invariant classes or anthropological classifications of social functions described by him: Jupiter, the ruling sovereign or sacred function; Mars, the armed struggle or military function, war; and Quirinus, the function of production, commerce and exchange. While not contesting the apparent universal presence of these three social classifications, Serres does stress, in line with our discussion above, a vitally important mode of their presence: that 'the invariance of these classes is not of the essence' (Serres, 1995a, p. 82). The forms of these three classes or structures are not ideal in the Platonic sense, they do not exist in some manner prior to the structures they give birth to. Rather they are emergent from their background conditions, they are islands of order within a sea of disorder, they are themselves born:

> ... born of the *noise* from which those three gods, these three concepts, these three objects, these three theoretical classes, these three social groups are born. History is not born of provinces, but of circumstances (Serres, 1995a, p. 100).

That these circumstances or environmental conditions consistently allow for the emergence and repetition of the same but evolving sets of basic forms is, I want to argue, probably the key concept to understanding the methodology of Serres. It is this repetition that we experience as the folding of time – we experience the same self-organization and the same emergent social forms as different social groups across both different geographical spaces and different chronological times have done, not because there exists some Platonic Form of which they are copies, but because energy and information flows taking the paths of least resistance have found these forms to be the most stable, given the conditions of the prevailing milieu. Time is folded and crumpled because life, existence, is topological rather the geometrical. This 'science of nearness and rifts' that allows such juxtapositions is topology, and it is opposed to 'the science of stable and well-defined distances ... called metrical geometry.' Serres explains with the metaphor of a folded and crumpled handkerchief: 'it's simply the difference between topology (the handkerchief is folded, crumpled, shredded) and geometry (the same fabric is ironed out flat)' (Serres et al., 1997, p. 60).

The repetition, or, dare I suggest, the eternal return of these basic patterns or forms is best discovered through synthesis rather than analysis, through a comparative methodology. Serres notes that 'the sailors of yesteryear are the only ones who remember that you can't reach your destination with just one sea-mark; you need at least two – it's an error to take only one alignment reading, in a single direction' (Serres et al., 1997, p. 178). Given a compass, a map, and two sea-marks, through a process of triangulation, your position is indicated at the place where the two angles converge. In *The Troubadour of Knowledge*, he makes a similar reference when he states that '[m]any sets are necessary, and that they must cross each other in the centre of the compass, so that meaning/direction will spring forth' (Serres, 1997, p. 18). This, in a very general sense, is what Serres means by the need for a third position; a position derived from the triangulation of at least two other positions; a methodology for deriving knowledge in general. Serres also points to the discovery by Kepler that stars follow elliptical orbits, not circular ones, and that, therefore, they need at least a second, if not 'several dark foci'. This means that the 'real centre of each orbit lies precisely in a third place, just between these two foci – the shinning globe and the dark point' (Serres, 1997, p. 37). He extends this metaphor to point out, in line with his comparative methodology, that knowledge requires at least two sources of light; that a single source of light, of knowledge, blinds us to the second "dark focus" – that a single source of light obscures either through its brightness or through the shadows it creates: 'At least two sources of light are necessary', he says, 'if not, what's presented is simply a position, which rapidly becomes a directive that is imperialistic, necessary, obligatory', and adds that 'the best light is obtained in the mingled region of interferences between the two sources' (Serres et al., 1997, pp. 178–79). This chiaroscuro, as he often terms it, picking up on the artistic term for the distribution of light and dark, represents the space occupied by the crossbreed, the half-breed, the third-instructed – the roaming seeker of comparative knowledge and understanding. So, through a rather circular route, we have again arrived at Deleuze's nomadology.

At the beginning of the previous paragraph, I implied a link between this repetition of a self-similarity of form and Nietzsche's concept of the eternal return. In *Difference and Repetition*, Deleuze attempts to enfold this much discussed and provocative concept into his own thinking. He argues, as we have discussed, that identity is a secondary principle, not the primary principle of the tradition, and that such a 'Copernican revolution ... opens up the possibility of difference having its own concept, rather than being maintained under the domination of a concept in general already understood as identical'. He adds that 'Nietzsche meant nothing more than this by eternal return'. In other words, that identity within the eternal return is a secondary power to that of difference, that identity is 'produced by difference, is determined as "repetition"'. The eternal return, on Deleuze's reading, is the return of the different and 'consists of conceiving the same on the basis of the different'.

But, and this is important for my argument, 'Only the extreme forms return' (Deleuze, 1994, pp. 40–1). Both writers, I would like to suggest, see the emergence and repetition of certain "extreme forms" as being of great significance, providing that their actual form and any notion of identity takes a back seat to the powers of difference that produced them. Deleuze explains this through the use of a very technical vocabulary, while Serres attempts a practical demonstration. It is through this comparative methodology that the repetition of emergent patterning can be disclosed, and it is this emergent periodicity or patterning that Serres refers to as time.

I would, though, like to highlight a particular methodological metaphor used by both writers, and one that has crept into my own description above: that concerning the use of maps. In *A Thousand Plateaus*, Deleuze and Guattari write:

> The rhizome is altogether different, a map and not a tracing. The orchid does not reproduce the tracing of the wasp; it forms a map with the wasp, in a rhizome. What distinguishes the map from the tracing is that it is entirely oriented toward experimentation in contact with the real. The map does not reproduce an unconscious closed in upon itself; it constructs the unconscious. It fosters connections between fields, the removal of blockages on bodies without organs, the maximum opening of bodies without organs onto a plane of consistency (Deleuze and Guattari, 2004, p. 13).

Here a tracing is aligned with representation and the codification of hierarchical thinking, while the production of a map is expressed as the experimental and active production of contacts and connections that allow for movement and escape. Serres often uses the term "map" to describe what he produces. For him, his books are guides for future travellers. Philosophy, he says, 'is an anticipation of future thoughts and practices', and 'not only must philosophy invent', he continues, but it must invent 'the common ground for future inventions. It's function is to invent the conditions of invention'. (Serres et al., 1997, p. 86, original emphasis). Using the notion of maps, however, needs a warning: the landscapes that we are negotiating are fluid, turbulent, complex and multiple, and the structures produced, the maps, are also fluid and reflect the relations that allow for the emergence of objects rather than the objects themselves. Serres has likened this exploration of relations, of prepositions or the spaces between, to negotiating the complex and fractal landscape/sea scape of the 'shores, islands, and fractal ice floes' of the Northwest Passage (Serres et al., 1997, p. 70). He is, though, cautious with his use of the term, in one instance preferring the image of a maritime chart – 'an ocean of possible routes, [which] fluctuates and does not remain static like a map. Each route invents itself' (Serres et al., 1997, p. 70), but on other occasions he likens it to the emergence of patterns: '... once estab-lished, thousands of relations, here, there, everywhere – after a while, when you step back and look, a picture emerges. Or at least a map. You see a gen-eral theory of relations ...' (Serres et al., 1997, p. 112). Elsewhere, he likens what he is composing to a weather map, complete with its 'turbulences, over-lapping cyclones and anticyclones' (Serres et al., 1997, p. 122) and the weav-ing together of networks to the drawing up of a road map.

I have also, throughout this paper, implied a connection between both writers and complexity science. Making such a connection explicit would have been a luxury not afforded by the space at my disposal; however, one brief reference is worth making.[6] In a recent paper, Francis Heylighen notes that 'complex systems such as organisms or minds have evolved internal models of the environment. This allows them to try out a potential action "virtually", in the model, and use the model to decide on fitness' (Heylighen, 1999, p. 16). These models are mental maps. The production of these maps is best achieved, Serres suggests, through '"comparativism" rather than sequential thinking' (Serres et al., 1997, p. 73), a process that requires intu-ition and imagination: 'Even in the sciences the imagination does the ground breaking' and 'Intuition is, above all things in the world, the rarest, but most equally distributed among inventors – be they artists or scientists. Yes, intu-ition strikes the first blows.' In other words, both Serres and Deleuze, in their own ways, argue that consciousness or self-consciousness is a self-organizing creative process that, when not restricted by the stasis of ready-made forms or objects, when not held captive by Platonic Forms, the State, by representative thinking in general, compares, simultaneously, a vast amount of data and finds patterns that connect it to its environment or to other experiences or maps, a process that is first achieved by our imagina-tion and intuition, a process that discovers those turbulent and fluid forms that provide the virtual background to our actual experiences – that discovers, in the repetition of these forms, time itself!

Serres' methodology, while appearing erratic, actively demonstrates the maps it attempts to produce; maps that guide our interpretation or under-standing of our world through their uncovering or disclosure of the repeti-tion of certain emergent patterns that reveal a deep self-organizing principle in nature; maps that guide our way through his writings. But the important point is that these maps need to be of our own construction. Our under-standing of his work is achicved in the same way that our knowledge and understanding of our world are created through our experiencing the repetitions and recurrences of life – in experiencing and making connections between the differential repetitions. We develop the same skills. If he just "told us", he would be representing the "truth", presenting us with statues that slow down to the point of stasis our relationship with our milieu, and in so doing we would be unable to discern the emergence of form. This emergent, rhythmic patterning, out of a background *noise*, is time – or rather, as these patterns are multiple, are times. Our ability to both navigate and actively reflect on these processes, our consciousness and self-consciousness, are themselves born of, are emergent from, the self-same processes, and self-organize in the same dynamic non-linear way. If we follow Serres lead and attempt to 'think the multiple as such', and adopt a similar comparative methodology, we would remove the constraints imposed upon consciousness by our rigid and static concepts of linear logic and our belief in the existence of pre-formed unities, and we would facilitate the development of our "natural", self-organizing and creative processes, processes that rely on the imagination and intuition, processes capable of reproducing the same fractal patterning from which they are emergent.

Notes

[1] This is the key book for understanding his ontology. Deleuze notes, in the Preface to the English Edition, that 'All he has done since is connected to this book, including what I wrote with Guattari'.

[2] For a more detailed exploration of Serres' attitude to analysis and abstract thinking, see his *The Five Senses*.

[3] See Serres' *The Birth of Physics* for a detailed exploration of Lucretius' *On the Nature of the Universe* and ancient atomism.

[4] In *Being and Event*, Badiou attempts to explain multiplicity through the utilization of the Zermelo-Fraenkel axioms of set theory. While this formalization is in opposition to the methodology of Serres, Badiou's description of the void is remarkably close to Serres' description of *noise*.

[5] In particular, see Lévi-Strauss' *Structural Anthropology*.

[6] For a good general introduction to complexity science and its relationship to philosophy – particularly philosophy within the post-structural flow of contemporary though – see Cilliers' *Complexity and Postmodernism*.

Bibliography

Badiou, A. (2007), *Being and Event*. London: Continuum.

Ball, P. (1999), *The Self-Made Tapestry: Pattern Formation in Nature*. Oxford: Oxford University Press.

Buchanan, M. (2003), *Small World*. London: Phoenix.

Cilliers, P. (1998), *Complexity and Postmodernism*. Abingdon: Routledge.

Deleuze, G. (1994). *Difference and Repetition*. London: The Athlone Press.

Deleuze, G. and Guattari, F. (2004), *A Thousand Plateaus*. London: The Athlone Press.

Goodwin, B. (2001), *How The Leopard Changed Its Spots*. Princeton: Princeton University Press.

—(2007), *Nature's Due*. Edinburgh: Floris Books.

Heylighen, F. (1999), 'The science of self-organization and adaptivity' (published by Principia Cybernetica Web at http:// pespmc1.vub.ac.be/papers/EOLSS-Self-Organiz.pdf).

Lévi-Strauss, C. (1963), *Structural Anthropology*. New York: Basic Books.

Lucretius (1997), *On the Nature of the Universe*. Translated by R. Melville. Oxford: Oxford University Press.

Serres, M. (1995a), *Genesis*. Michigan: The University of Michigan Press.

—(1995b), *The Natural Contract*. Michigan: The University of Michigan Press.

—(1997), *The Troubadour of Knowledge*. Michigan: The University of Michigan Press.

—(2000), *The Birth of Physics*. Manchester: The Clinamen Press.

—(2008), *The Five Senses*. London: Continuum.

Serres, M. and Latour, B. (1995), *Conversations on Science, Culture and Time*. Michigan: The University of Michigan Press.

Solzhenitsyn, A. (2003), *Cancer Ward*. London: Vintage.

Chapter 3

Michel Serres: From the History of Mathematics to Critical History

David Webb

In the closing lines of *The Birth of Physics*, Michel Serres calls for the invention of 'liquid history' (Serres, 2000, p. 191; 1977, p. 237). The book itself argues passionately that forms of thought based on the fixed outlines and movement of solids should be displaced by forms of thought modelled on the complex dynamics of fluid flow. In thinking about the significance of Serres' work on history, it would therefore be tempting to take up this theme and set out the ways in which his writing exemplifies the adoption of a model of fluid flow in relation to history and to writing about history. However, there is another theme in *The Birth of Physics* that is at once crucial for the reading he develops there, and is reflected throughout his work, and it is primarily with this that I want to deal here. His case for treating the atomist physics presented by Lucretius in *On the Nature of the Universe* as a rigorous science, rather than a work of poetic fancy, rests on the way he matches the imagination and philosophical richness of its verse form to the mathematics of Archimedes. Together, Serres proposes, they provide a materialist account of the emergence of physical form that incorporates the principles of complexity and of non-linear dynamics, and which goes on to provide the basis for a description of nature, but also of the mind, society, morality, culture and more besides. Although the application of complexity theory outside of the natural sciences has become almost routine, it is worth reflecting on the possible consequences of such a move. There is, for example, a risk that it may encourage a form of reductionism, albeit non-deterministic, that prolongs an old prejudice against the possibility, or at least the status, of the human sciences. One of the virtues of Serres' work is the way it resists such an interpretation by revealing channels of communication between different discursive regions. In this paper I have traced the development of this resistance back not only to Serres' early advocacy of structuralism, but also to the way themes central to structuralism were modified as a result of Serres' engagement with work on the historical character of mathematics by philosophers such as Jean Cavaillès. These changes prepared the way for a distinctive sense of history to emerge, which has been a consistent feature of Serres' writing. However, the extension of this sense of history beyond mathematics and purely formal discourses required a crucial contribution from atomism, which is where we come to the idea of 'liquid history'. In fact, we shall see that perhaps the most significant thing about the sense of history that Serres advocates in *The Birth of Physics* is the way it generalizes a dissolution of the distinction between transcendental conditions and empirical events. Not only does Serres achieve this without falling into a simple naturalization of philosophy, he also opens up the possibility of a distinctive form of critical history.

The story involves too many steps for me to cover them all here with the care they deserve; my aim is simply to set out what I regard as key elements in Serres' development of a conception of history.[1]

The importance of mathematics in other forms of discourse, and in history in particular, featured in Serres' writing from very early on. In the Introduction to *Hermès I: La Communication*, a piece written in 1961, Serres already proposes that a structural analysis drawing heavily on mathematical formalism can make an important contribution to historical, literary and philosophical critique (Serres, 1968a, p. 33). In this respect, he was writing as an enthusiastic supporter of structuralism. Indeed, François Dosse suggests that Serres was 'without doubt the first philosopher to define an explicitly structuralist global programme in the field of philosophy' (Dosse, 1992, p. 115; 1997, p. 89). It is easy to see why, if one reads the first chapter of *Hermès I*, 'Structure et importation: des mathématiques aux mythes,' in which Serres wholeheartedly endorses the structuralist emphasis on the formal at the expense of the attribution of meaning to individual elements in cultural and historical life, and sees no obstacle to the extension of this method beyond the fields of linguistics and anthropology in which it had already been deployed with conspicuous results. However, he is also sensitive to a question regarding the conception of form and its application. The contemporary conception of critique (at the beginning of the 1960s) could, writes Serres, be described as moving at the limits of a difficult relation between what he calls the classicism of a formal discourse concerned with truth, and a romanticism that aims to explore the meaning of our pluralistic historical and cultural life via its symbolic expression. In structuralism, Serres sees an opportunity to move this conception of critique forwards, beyond what remains an uncomfortable conjunction of contrasting methodologies. However, there are several obstacles to achieving this, and by no means the least of these is the difficulty of overcoming the distinction between two very different kinds of analysis. Classicism aspires to a mathematical conception of order that stands apart from the contents to which it gives form. By contrast, writes Serres, symbolic analysis aims to construct 'a concrete model' within the field of historical and cultural life under analysis, referring to its specific contents rather than to its order (Serres, 1968a, p. 22). The contents themselves are understood as repetitions of a symbolic model, rather than as copies of an ideal form. The analyses of Hegel, Nietzsche and Freud are in this sense symbolic and archetypal, appealing to figures from mythical history such as Apollo, Dionysus, Ariadne, Zarathustra, Electra and Oedipus; the meaning of a cultural phenomenon is established 'when one can show that it is a re-commencement, that it reiterates the archetype, that it realizes it anew, that it makes it pass from myth to history, from the eternal to the evolutionary' (Serres, 1968a, p. 23). However, Serres notes that the language of symbols only partially breaks with the notion of ideal forms, since the symbolic is in effect a translation of such forms into an historical dimension of myths and archetypes (Serres, 1968a, pp. 22–3). There is a difference between methodologies, then, but not one that is decisive; and the pursuit of meaning in cultural and historical life appears to remain tied to a form of idealism it sought to avoid.

This is Serres' summary of the position in the period up to the time he was writing. However, at that time a new possibility for a form of critical history had arisen from work in the philosophy of mathematics, involving a new perspective on the idea of a meta-language and thereby a new relation between levels of analysis. To see how Serres approaches this from the situation described so far, one has to note that for him what is most characteristic of the appeal to symbols and myths is less the particular symbols and myths chosen, than the fact that a choice exists at all and that there is a variation between the symbols and myths chosen. The appeal to figures from mythical history was, he observes, a feature of a strand of the nineteenth century, but even in that period alternatives existed, and one's choice depended on the kind of question asked; that is, on the field of study. If one were to pose the problem of the true, one would have mathematics as a guide; if one were to pose the problem of experience, it would be mechanics, physics or the philosophy of nature; and if one were to consider the meanings within cultures, 'one would have the whole ensemble of archetypes provided by the immemorial memory of humanity' (Serres, 1968a, p. 24). The fact that one can choose different myths according to the field one wishes to analyse leaves open the question of the relation between them and of the reason for associating a given field with a given myth or set of myths. The work of Gaston Bachelard, which Serres places at the centre of this chapter, throws a significant light on this question.

In the late 1930s, Bachelard began a series of studies on the poetic imagination, which he envisaged as divided into two contrasting kinds. To the
imagination engaged in the invention of new forms, he counterposed an
imagination with an affinity for the material elements. From this second
kind arise images prompted by fire, water, air and earth; images that encap-
sulate something distinctive of a given element without recourse to the
unity set in place by form. These are, writes Bachelard, 'direct images of
matter' (Bachelard, 1942, p. 8), which occur as a variety of psychic states
that change little or not at all over long spans of time. As a consequence,
the images themselves have an archetypal quality. Still or slow moving water,
for example, conjures images of death; fire combines life and death. What
interests Serres in this poetics is the way Bachelard's writing on the four elements can be seen as a variation of the model familiar to us from the past.
However, it is in his view an exceptional variation and for two reasons. First,
the four elements take over the roles of figures from mythical history; for
example, Empedocles and Prometheus are treated as particular manifestations of fire; Ophelia as a manifestation of water. This establishes a level of
generality that encompasses, and so forecloses, further possible variations.
Moreover, and this is the second point, relating mythical figures in culture
to the elements of ancient natural history, which are themselves almost
mythical, has a dramatic consequence.

> [I]n a dazzling short-circuit, this ensemble of choices is at once designated
> (according to a chiasmatic diagram) as the original source [l'originel] of
> clear scientific models, in a psychoanalysis of objective knowledge, and as
> the original source of symbolic cultural archetypes, in a psychoanalysis of
> the material signifying imagination (Serres, 1968a, p. 24).

With the generalization of the myths chosen, those of human life and those
of nature converge and what had previously been exclusively the symbolic
world of cultural meaning is, at least potentially, opened to the formal clarity of the sciences.[2] The gap between classicism and romanticism thereby
closes, at least to some degree. For Bachelard, it does not close entirely, as
the two forms of imagination remain fundamentally distinct. Serres, on the
other hand, appears to treat the move as an indication that it is possible to
think together the human world of symbolic meaning and the natural world
of order and truth, whose paradigm remains mathematical formalism.
Structuralism would be the methodology allowing one to do this, and
thereby to move beyond the separation of fields of study that Serres
described earlier, each marked by the choice of a different set of myths. In

this way, it should be possible to introduce a formal language describing the relations between the elements of any given myth; a formal account that allows a translation not just between the myths of different cultures relating to a particular practice, but also between the myths informing different cultural discourses. This suggests the possibility of moving between the discourses concerned with truth, experience and cultural meaning; something that became a hallmark of Serres' writing.

There is, it seems to me, an ambiguity in Serres' presentation of this form of history that arises with the convergence of human life and nature. On the one hand, the opportunity appears to belong to structuralism, as the discourse best placed to deliver a formal analysis over a new extended range, albeit one perhaps modified in certain respects. On the other hand, the very possibility of such a new form of history appears to arise as a direct consequence of Bachelard's introduction of the four elements into the analysis of historical and cultural life (or at least into an account of a form of imagination). To this extent, the balance tips away from structuralism as such. Rather than simply being allowed to extend its range, its resources appear to be appropriated to a new task. On this reading, the singularity of meaning embedded in historical life is not to be so freely handed over. Later, it is clear that Serres came to have strong reservations over the idea of a formal discourse having the scope that he appears to have envisaged in this early text. In *Genesis,* he reflects on how, after a long pursuit of ontological unity and simplicity with the tools of reason failed either to master or adequately to articulate the multiplicities that remained dispersed both within them and outside them, we have been "obliged" to turn our attention from beings to the relationships between them; a description that is perhaps not unique to structuralism, but which certainly includes it. Tellingly, Serres then adds a note of caution: 'We have supposed this was a decisive and necessary step forward, but perhaps it was only a detour' (Serres, 1982, p.17; Serres, 1995, p. 3).

Returning to the context of Serres' early advocacy of structuralism, the difficulty with a formal analysis of the relations between different discourses is that the relation between form and contents remains too close to a traditional idealism. At the level of symbolic meaning, the model is to be constructed within the field analysed, while at the level of structural analysis the model appears to transcend the contents of a given field precisely insofar as it allows one to identify an invariance between elements in the structure of distinct fields. In effect, either there remain two models, or there is an ambiguity insofar as the model is at once indigenous to the field in question and yet also suspended beyond it, drifting somehow independently from the concrete cultural meanings that move in from different quarters to fill it. The upshot is that if the model is to work in the way Serres describes, for there to be a new relation between form and the concreteness of cultural life, the very conception of form and its relation to content, to the concrete, has to be thoroughly revised. This is something that Serres appears already to acknowledge in *Hermès I* when he writes that the task handed down to us by Bachelard is twofold: first, to write a new account of scientific rationality, a new epistemology; second, to undertake a new form of critique directed at historical and cultural life. The second, he adds, is underway (a reference to Lévi-Strauss, but also to Michel Foucault), but cannot be carried through properly until progress is made with the first, and this remained (at the time Serres was writing) a task for the future. I now want to look at what Serres hoped to gain from the development of such an epistemology.

Modern mathematics and modern science had begun to provide a new conception of formal thought and its possibilities, but in the absence of a thorough reflection on these developments, the critique of historical and cultural life was faced by two unsatisfactory options: either to continue as before, trying to fold together conceptions of form and content that are fundamentally distinct in nature, and thus to remain within an essentially Kantian framework that was beginning to appear a constraint for the human sciences, or else themselves to piece together an incomplete picture of the new possibilities presented by formal thought, in order to employ them in their own analyses.[3]

The changes that Serres has in mind arose from developments in mathematics. For some time, he writes, it has been the case that epistemology has no longer been a prescriptive 'science of sciences,' but rather a discourse in a meta-language that describes a particular "regional" scientific practice (Serres, 1968a, p. 66). One would expect that once this discourse relinquished the authority and universality traditionally characteristic of a meta-language, it would have to explain the principle of its coherence, and above all the nature of its relation to the scientific discourse it describes. However, in the case of mathematics, there is a simple and emphatic response: this epistemological meta-language does not exist, 'for mathematics has sufficient meta-languages to speak of itself, to describe itself, and even to found itself' (Serres, 1968a, p. 66). Epistemological truth is itself descriptive and speaks a meta-language that is the same as the language it describes. As Serres puts it, epistemology is "imported" entirely into the field of mathematics itself (Serres, 1968a, p. 67) and there is, then, no theory of mathematics beyond mathematics itself. To explain how this works fully, it is helpful to turn briefly to the work of Jean Cavaillès.

If Cavaillès's interest centred the foundation of mathematics, his primary concern was that its status as a deductive science should not compromise its capacity for innovation and thereby its authentically historical character. Yet precisely this, it seemed to him, was the inevitable consequence of placing the foundation of mathematics in any fixed formal structure, whether this be logic, an axiomatic base, or the structure of transcendental consciousness. Instead, Cavaillès sought to demonstrate that mathematics could, and should, be viewed as a wholly autonomous formal discipline grounded in its own distinct historicity. On his way to formulating this proposal, Cavaillès broke with what he identifies as the Kantian principle that the ground of the formal unity of our experience precedes the act through which that experience is constituted. One is led to accept this precedence, he suggested, by regarding the division between form and matter as fundamental, such that form remains immune from the effects of variation in material content. However, it supports a view of change as a series of material variations on form that remains essentially fixed in advance and thereby sets the bounds of any possible change at the material level.

To move away from this requires a consideration of how change occurs, and this means, to stay within a Kantian perspective, to understand how the rules that govern synthesis occur, how they determine the appearance of concrete things and how they themselves may change. To begin with the first of these questions, for Kant, it is the transcendental imagination that brings a manifold of intuitions under the unity of a concept by the transcendental. However, Cavaillès is unwilling to go down this route, and moreover thinks that there is no necessity to do so, at least not as long as one is dealing with mathematics. In his view, the division between form and content may be fundamental to empirical experience, but not to the construction of mathematical objects, since these are not synthesized from intuitions. At any given stage of mathematical thought, concepts from earlier stages themselves become the objects of reflection and the material from which new concepts and objects are constructed. As a consequence, there is no fundamental, or ontological, distinction between concepts and objects. With the fall of this division, a change occurs to the constraints on thought that previously arose from the tension between formal rules and the object they disclose. As long as this division is in place, thought will meet its limits either in the unchanging nature of its formal conditions, or in a resistance arising from the material there to be thought (or represented). Where objects are constructed from the formal apparatus of thought itself, the constraints on thought cannot be externally imposed. This by no means entails that an 'anything goes' approach. On the contrary, Cavaillès is concerned with how deductivity can survive within a historically developing discipline. Closely connected with this, for Cavaillès, is the question of the unity that mathematics must have if it is to preserve its status as a science. Cavaillès proposes that this unity can be found in the very movement of the historical development of mathematics, which he describes as 'an unstoppable conceptual becoming (Cavaillès, 1994, p. 505). Mathematics therefore has no need for any transcendental condition or metaphysical ground to determine the proper bounds of its legitimacy, since it performs these functions itself. If mathematics has an essential nature, it is determined by its own development, by the continuity spanning its history, with all its bifurcations and revisions. The unity of this movement also determines the historically specific limits of what is possible at any time. And yet in doing so, it is already indicating the direction in which thought must, with a necessity that only reveals itself retrospectively, step into a future that is still unknown and undertake what existing rules declare impossible. Each stage in a problematic is prepared by the last, even as its construction modifies the limits of possibility that determined the stage from which it emerges. In this way, Cavaillès proposes a view of form as itself the outcome of a process whose development is governed by rules determined anew at each stage. Even if we think we are looking at a change in a higher order determination of mathematical concepts and objects, in fact we are always dealing with a specific change that has emerged from a well-defined series of antecedent operations. Movement is always of the whole of mathematics (Cavaillès, 1994, p. 556), and is to be understood as the revision of everything that has come before (Cavaillès, 1994, p. 560). To see the development of a mathematical problematic as a perpetually re-opened breach into the future is quite different to seeing it as the adjustment of a structure towards an equilibrium with itself, and the difference springs from the recognition that the structure is itself the vehicle of change. The situation in which the formal conditions that determine the possible objects of mathematics, the path its development, and thereby the unity from which it draws its scientific character, are all set by mathematics itself is precisely that described by Serres when he writes that mathematics has taken over the role of its own epistemology. As Cavaillès clarifies, it is from the ongoing reflection on its own concepts and methods that mathematics moves forward; or as Serres writes, '[T]he epistemological intention of modern mathematics has been the condition and the motor of its development' (Serres, 1968a, p. 67).

There are two important observations to make about this conception of the historical character of mathematics. The first is that mathematics exemplifies the possibility of a formal discourse that is at the same time essentially historical, which in turn shows that the formal character of such a discourse need not be modelled on the classical ideal of 'order'; or, to put this the other way around, the example of modern mathematics shows that history is not confined to the realm of symbolic expression. The second observation is that mathematics constructs its objects within the field under analysis; something that Serres recorded as necessary if structuralism were to avoid relying on a pre-given or antecedent (ideal) form that determines the truth of the field in question. This is achieved, as noted above, by problematizing its own concepts, such that mathematics can be said to construct its form from its own content, and the rules that determine the possibilities of each stage are themselves in evolution; not in a gradual approach to an ideal form, but in an ongoing dynamic involving a continual exchange between formal conditions and the content, or meaning, they determine. It is true that Cavaillès describes this exchange as dialectic, but one should not assume that it is therefore easily assimilated to a form of Hegelianism. Under the influence of figures such as Jean Hyppolite and Alexandre Kojève, French thought in the 1930s and 1940s was no stranger to Hegelian philosophy, but for Cavaillès there is no teleology at work in the historical development of mathematics, the process is not driven by negation and there is no impulse towards self-recognition and the identity it secures. Rather, even within the bounds of the unity of a deductive science, Cavaillès endorses a methodology of continual problematization in something akin to a spirit of experimentation.[4]

Taken together, these two points suggest that modern mathematics provides the epistemology required to sustain the new form of historical and cultural critique that Serres could sense just beyond the horizon at which, in Bachelard, the myths of nature and of human life coincide. However, while mathematics indicates a possible future, it does not in itself solve all of the problems associated with the development of a critical discourse of such a kind. In particular, for all the talk about coincidence and the problematization of concepts, the relation between form and meaning is still far from clear. The difficulty is perhaps less acute in the case of mathematics, where concepts and objects are ontologically more proximate to one another, but if the approach outlined in relation to mathematics is to be extended to historical and cultural life, the old distinctions between the currency of thought and its object begin to reassert themselves. In order for the transformation that Serres envisages to occur, an explanation is needed of the relation between form and that which becomes meaningful through the acquisition of form, and moreover it should convey the ontological proximity of the two aspects (in Deleuze's terms, it should be set out in terms of the univocity of being). In fact, to return to the beginning of this paper, Serres has just such an explanation available in the Lucretian atomism he explores in *The Birth of Physics*.

At one level, *The Birth of Physics* is simply an extended meditation on *On the Nature of the Universe*, written by Lucretius in the first century BC, which was itself a presentation of the philosophy of Epicurus, written roughly 300 years before that. Yet as a meditation, it is also an irrepressibly passionate book, enlivened by rushes of excitement and expressions of praise, frustration and sometimes fury, through the course of which Serres composes a defence of a philosophy firmly at odds with idealism of every kind, and, one must therefore presume, its legacy in the authority commonly accorded to the priority of form as this is usually understood. And of course, it does this by calling on the support of mathematics, in the guise of Archimedes, as a neglected counterpart to the verse of Lucretius. Serres argues that the works of Archimedes provide a mathematical language that describes precisely similar themes and phenomena in a complementary way: equilibrium and disequilibrium, fluid flow, large populations, helixes, conic sections and, above all, indeterminacy. Since Lucretius, having begun with an explication of the principles of atomism, moves on to deal with the formation of worlds, meteorological phenomena, society, the body and sexual reproduction, the mind and ethics (the main themes alone), Serres' work amounts to a claim that the scope of the role accorded to mathematics can be extended to include phenomena in cultural and historical life.

Lucretius describes an infinite universe in which there are just atoms and void. Although the universe has no beginning as such, there is an 'initial condition' in which atoms rain down through the void in parallel lines, and as a consequence there is a kind of blank chaos. However, the laminar flow is disrupted, which brings the atoms into contact with one another, leading in turn to turbulence and thus to the formation of vortices and relatively stable pockets of order sustained by the iteration of a cycle. The iteration is never exact, and over time the order is destined to break down, releasing the atoms back into the wider flow. The initial disruption arises by virtue of a minimal deviation in the path of an atom, the clinamen, which occurs spontaneously 'at an indefinite time and place' (Lucretius, 1999, Book II, pp. 218–19). Because Lucretius declares it impossible to identify a true cause of the clinamen, it has historically been regarded with suspicion as something like an ad hoc hypothesis to account for the emergence of order, yet without providing an adequate explanation; as if the clinamen were an irresponsible rogue usurping the place rightly held by either God or physical law. The criticism is an unfair one for several reasons, of which I shall mention two. First, the clinamen does not fall accidently beneath the threshold of perception and measurement, as if, in spite of appearances, there is an unbroken causal chain that improvements in our instruments of measurement will reveal. Rather, it marks an irreducible complexity in dynamic systems. While phenomena can be explained by the movement of atoms, this movement itself cannot be resolved into a final law-governed description. There is "knowledge" of this pre-phenomenal stage, but not "science" (Serres, 2000, p. 122; 1977, p. 152). Second, and this point follows from the first, prior to the emergence of order in the vortices that form within the more general chaos, there is no discernible law at all. It is, writes Serres, only when relations are established that we can speak of a law manifest in their regularity: 'As soon as a phenomenon appears, as soon as a body is formed, a law can be expressed' (Serres, 2000, p. 122; 1977, p. 152). This approach entails a change in the conception of law. Rather than a law setting a universal condition governing all possible appearances of a given kind (*foedera fati*), it describes a regularity that has emerged from the process or processes to which the law itself applies (*foedera natura*). The difference is decisive, in part for reasons to do with Lucretius's promotion of peace and an Epicurean ethic in contrast to what he regards as the martial associations of the view of law as a universal condition.[5] However, it is also decisive because it closes the (ontological) gap between form and what is determined by form, and thereby speaks to concerns over the appropriateness of the idea that form is "constructed" within the field under analysis. Insofar as law, or form, is a regularity emerging from the field itself, it is not fundamentally distinct from what conforms to it and construction amounts to the recognition of what is already implicit within the phenomenon itself. There is, therefore, no need to explain the coincidence between form and the meaning, as though it were a union of heterogeneous elements.

The point can also be made in two further ways, which are not incompatible with one another. If one follows Lucretius in his description of atoms as letters that combine to form larger assemblages that have both meaning and a regular structure (Lucretius, 1994, II, pp. 687–97, pp. 1013–21). As in the case of atoms, there are no laws to determine how such assemblages should be formed prior to their actual emergence: 'as soon as the text or the word appears, there appear laws of good formation, of combination, of conjugation' (Serres, 2000, p. 123; 1977, p. 152). As Serres adds, law is a repetition of what is already there, and 'From fact to law, the distance is null' (Serres, 2000, p. 123; 1977, p. 153). Things appear bearing their own language, not merely inscribed upon them, but woven seamlessly into the very fabric of their bodily nature, of their appearing at all. This is a point to which I will return shortly. In addition, one can look at the transformation in the notion of form directly. Serres notes that in *Problems of General Linguistics*, Emil Benveniste observes that a flow of water cannot form a rhythm, because the flow is continuous and uniform, whereas rhythm requires repetition or a turn of the water back upon itself. Yet for the early atomists Leucippus and Democritus, rhythm signified form. If Benveniste were right, flow cannot itself constitute form, which must therefore be given to the flow from outside (Serres, 2000, pp. 153–54; 1997, p. 190). Of course, Serres disagrees, proposing instead that rhythm is the form adopted by atoms as they conjoin in the first vortex or whirl (Serres, 2000, p. 154; 1977 p. 154). This means that whereas Benveniste places himself in a Platonic tradition by believing that form must be impervious to flow, which is its job to shape and make meaningful, Serres endorses the atomist view that flow itself composes form, and form is implicit in flow.

The discourse of atomism is important for Serres in that it provides a way of extending the changes that modern mathematics introduced regarding the relation between form and meaning beyond the field of mathematics itself. If, in mathematics, change occurs through the turning back of mathematics upon itself via the problematization of its own concepts, which Serres also describes as the importation of epistemology into the field of mathematics itself, in atomism there is a recursive pattern as events occur according to a law that will in turn be modified by events in the future. The law provides a model that is reiterated in and by the events whose order it describes, but not a hard and fast condition of possibility of such events, which will vary over the course of a series of iterations, sometimes more so and sometimes less. As Serres wrote apropos of structuralism back in 1961, the model is repeated in a series of variations through which it becomes history. The vital thing is to see that this involves the coalescence of a form, and not the embodiment, incarnation or actualization of a pre-existing ideal.

In the chapter in *The Birth of Physics* entitled 'History', Serres describes and then seeks to resolve a challenge presented by the research he had been undertaking. Summing up his findings – the extent to which Archimedes and Lucretius prefigured modern science, with its concern for applied knowledge, and the motifs of planes, equilibrium, inclination – he interrupts himself, 'Sudden anxiety: what is history about?' (Serres, 2000, p. 159; 1977, p. 196). With no response ready, he continues recording further consistencies and continuities: the science of conic sections, infinitesimals, the fall, the spiral. As a historian, and in particular as a historian of science, Serres expected to find radical change, shifts of paradigm, breaks and discontinuities (not least by virtue of his having assimilated the work of Bachelard). Yet this is not what he finds. His prejudices would have been confirmed if he had discovered that ancient science has little interest to offer its modern counterpart; or even that ancient science harboured a distinctive and potentially rich conceptualization that had been eclipsed by the rise of a thoroughly distinctive modern science. Either way, there would still be discontinuity. What he discovers is a way of thinking at once different from the prevailing orthodoxies of philosophy, yet unmistakably present in a long series of variations along the length of the history of science, both modern and pre-modern. Galileo, Newton, Laplace, Carnot, all frame variations on the model traced by Archimedes and Lucretius, in spite of the fact that this debt we bear to the ancients has been largely concealed. Look closely, he argues, and continuities appear that one never suspected.

At least in part, Serres suggests, the discomfort of this unexpected outcome arises as a result of an impoverished conception of time as a line, and history as a curve, ascending or descending, continuous or discontinuous. Such a view encourages the adoption of relatively simple patterns of development and exchange from one context to the next, but also of relatively simple patterns of discontinuity. What he realizes is that apparent continuities he has discovered are not adequately represented by such a way of thinking. His initial alternative is to suggest a geophysical model according to which the rapidly changing surface of the landscape conceals deeper strata that are by comparison almost invariant, their pace of change being so gradual as to be nearly imperceptible. Nonetheless, the different strata are connected and patterns at the surface can be accounted for by the configuration of what lies beneath it. On this reading, the atomist principles of equilibrium and disequilibrium, descent, and flow, constitute the deeper geophysical structure of our knowledge, and the model has the advantage of allowing at least some sense in which different times may be overlaid one on top of the other such that the deeper level is in fact never left behind as a distant past beyond the range of possible influence on the present. But the model does not go far enough in this respect and Serres concludes that it is limited insofar as its contours mirror time, yet 'it keeps us from thinking time as such' (Serres, 2000, p. 163; 1977, p. 201). To overcome this obstacle, an approach that allows a more complex picture to emerge is required.

We recognize several [times]: the irreversible, that of entropy, the fall towards disorder; that, on the other hand, which goes against the current, that of negentropy; the reversible, that of clocks, of the solar system, of our dating, that we have so long taken for that of history ... Now what we are seeking in order to understand history, and not only that of the sciences, is a model that associates, combines and integrates these times. (Serres, 2000, p. 163; 1977, p. 201)

Fortunately, a model is readily at hand. With the abandonment of the geo-physical model, change and relative stability are no longer drawn apart into separate strata. In fact, for Serres, they are both present together in all things, as are the entropic descent into disorder, the emergence of new forms out of instabilities on that descent, and the resistance that sees forms persist for a while. 'Any object in the world', he writes, 'can therefore serve as the model that I'm looking for' (Serres, 2000, p. 163; 1977, p. 201). To understand history, then, is to read these times inscribed in the model that each thing is as it emerges bearing its own language. Indeed, history is the combination of these various times, the rhythmic pattern formed by their interference, and as one reads the language of a thing, one is directed beyond it to the currents, counter-currents, relations, and influences that shape it, and to the dissipations and deformations that undo that shape, sending it spiraling towards its end as a single entity. From each thing, one can read its history, the law of its emergence and of its relations with other things (for the history of a thing is of course never the history of that thing alone).[6]

The law of a thing's emergence is not equivalent to the conditions of possibility underpinning its appearance, for two reasons. First, a condition of possibility underpins any appearance of a given phenomenon as the actualization of a possibility that can be repeated exactly at another time and place, whereas the law of a thing's appearance, as Serres intends it, prepares the unique appearance of particular thing. There is no possibility that can be actualized again. Indeed, not only will the thing in question not appear again in the same way, but also the conditions that prepared its appearance will themselves have changed. Second, the law of a thing's appearance is itself complex. For while the appearance of a thing may be conditioned by events that are local to it in space and time, these events in turn would have been shaped by patterns or regularities that are estab-lished at different scales. Historical events that are distant in a linear or chronological sense from a given moment of time may shape the patterns that continue to influence that moment, even where there is no chain of cause and effect between them. To borrow the analogy of the river often used by Serres, the tiniest movements of a pocket of water will depend not only on the currents flowing around it, but also on the patterns of flow at successively higher scales. This confidence in the translation of form may be regarded as a legacy of Serres' early enthusiasm for structuralism. However, form is not translated perfectly, for as the linear chain of cause and effect becomes more complex, it is no longer characterized by irreversibility: 'the source and the reception are at once effect and cause' (Serres, 1968a, p. 20). This leads to a breakdown in the idea of a temporal sequence, to feedback loops, noise and to a form of temporal pluralism. The thing, as the model from which different times and their inter-relation may be read, allows one to trace both the surface detail of events and what according to the geophysical model Serres called the deep archaeological strata. As Serres notes, the very gradual pace of change in the deeper strata may appear to our more short-lived and accelerated sensibilities to be an invariance in the deeper underlying model of flow, inclination, descent and so forth. Nonetheless, there is change here too, meaning that the most basic laws governing the appearance of a thing will themselves be a part of the historical process.

In the early essay on structuralism, Serres proposed that a new form of historical critique was ready to emerge, if developments in the epistemology of mathematics were acknowledged appropriately. One can now see that to adopt a critical approach to history means to search out the conditions that govern the appearance of a given unique event, not in general principles, but in a combination of the empirical history of events local to it in space and time, and wider patterns of events that extend across history in potentially unpredictable ways. The patterns themselves, though composed of individual events and the appearance, development and dissolution of actual things, are not themselves things that appear as objects of a possible experience, and in this respect they retain something of the a priori about them. In Serres' own work, one can see this in his interpretation of Zola, where the Rougon-Macquart novels are read in terms of a model of thermodynamics and the flow of heat.[7] The elements of the story are understood in terms of their relation to other elements, and the pattern of relations itself is understood through a thermodynamic model, which is in turn a recent reworking of a much older conception of flow, descent and entropy. Whether one begins with a character in the book, or with the book itself, the law by virtue of which it appears and has meaning derives from a larger network of relations established by series of antecedent events at different scales. The scope for a critical history is illustrated by an example concerning space rather than time, in which Serres reflects on the way that his own body does not exist in a simple homogenous space.

> It works in Euclidean space, but it only works there. It sees in a projective space; it touches, caresses and, and, feels in a topological space; it suffers in another; hears and communicates in a third; and so forth, as far as one wishes to go. (Serres, 1983, p. 44)

A culture 'constructs in and by its history' a characteristic pattern according to which such spaces intersect with one another, but it is still up to the individual to establish actual connections between different spaces by negotiating a passage between them: 'whoever fails or refuses to pass like everyone else through the crossroads of these multiple connections ... is treated as ill-adapted or delinquent or disoriented' (Serres, 1983, p. 45).[8] A careful reading of the body will reveal the network of spatial forms and relations within which it exists; forms that do not themselves stand in the world alongside other things, yet for all that remain unmistakably historical by virtue of the appearance of particular sciences at particular times, and by virtue of the changes that the sciences themselves undergo with time. From the model of the individual thing, one can read the laws of its emergence, which themselves emerge and evolve at different levels and at different paces. History is an indispensible medium for this sense of critique, which begins with the model of the thing itself and from there, traces a complex system of relations and regularities (rules), spatial and temporal, which determine its existence. The importance of history for this critique is not confined to it being the context in which the relations occur. Because there is no model given once and for all, the relations in and by which a given thing exists cannot be traced simply by laying a pre-given model on the field under analysis. To trace the relations in and by which a given thing exists is to find in them a pattern, and then to explore the emergence of that pattern itself, its existence as the reiteration of a pattern or form that had already occurred elsewhere and had communicated its laws to other localities. For Serres, these models are predominantly those of fluid flow, of 'liquid history'. Yet there is no general or ideal model that remains invariant at the highest level; not even that of fluid flow itself. There are only variations, until even the "theme" appears to be one more variation among others (Serres, 1997, p. 149).[9] To explore these variations is to reveal existing channels of influence (some of which may be more widely acknowledged than others), but it is at the same time to strengthen some, to weaken others and thereby to intervene in the pattern of their descent. This is the sense in which the history one researches and writes has a critical function for Serres, as a work that reveals the conditions of our own existence while also contributing to the changes by which those conditions are overtaken.

Notes

¹ I have addressed some of the themes completely discussed in this paper more fully elsewhere. See Webb, D. (2004), (2005), (2006).

² Serres writes that Bachelard presents us with a generalized psychoanalysis in which the unconscious body is replaced by unconscious nature (Serres, 1968a, p. 26).

³ In *The Order of Things*, published just a few years later, Foucault identifies what appears to be a methodological impasse in the dichotomy between positivism and an attempt to ground knowledge either in the transcendental structures of consciousness, or in a philosophical anthropology of some kind, with neither approach proving up to the task (Foucault, 1966, pp. 323–333; Foucault, 1970, pp. 312–322). In 1940, Bachelard had already proposed a 'non-Kantianism' that, while remaining Kantian in inspiration, moved beyond its classical formulation (Bachelard, 2002, p. 15). In different ways, phenomenology and hermeneutics had both explored the possibility of dealing with cultural and historical meaning independently of a Kantian framework.

⁴ This is something that is reinforced by Serres in his own critique of dialectic and his proposal that one moves from a linear model to a tabular model in which each point is connected to multiple others in a network of connections of different weightings. This idea of networks comes from mathematics, and in particular from the idea of graph theory that goes back to Euler and in the view of many, including Serres, to Leibniz. See Serres (1968a), pp. 11–20; (1968b), pp. 13–8.

⁵ See Webb, (2006).

⁶ One can see here how easily almost the whole of the account that I have given here could have been developed out of Serres' relation to Leibniz alone. See, for example, note 3 to the 'Introduction' in Serres (1968a), in which Serres writes that in Leibniz one can find a classical method, a symbolic method and a structural method.

⁷ See the essay 'Language and space: from Oedipus to Zola' (Serres, 1983), but and also the esssay 'Turner translates Carnot', in which Serres pairs Turner's art with the physics of Carnot (Serres, 1983).

⁸ One inevitably thinks of Michel Foucault here. Serres' text was originally published in 1975, the same year that *Discipline and Punish* appeared in French, and some time after Foucault had begun to explore marginal forms of subjectivity.

⁹ That there are only variations and no originals might suggest that for Serres meaning circulates in the free play of signification. This was always perhaps a crude characterization of a strand of post-structuralism, but it is entirely inappropriate in relation to Serres, for whom there are clear constraints to thought that arise from the phenomenal world itself. The idea that meaning can circulate freely in language could only take hold where language itself is a self-contained formal system, which is precisely what atomism denies. In fact, it would not be inaccurate to describe history as the exploration of these constraints.

Bibliography

Bachelard, G. (1938), La Psychanalyse du Feu. Paris: Librarie Gallimard.

—(1942), *L'Eau et les Rêves*. Paris: Jose Corti.

—(1964), *The Psychoanalysis of Fire*. Boston: Beacon Press.

—(2002), *La Philosophie du Non*. Paris: Presses Universitaires de France.

Benveniste, E. (1971), *Problems of General Linguistics*. Miami: University of Miami Press.

Cavaillès, J. (1994), *Oeuvres Complètes de Philosophie des Sciences*. Paris: Hermann.

Dosse, F. (1997), *History of Structuralism I: The Rising Sign 1945–1956*. Minneapolis: University of Minnesota Press.

Foucault, M. (1970), *The Order of Things*. London: Routledge.

—(1991), *Discipline and Punish: The Birth of the Prison*. London: Penguin Books.

Lucretius (1999), *On the Nature of the Universe*. Oxford; New York: Oxford University Press.

Serres, M. (1968a), *Hermès I: la Communication*. Paris: Les Èditions de Minuit.

—(1968b), *Le Système de Leibniz et Ses Modèles Mathématiques*. Paris: Presses Universitaires de France.

—(1977), *La Naissance de la Physique: dans le Texte de Lucrèce*. Paris: Les Èditions de Minuit.

—(1983), *Hermès: Literature, Science, Philosophy*. Baltimore: Johns Hopkins University Press.

—(1995), *Genesis*. Ann Arbor: The University of Michigan Press.

—(1997), *The Troubadour of Knowledge*. Ann Arbor: The University of Michigan Press.

—(2000), *The Birth of Physics*. Manchester: Clinamen Press.

Webb, D. (2005), 'Cavaillès and the historical a priori in Foucault', in S. Duffy (ed.), *Virtual Mathematics: The Logic of Difference*. Manchester: Clinamen Press, pp. 100–17.

—(2004), 'Cavaillès, Husserl and the historicity of science'. *Angelaki*, Vol. 8, No. 3, pp. 59–72.

—(2006), 'Michel Serres on Lucretius: atomism, science and ethics'. *Angelaki*, Vol. 11, No. 2, pp. 125–36.

Chapter 4

Deleuze, Foucault and History

Paul Patton

In the interviews that accompanied the publication of his *Foucault*, Deleuze expresses his great admiration for Foucault and describes his thought as 'one of the greatest of modern philosophies' (Deleuze, 1995, p. 94). While he acknowledges that he and Foucault wrote in the service of different ends and employed very different methods, he nonetheless points to strong affinities between their respective approaches to philosophy: a lack of interest in origins and a distaste for abstractions such as Reason, the Subject or Totality; a concern to analyse assemblages or apparatuses at varying levels of concreteness; a shared interest in cartographic description that sought to disentangle the various kinds of line that run through social and subjective space (Deleuze, 1995, p. 86). Above all, he suggests, they shared an interest in the emergence of the new. This was what separated them from the philosophical tradition that sought to discover the universal or eternal character of things: 'We weren't looking for something timeless, not even the timelessness of time, but for new things being formed, the emergence of what Foucault called "actuality"' (Deleuze, 1995, p. 86).

This shared interest in the emergence of the new meant that both philosophers made extensive use of history and historical materials. However, in both cases, their relationship with history is an unconventional one that separates them from the practice of historians concerned to accurately record the past. Thus, in his 1990 interview with Antonio Negri, Deleuze explains that he had become 'more and more aware of the possibility of distinguishing between becoming and history' (Deleuze, 1995, p. 170). In *What is Philosophy?*, he elaborates this distinction by contrasting sharply the intellectual activities of philosophy and history: philosophy creates concepts that express pure events, while history only grasps the event in its effectuation in states of affairs or lived experience: 'the event in its becoming, in its specific consistency, in its self-positing as concept, escapes History' (Deleuze and Guattari, 1994, p. 110).

In terms of this intellectual division of labour, he aligns Foucault with philosophy, suggesting that Foucault used history, but only for the a-historical purpose of diagnosing and reinforcing certain kinds of becoming-other in contemporary societies: 'If Foucault is a great philosopher, it is because he used history for something else: as Nietzsche said, to act against time and thus on time in favour, I hope, of a time to come' (Deleuze, 2007, pp. 350–52).[1] Deleuze sometimes suggests that Foucault was not a historian, even though the study of historical materials was an important part of his method:

> Foucault's a philosopher who invents a completely different relation to history than what you find in philosophers of history. History, according to Foucault, circumscribes us and sets limits, it doesn't determine what we are, but what we're in the process of differing from; it doesn't fix our identity, but disperses it into our essential otherness ... History, in short, is what separates us from ourselves and what we have to go through and beyond in order to think what we are. As Paul Veyne says, actuality's something distinct from both time and eternity. Foucault is the most 'actual' of contemporary philosophers, the one who's most radically broken away from the nineteenth century (which is why he's able to think the twentieth century). Actuality is what interests Foucault, though it's what Nietzsche called the inactual or the untimely; it's what is *in actu*, philosophy as the act of thinking (Deleuze, 1995, pp. 94–5).

Deleuze's characterization of Foucault in these passages closely resembles the terms in which he describes his own conception of philosophy. However, as I propose to show in what follows, this characterization of Foucault is profoundly misleading. His conception of philosophy is not the same as that of Deleuze. He has a different usage of the term "actuality" and a different relationship with history.

History and Actuality

Deleuze argues that he and Foucault shared a common interest in seeking answers to a question peculiar to twentieth century philosophy: 'How is it possible that something new is produced in the world' (Deleuze, 2007, p. 349)? His own manner of answering this question is clearly spelled out in *What is Philosophy?* It is the event in its becoming that is the condition of novelty or change in the world. The concepts that philosophy creates give expression to the pure event or eventness that is a part of every event but that also escapes or exceeds its actualization. Since history only refers to the event as actualized, the study of history can never really come to grips with the condition of possibility of newness in the world. For that, we need a different approach that Deleuze outlines with reference to Charles Péguy's *Clio* (Péguy, 2002). Péguy shows us

> that there are two ways of considering events, one being to follow the course of the event, gathering how it comes about historically, how it's prepared and then decomposes in history, while the other way is to go back into the event, to take one's place in it as in a becoming, to grow both young and old in it at once, going through all its components or singularities' (Deleuze, 1995, pp. 170–171).

The latter approach is the one followed by Deleuze and Guattari's philosophy when it creates concepts that express pure events or becomings, such as the concept of nomadic lines of flight, the concepts of relative and absolute deterritorialization, or the concept of a ritornello. These pure events are the real object of philosophy precisely because, like Nietzsche's untimely as construed by Deleuze, they embody the conditions of the emergence of the new (Patton, 2010, p. 99).

In *What is Philosophy?*, Deleuze compares his own approach to philosophy with that of Nietzsche and Foucault in suggesting that what matters for all these philosophers is not so much the present but the actual, where this is understood to mean what we are in the process of becoming. He argues that, whereas he and Guattari identify becoming as the source of change, in the same way that Nietzsche identifies the untimely (*l'inactuel* or *l'intempestif*), Foucault identifies what he calls the actual (*actuel*). He does not mean *actuel* in the ordinary French sense of this word, which refers to that which is current or present, but rather something much closer to Nietzsche's untimely. It is in this sense, according to Deleuze, that we must understand Foucault's use of the term. It is not a question of what already exists or is present in a given historical moment, but of what is coming about, of what is in the process of becoming. Thus, he argues that

> When Foucault admires Kant for posing the problem of philosophy in relation not to the eternal but to the Now, he means that the object of philosophy is not to contemplate the eternal or to reflect history but to diagnose our actual becomings (Deleuze and Guattari, 1994, p. 112).

Deleuze defends his assimilation of Foucault's *actuel* to Nietzsche's untimely and his and Guattari's becoming by reference to a passage in *The Archaeology of Knowledge* in which Foucault draws a distinction between the present (*notre actualité*) and 'the border of time that surrounds our present, overhangs it and indicates it in its otherness' (Foucault, 1972, p. 130). In *What is Philosophy?*, he suggests that this border between the present and the future is what Foucault means by the actual: 'for Foucault, what matters is the difference between the present and the actual. The actual is not what we are but, rather, what we become, what we are in the process of becoming – that is to say, the Other, our becoming-other' (Deleuze and Guattari, 1994, p. 112). He is right to suggest that, in the passage from *The Archaeology of Knowledge*, Foucault draws a distinction between the present and the border of time that surrounds it and indicates its difference from what has gone before. However, he is wrong to suggest that this border is what Foucault calls the actual. Foucault does not use this term in the manner that Deleuze suggests. His text actually contrasts this border region with 'our actuality':

> The analysis of the archive, then, involves a privileged region: at once close to us and different from our actuality, it is the border of time that surrounds our present, which overhangs it, and which indicates it in its otherness; it is that which, outside ourselves, delimits us. (Foucault, 1972, p. 130; translation modified).[2]

Foucault's remark occurs in the context of a discussion of the overall system or arrangement of the different discursive practices present in a given society at a given time. Each discursive practice is defined by a set of rules that govern the emergence of things said (*énoncés*) in a given domain. These rules constitute an historical a priori of statements considered as events, that is, as things actually said. The totality of such sets of rules governing the discursive formations in a given culture at a given time is what Foucault calls the archive. It is 'the law of what can be said, the system that governs the appearance of statements as unique events' (Foucault, 1972, p. 129). Given that all statements, including those of the archaeologist of discourse, are subject to such rules governing what can be said, Foucault's problem here is to explain how and when it becomes possible to describe such an archive. It is clearly not possible to describe the archive within which we speak and write. However, it is possible to describe the archive of those discourses that are no longer our own. In this sense, a condition of possibility of the archaeology of discourse that Foucault undertakes is 'the discontinuity that separates us from what we can no longer say and from that which falls outside our discursive practice' (Foucault, 1972, p. 130). It is of this discontinuity, this difference, that Foucault speaks in referring to the 'border of time' that surrounds our present (*notre actualité*).

The extent of Deleuze's creative misinterpretation of Foucault's remark from *The Archaeology of Knowledge* is even more apparent in the extended commentary on this passage provided in 'What is a Dispositif?' (Deleuze, 2007, pp. 343–52). Here, Deleuze goes further than the mere transposition of the term "actuality" so that it becomes identified with the border of time that surrounds our present. He suggests that this border that surrounds the discursive present in which we speak and write is not simply a backward-looking difference that allows us to identify and describe the archive of discursive practices that are no longer our own, but a difference endowed with a forward-looking momentum. On his account, it acquires the positive meaning of a becoming, in the sense of what we will become in the future:

> The novelty of a dispositif in relation to those that precede it is what we call its actuality, our actuality. The new is the actual. The actual is not what we are but rather what we are becoming, what we are in the process of becoming, that is to say the Other, our becoming-other. In every dispositif we must distinguish what we are (what we are already no longer) and what we are becoming: the part of history and the part of the actual. History is the archive, the design of what we are and cease being while the actual is the sketch of what we will become (Deleuze, 2007, p. 350 translation modified).[3]

In Foucault's text, the border of time that separates us from what we can no longer say is a becoming only in the most negative and minimal sense of the term. In Deleuze's commentary, it has been turned into the actual in the sense of what we are becoming or what we will become. A problem with this forced interpretation of Foucault is that we search in vain in his published works for analyses of what is coming about or we are becoming. In terms of Deleuze's hypothesis, *Discipline and Punish* should have analysed what prisons are in the process of becoming rather than confining itself to the analysis of the disciplinary techniques of power that they have embodied since the early nineteenth century. Deleuze's response to this problem is to suggest that we need to enlarge our understanding of Foucault's oeuvre to include not only his books but also his interviews. The books that address a particular archive, whether in relation to madness, the clinic, disciplinary power or sexuality, are only half the story: the other half is made explicit in the interviews that Foucault gave alongside the publication of his major works, in which he comments on the bearing of his historical studies on current problems. In this manner, Deleuze draws a distinction between Foucault's analysis of particular aspects of the archive, which are presented in his genealogical and archaeological studies, and his diagnoses of what the present is becoming, which are presented in interviews:

> What are madness, prison, sexuality today? What new modes of subjectivation do we see appearing today that are certainly not Greek or Christian?.... Foucault attached so much importance to his interviews in France and even more so abroad, not because he liked interviews but because in them he traced lines of actualization that required another mode of expression than the assimilable lines in his major books. The interviews are diagnoses (Deleuze, 2007, p. 352).[4]

At this point, over and above mere textual distortions, we can begin to see the distance that separates Foucault's relationship with history from Deleuze's account of that relationship. Let us begin by comparing Deleuze's account of how Foucault's histories of the present aim to capture the form of society that is emerging with Foucault's own description of his philosophical orientation in several versions of his lecture on Kant's 'What is Enlightenment?' (Foucault, 2007).

Philosophy versus Genealogy

It is no exaggeration to say that Foucault invented a new practice of philosophy. His major works traced the emergence of concepts, institutions and techniques of government that helped to delineate the peculiar shape of modern European culture. They include a history of madness; an account of the birth of clinical medicine at the end of the eighteenth century; an archaeology of the modern sciences of language, life and labour; a genealogy of the modern form of punishment; and fragments of a history of sexuality. These are all historical studies by virtue of the kinds of claim advanced and the documentary evidence adduced to illustrate and support them, but they do not conform to established rules of historiographical method and often invent new objects of historical research. The title that Foucault chose for his chair at the Collège de France – professor of the history of systems of thought – provides a clue to the distinctive nature of his research. By "thought" he meant, first, the forms of theoretical and conceptual reflection developed within philosophy and the human sciences. His early work dealt with the history of psychopathology and clinical medicine in a manner that owed much to the approach of French philosopher-historians of science such as Bachelard and Canguilhem. However, Foucault also took "thought" to encompass the forms of rationality embedded in the everyday practice of administrators, doctors, priests and private individuals, as well as the reason expressed in technical manuals, projects for institutional reform and the writings of moralists and theorists of government. His "histories" of madness, criminal punishment and sexuality sought to expose the singularity of these forms of experience that involve thought in both the above senses. The history of systems of thought thus defines an approach to the workings of a culture rather than a specific level within it.

While the exhumation of particular systems of thought requires historical research, the demonstration of their historical character is a matter of philosophical critique. Foucault's conception of philosophy as critical history of thought is indebted to both Kant and Nietzsche: it involves analysis of the conditions of possibility of particular systems of thought. However, in contrast to Kantian critique, it does not take for granted their status as knowledge, nor does it assume universal or eternal a priori conditions of knowledge. Rather, it assumes only the fact that certain statements are made and that they function as knowledge within a given period. Foucault's archaeology seeks to uncover the historical a priori conditions of knowledge in empirical domains such as language, political economy and criminal anthropology.

In a text extracted from his first lecture at the Collège de France in 1983 and published in English under the title 'What is Revolution?', Foucault characterizes Kant as the founder of the two critical traditions that divide modern philosophy. On the one hand, he founded the critical tradition that seeks the universal conditions of the possibility of knowledge; on the other hand, he founded the critical tradition that asks the question: 'What is our actuality? What is the present field of possible experiences?' (Foucault, 2007, pp. 94–5). Foucault situates his own work in the latter tradition, alongside that of Hegel, Nietzsche, Weber and the Frankfurt School, which he describes as oriented towards 'an ontology of ourselves, an ontology of the present' (Foucault, 2007, p. 95). In a text published in English the following year as 'What is Enlightenment?', he characterizes the Kantian critical ontology of the present as an attitude, ethos or philosophical life in which 'the critique of what we are is at one and the same time the historical analysis of the limits that are imposed on us and an experiment with the possibility of going beyond them' (Foucault, 2007, p. 118). In this text, as in the former, he contrasts this critical attitude towards the present with the search for universal formal structures in the manner of Kant's critiques of pure and practical reason. For Foucault, criticism of the present is a matter of working on the limits of our present, where this means working on strategically chosen points with the aim of separating out 'from the contingency that has made us what we are, the possibility of no longer being, doing, or thinking what we are, do or think' (Foucault, 2007, p. 114). In this manner, Foucault's historical studies are intended to assist the criticism of systems of thought and practices informed by them. The critical force of this "genealogical" history emerges in relation to present social movements. It provides indirect responses to questions such as the following: What else could we do with criminals, but imprison and attempt to rehabilitate them? How can we understand the social relations between the sexes other than as the product of natural differences? How could we regulate our sexual behaviour other than by discovering and accepting the truth about our desire? Such criticism, Foucault suggests, 'does not mark out impassable boundaries or describe closed systems; it brings to light transformable singularities' (Foucault, 1984, p. 335).

For Nietzsche, moral interpretations of phenomena are among the most important means by which human beings act upon themselves and others: it is by such means that one can arouse pity in others, or experience one's own actions as cowardice or humility according to whether one lives in the moral culture of ancient Greece or European Christianity. Like Nietzsche, Foucault refuses any form of philosophical anthropology. He rejects the idea that there is a universal human nature, even while supposing the existence of a distinctively human body endowed with particular forces and historically constituted capacities for action and self-interpretation. The systems of knowledge, moral judgment and government that he studied in relation to such things as mental illness, punishment and sexuality are important elements of the interpretative framework within which Europeans have acted upon their own actions as well as those of others. In this sense, the thought of which Foucault writes the history may be found in every manner in which individuals speak and behave: In this sense, Foucault comments, 'thought is understood as the very form of action' (Foucault, 1984, p. 335). His own studies of the history of Greek and Roman ethical thought are instances of thought thinking its own past in order to free itself from what is currently thought and to be able to 'think otherwise' in the future (Foucault, 1985, p. 9).

Much of Foucault's work may be seen to follow in the footsteps of Nietzsche's way of writing a genealogy of the present. He reinterprets past practices, institutions and forms of knowledge, but always from the perspective of a hitherto unnoticed distance from that past. His genealogies describe the discursive and non-discursive formations (*dispositifs*) from which we are separated by hitherto imperceptible fractures in the hermeneutical frameworks within which we live and experience the historical present. In this manner, he shows up the madness of incarcerating the insane, the arbitrariness and injustice of imprisoning convicts, the irrationality of making our identity as subjects that depend upon our sexual behaviour. In terms of his own retrospective account of his genealogical method in 'What is Enlightenment?', these are all examples of practices that were previously considered unproblematic or unavoidable but that we can now perceive as contingent and open to change (Foucault, 1997, p. 315). Foucault describes the aim of his genealogies as pursuing this break with the past in a manner that might serve as a condition for further change. However, he rarely takes the further step, attributed to him by Deleuze, of attempting to outline the direction of change in the present.[5]

Becoming Control Society

The distance that separates Deleuze and Foucault's relationship with history is clearly manifest when we compare Deleuze's characterization of Foucault in his own attempts to pursue what he presents as a Foucaultian form of criticism of the present. For the most part, Deleuze does not undertake the same kind of historical reinterpretation of the present that we find in Foucault. One exception to this is the diagnosis outlined in his 'Post-script on Control Societies', and in his 'Control and Becoming' interview with Negri, where he describes the present as the initial stages of a newly emerging 'control society'.[6] Deleuze presents his diagnosis as though it corresponded to or continued Foucault's method of undertaking an analysis or an archaeology of the present. In fact, it corresponds far more to the manner in which Deleuze presents Foucault's diagnostic method than it does to anything Foucault wrote.

Deleuze offers a diagnosis that builds upon Foucault's discussion of political technology in *Discipline and Punish*, suggesting that this moment is witness to the birth of a society characterized by the predominance of a new type of political technology. Just as the modern society described by Foucault in *Discipline and Punish* was characterized by a diagram of disciplinary power, so the new society emerging at the end of the twentieth century is characterized by a diagram of control. Foucault identified an historical series in which distinctive kinds of society are defined by a particular diagram of power: sovereign society gave way to disciplinary society. Control society comes next in the series. This diagnosis stands in stark contrast to the account of the present given in his 1972 discussion with Foucault, 'Intellectuals and Power', where Deleuze saw the political present as a period of repression after the social upheavals of 1968 and its immediate aftermath (Deleuze, 2004, p. 201). He described this present not only as a response to what occurred in May 1968, but as the concerted preparation and organization of the immediate future by reinforcing the social structures of confinement. His diagnosis at this point effectively anticipated the New Philosophers in describing the present period with reference to Foucault's discussion of "confinement".

More importantly, this diagnosis raises the question of what is meant by "control" in the context of specific diagrams of power? How does it differ from disciplinary power? In the first place, in the light of Foucault's later clarification of his concept of power, we can say that insofar as it is the name of a particular technique for the exercise of political power, it involves a certain kind of action upon the action, or the field of possible actions, of others (Foucault, 2000, pp. 326–48). Control power is different from disciplinary power at the level of its primary material, its means, modalities and ends. At the level of primary materials, control does not operate on the individual-mass couple but on the one hand on "dividuals" and on the other hand on samples or databanks. Unlike disciplinary society, control societies do not form individuals to fit certain moulds in order to produce docile bodies, obedient subjects and so on. Rather, they extract dividuals that do not correspond to whole persons. A dividual is not a person but a certain number of functional aspects of an individual, each one responding to particular criteria or defined in relation to particular ends. It is a bundle of aptitudes or capacities such as the financial means that ensure a capacity to repay a bank loan or the scholarly aptitudes that guarantee entry into a given programme of study. A multiplicity of dividuals do not constitute a mass but rather a sample or a databank that can be analysed and exploited for commercial, governmental or other ends.

At the level of the means of its exercise, control makes use of passwords rather than order-words. Individuals are associated with an increasingly long and potentially endless chain of passwords, including passwords for their computers and computer software, email servers, assorted bank and credit card logins, medical insurance, online shopping, travel agencies and online tickets, journal and newspaper subscriptions, professional associations and so on. In contrast to disciplinary societies, control societies do not establish institutional spaces of confinement. Rather, they establish series of thresholds through which one can only pass with the right password. They establish different kinds of penalties as alternatives to imprisonment, such as fines, community service, compulsory rehabilitation and so on. They establish home medical care instead of hospitalization, lifelong education and training instead of schools and colleges, and enterprises of various kinds instead of factories. Control operates in the open air rather than in confined spaces, by means of various new technologies, especially digital and electronic technologies. To take an example that has emerged since Deleuze wrote his "Post-script", consider the manner in which GPS location has become utilized in a whole series of devices, from personal direction-finders to electronic bracelets and other tracking devices. In the words of one commentator: 'GPS represents the final stage of this evolution. Even the electronic bracelet remains essentially disciplinary, transforming the home into a prison and trapping the condemned as though in his apart-ment burrow. By contrast, mobile technologies of surveillance in real time liberate the individual. They liberate his energy and his desire so that he can work at his own always ephemeral and perfectible integration' (Razac, 2008, p. 61).

At the level of the modality of action, control mechanisms do not impose particular moulds according to the nature of the institution in which they are employed, producing a certain kind of subject, body or relationships. Rather, they involve the continuous modulation of behaviours or perfor-mances in and by means of their relationship with one another. In turn, this implies a series of replacements in different domains of social life. For example, in the judicial sphere, acquittal is replaced by unlimited deferral of judgment, just as in the economic sphere the manufacture of products is replaced by the sale of services or immaterial products and in the educa-tional sphere examinations are replaced by continuous assessment. In each case, it is a question of abandoning disciplinary modalities in favour of other means of acting upon the action of people.

Deleuze's reference to Foucault in elaborating this concept of control society raises a number of problems. The first is that, as he reminds us, Foucault was among those who pointed out that we no longer live in an age of discipline: 'he was actually one of the first to say that we're moving away from disciplinary societies, we've already left them behind' (Deleuze, 1995, p. 178). In the course of the 1977 interview, 'The Eye of Power', Foucault noted that 'disciplinary power was in fact already in Bentham's day being transcended by other and much more subtle mechanisms for the regula-tion of phenomena of population, controlling their fluctuations and com-pensating their irregularities' (Foucault, 1980, p. 160).[7] According to this diagnosis of the present that Deleuze presents as both Foucault's and his own, disciplinary society is already disappearing. The techniques of disciplinary power are in crisis and institutions such as the school, factory, hospital, army and prison have more or less reached their use-by date:

> It is simply a matter of nursing them through their death throes and keeping people busy until the new forces knocking at the door take over. Control societies are taking over from disciplinary societies (Deleuze, 1995, p. 178).

However, it is one thing to say that disciplinary techniques have long been giving way to other mechanisms of government of both individuals and populations. It is another thing to say that the diagram of disciplinary power is currently giving way to the control model. It is true that in his lectures in the years that followed the publication of this book, Foucault did focus on other technologies of power that emerged alongside disciplinary techniques in the course of the eighteenth century, such as mechanisms of security. Razac suggests that Foucault's analyses of 'security apparatuses' in the course of his 1977–1978 lectures, *Security, Territory, Population*, played a more or less implicit role in Deleuze's characterization of control society (Foucault, 2007b). The basis for this suggestion lies above all in the mode of regulation of a given material that is common to Foucault's security apparatuses and Deleuze's control societies: 'continuous modulation and the treatment of the object of power adapt in real time to what actually occurs' (Razac, 2008, p. 40). At the same time, however, Razac points to the historical difficulty raised by this suggestion: Foucault situates the emergence of techniques of security at the end of the eighteenth century, whereas Deleuze situates the transition to control societies in the latter half of the twentieth century.

Moreover, the study of mechanisms of security led Foucault in an altogether different direction towards that suggested by Deleuze's account of control society. Rather than a continuation of the series of diagrams of power on the model of that suggested for disciplinary society, Foucault turned towards the analysis of different forms of governmentality and a genealogy of liberal and neo-liberal government. This project led him in the direction of a more refined study of the different means by which states sought to act on the actions of people. In terms of Foucault's study of different forms of governmentality, the idea that a society might be defined by a single diagram of power in the manner that he had suggested in *Discipline and Punish* no longer played a role. One of the polemical refrains of Foucault's lectures on liberal and neo-liberal governmentality is a plea for realism instead of the kind of political criticism that interprets the present by reference to already given concepts. Deleuze's *Foucault* is based not only upon an earlier moment of Foucault's thought, namely his analysis of the diagram of disciplinary power, but also upon a philosophical conception of history that does not have the same commitment to realism. Foucault's aim was to show the historical specificity of forms of discourse or techniques of power and government in order, as he says, 'to let knowledge of the past work on the experience of the present' (Foucault, 2008, p. 130). For Deleuze, it is the philosophical concept rather than historical knowledge of the past that is supposed to act upon our experience of the present. In the end, he and Foucault held very different views of the relationship between philosophy, history and criticism of the present.

Notes

[1] See also Deleuze, 1986, p. 119 and Deleuze, 2007, p. 246. In these remarks, Deleuze alludes to a passage from Nietzsche's essay 'On the uses and disadvantages of history for life', that he frequently invokes in relation to his own conception of philosophy. See Nietzsche, 1983, p. 60; Deleuze, 1990, p. 265 and Deleuze, 1994, p. xxi. Craig Lundy points out that Deleuze invariably fails to mention the first half of Nietzsche's sentence in which he speaks as a philologist. This is but one of many indications of the extent to which Deleuze creatively misconstrues Nietzsche's concept of the untimely (Lundy, 2009, p. 202).

[2] The original reads: L'analyse de l'archive comporte donc une région privilégiée: à la fois proche de nous, mais différente de notre actualité, c'est la bordure du temps qui entoure notre présent, qui le surplombe et qui l'indique dans son altérité; c'est ce qui, hors de nous, nous délimite (Foucault 1969: 172).

[3] The original text reads: La nouveauté d'un dispositif par rapport aux précédents, nous l'appelons son actualité, notre actualité. Le nouveau, c'est l'actuel. L'actuel n'est pas ce que nous sommes, mais plutôt ce que nous devenons, ce que nous sommes en train de devenir, c'est-à-dire l'Autre, notre devenir-autre. Dans tout dispositif, il faut distinguer ce que nous sommes (ce que nous ne sommes déjà plus), et ce que nous sommes en train de devenir: la part de l'histoire, et la part de l'actuel. L'histoire, c'est l'archive, le dessin de ce que nous sommes et cessons d'être, tandis que l'actuel est l'ébauche de ce que nous devenons' (Deleuze, 2003, p. 322).

[4] Similar claims about the role of interviews as an integral part of Foucault's oeuvre are presented in Deleuze, 1986, p. 115; Deleuze, 1995, p. 106.

[5] One occasion on which Foucault did discuss a transformation currently underway was in his 1979 lectures devoted to German neo-liberalism and American anarcho-liberalism. He made it clear that part of his reason for focussing on this emerging form of governmental reason and practice was that: 'The German model which is being diffused, debated and forms part of our actuality, structuring it and carving

out its real shape, is the model of a possible neo-liberal governmentality' (Foucault, 2008, p. 192).

6   The interview with Negri first appeared in *Futur antérieur*, no. 1, Spring 1990. The Post-script first appeared in L'autre journal, May 1990. Both are reprinted in *Negotiations* (Deleuze, 1995, pp. 169–176, 177–182). See also the comments in 'What is an act of creation' in *Two Regimes of Madness* (Deleuze, 2007, pp. 317–329).

7   Earlier in the same interview, he commented that 'the procedures of power that are at work in modern societies are much more numerous, diverse and rich' (Foucault, 1980, p. 148). See also *Dits et écrits*, Vol. III, 'La société disciplinaire en crise' (Foucault, 1994, pp. 532–34).

Bibliography

Deleuze, G. (1986), *Foucault*. Paris: Éditions de Minuit.

—(1988), *Foucault*. Edited and translated by S. Hand. Foreword by P. Bové. Minneapolis: University of Minnesota Press.

—(1990), *The Logic of Sense*. Translated by M. Lester with C. Stivale. Edited by C. Boundas. New York: Columbia University Press.

—(1994), *Difference and Repetition*. Translated by P. Patton. London: Athlone; New York: Columbia University Press.

—(1995), *Negotiations 1972–1990*. Translated by M. Joughin. New York: Columbia University Press.

—(2002), *L'Île Désert et Autres Textes, Textes et Entretiens 1953–1974*. Edited by D. Lapoujade. Paris: Éditions de Minuit.

—(2003), *Deux Régimes de Fous. Textes et Entretiens 1975–1995*. Edited by D. Lapoujade. Paris: Éditions de Minuit.

—(2004), *Desert Islands and Other Texts 1953–1974*. Translated by M. Taormina. Edited by D. Lapoujade. New York: Semiotext(e).

—(2007), *Two Regimes of Madness: Texts and Interviews 1975–1995*. Translated by A. Hodges and M. Taormina. New York: Semiotext(e) [Revised Edition].

Deleuze, G. and Guattari, F. (1991), *Qu'est-ce que la philosophie?* Paris: Éditions de Minuit.

—(1994), *What Is Philosophy?* Translated by H. Tomlinson and G. Burchell. New York: Columbia University Press.

Foucault, M. (1969), *L'Archéologie du savoir*. Paris: Éditions Gallimard.

—(1972), *The Archaeology of Knowledge*. Translated by A. M. Sheridan. London: Tavistock.

—(1977), *Discipline and Punish*. Translated by A. Sheridan, London: Allen Lane/ Penguin.

—(1980), *Michel Foucault: Power/Knowledge*. Edited by C. Gordon. Brighton: Harvester.

—(1984), *The Foucault Reader*. Edited by P. Rabinow. New York: Pantheon Books.

—(1985), *The Use of Pleasure: The History of Sexuality*, Vol. 2. New York: Random House.

—(1994), *Dits et écrits. 1954–1988.* Edited by D. Defert and F. Ewald. Vol. III, 1976–1979.

—(1997), *Essential Works of Foucault 1954–1984, Vol. 1, Ethics.* Translated by R. Hurley et al. Edited by P. Rabinow. New York: The New Press.

—(2000), *Essential Works of Foucault 1954–1984, Vol. 3, Power.* Translated by R. Hurley et al. Edited by J. D. Faubion. New York: New Press.

—(2007), *The Politics of Truth.* Edited by S. Lotringer. New York: Semiotext(e).

—(2007b), *Security, Territory, Population: Lectures at the Collège de France 1977–1978.* Translated by G. Burchell. Edited by M. Senellart. Houndmills, Basingstoke and New York: Palgrave Macmillan.

—(2008), *The Birth of Biopolitics: Lectures at the Collège de France 1978–1979.* Translated by G. Burchell. Edited by M. Senellart. Houndmills, Basingstoke and New York: Palgrave Macmillan.

Lundy, C. (2009), 'Deleuze's Untimely: Uses and Abuses in the Appropriation of Nietzsche', in C. Colebrook and J. Bell (eds), *Nietzsche and History.* Edinburgh: Edinburgh University Press, pp. 188–205.

Nietzsche, F. (1983), 'On the Uses and Disadvantages of History for Life', in *Untimely Meditations.* Translated by R. J. Hollingdale. Cambridge, UK: Cambridge University Press, pp. 59–123.

Patton, P. (2010), *Deleuzian Concepts: Philosophy, Colonization, Politics.* Stanford: Stanford University Press.

Péguy, C. (2002), *Clio.* Paris: Éditions Gallimard.

Razac, O. (2008), *Avec Foucault/Après Foucault: Disséquer la société de contrôle.* Paris: L'Harmattan.

Chapter 5

Ulyssean Trajectories: A (New) Look at Michel Serres' Topology of Time

Maria Assad

There is a Confucian saying that 'he who knows how to rekindle the past in order to understand the new, merits being called a master'.[1]

The fluid dimensions of a multi-layered discourse that Michel Serres, philosopher, mathematician and historian of the sciences, prefers to call a 'philosophy of circumstances', are the tools with which he fires up the past in order to enlighten our understanding of the present. Serres' works represent a discourse on the dynamical nature of time. His frequent use of fables and apologues adds to a sense of urgency for our era, and is expressed through a non-linear view of History. It becomes a resounding call for new thinking and novel action in particular texts, as in *Le Contrat naturel*, *Atlas*, and *Le Mal propre*. How we change our procedures and assess what it means to gain new knowledge ('le nouveau savoir') is mirrored in the dynamical non-linearity of Serres' writings and culminates in what he characterizes as an "exo-Darwinian" evolution of future possibilities outlined in daringly bold strokes in *Hominescence*.

At the very core of the work under consideration, and driven by a conscious effort to confront the problem of Evil, is Serres' unwavering search for a vital and non-oppositional (re)union of subject and object, joining historical consciousness and the material reality of the world. Where this search begins, under what epistemological magnifier it develops its strategies and evolves over time and where it continues today, is the topic of the following pages. It is a complex story with discursive trajectories that reflect the intricacies of the subject matter.

. . .

The first pages of *Atlas* signal a contradiction: 'Everything changes, but nothing changes' (Serres, 1994, p. 16). For Serres, however, it renders its own logic although violating the principle of identity (A = A, under the same conditions). Between the everything and nothing, Serres discovers a third space that swells into a vast atlas of virtual maps related to each other by passages through which new knowledge percolates, not in a straight Cartesian line, but in unexpected movements that resemble a 'zigzag path of grazing goats' (Serres, 1985, p. 94). *Atlas* is a discursive network of "multiples", non-linear systems, folds, and circumstances, themselves networks of other folds. A dynamical web appears where fluid mappings are the home of the seeker of "new knowledge", to whom Serres lends a face and a name: 'All is folds, and Gilles Deleuze is correct to say so' (Serres, 1994, p. 49).[2] Discussions around concrete examples of our physical world, thought processes that invariably change and multiply into passages tracing a virtual atlas of time maps, are interconnected like transversal relations similar to Riemann surfaces, with complex manifolds guiding the "nouveau savoir" with its inventive powers. The alternative, over and over repeated in Serres' writings, is collective stagnation and death, both physical and cultural.

Offering an unexpected fold among the bundles of world-maps, the last chapter of *Atlas* lays out a temporal atlas of Serres' major works, from the first study on Leibniz to *Atlas* itself, 18 texts in all. What begins with a double question, 'Passing through where, in order to go where?' (Par où passer pour aller où?) (Serres, 1994, p. 265), ends in a barrage of questions that attenuate any impression of authoritative certainty. Serres' technique is deceptively simple: Recognizable by their italics, keywords of the titles of his earlier works are woven into the contents of this chapter (pp. 265–74). Each title word becomes part of the syntax of a sentence, each advancing the topic of *Atlas* while simultaneously summarizing each prior work, here tersely, there expansively, even with a lengthy stitched-together citation out of *Genèse*, and ending with an invitation to 'leaf through *Atlas*, map by map' (Serres, 1994, p. 276).

The keywords of Serres' titles form yet another network within the virtual world-maps that are meant to guide through the ever-meandering passages of existence ('par où?') towards an unpredictable goal in movement ('aller où?'). The written history of Serres' non-linear view of time and History is concretized as an open-ended recording of his works up to 1994. Embedded in the many descriptive "mappemondes" of *Atlas*, this creative movement is part of the principal argument, namely that today's local systems develop over time into global entities and do so topologically rather than linearly, and that the routes they take are always chaotic, complex, unexpected and non-linear. The reader is invited to intuit these timelines in the form of an 'entrelac volumineux à la chevelure' (Serres, 1994, p. 270), a fine image that refers to either a voluminous tangle of hair or the tail of a comet.

Serres' title keywords act like folds, which further crumple the already sinuous line-bundles of *Atlas*. They cause the "end" of the tale to explode onto images (lightning, columns of fire, global conflagrations) that express topological mayhem: Each keyword is an outside referring to an earlier text, but becomes an inside of *Atlas* without abandoning its outside character. Inversely, the inside that is *Atlas* used as a keyword, becomes the outside of its own inside, and both at the same time. What opens up is a deep topological fold in the closest meaning that Gilles Deleuze assigns to this concept in *Le Pli*. It is a further stretching of what is already a complex discursive world-map of contingencies. *Atlas* thus becomes a Serresean mapping of space-time (p. 277), for in the crinkled and twisted virtual plane of *Atlas* appears the history of Serres' writings compressed into keywords waiting to emit their own non-linear discourses, like additional bundles ("gerbes") of timelines and spatial narrative routes.

It is an urgent invitation to go 'back to the future' and take a new look at some earlier Serresean texts. However, "earlier" and "more recent" are linear temporal categories that Serres replaces by the notion of a 'self-same time' (Serres, 1995, p. 46).

. . .

Published between 1968 and 1980, the five *Hermès* texts present Serres' attempt to identify and evaluate the growing alienation between human capacity for knowledge acquisition and the material reality of the world the subject is part of. Equally important, they lay the foundation for a long quest, far beyond their own contents, to find passages (*Le passage du Nord-Ouest*), meaningful communication (*La communication*), inventive interceptions (*L'interférence*), mutual transformations (*La traduction*) and creative disorder (*La distribution*) that, together, shape a tentative portrait of an epistēmē that may reconcile subject and object, thereby forming the promise of an organic and creative whole, which is later expressed as non-linear history. In these texts, movement as a concept is the driving metaphor. It informs a critical investigation that challenges the logo-centric tradition of Western thought, by gathering in a network of transversal relations unique readings of literary, philosophical, epistemological, artistic, scientific and mathematical works. Serres' method in the most recent of his essays has not changed much in this respect from his arguments in *Hermès*. Instead of rejecting outright any given concept, he examines it from a different point of view informed by movement or – increasingly as his argument proceeds – by complexity. Already in *La communication*, he proposes networking ("réseaux") to replace pure linearity of concepts, and to re-orient the laws of causality traditionally determined by the one-directional structure of cause and effect.

> At its most advanced application, [this network] can become an excellent organon of historic comprehension [...] Complexity is no longer an obstacle to knowledge or, worse, a descriptive judgement call; it is the best of stimulants for knowledge and experience. (Serres, 1968, p. 20)

With the *Hermès* essays, Serres' writings come closest to the philosophy of Gilles Deleuze. Although their language may differ, they share a critical approach to traditional philosophical systems, and practice what is often referred to as an epistemo-critique. Both reject the traditional principle of identity. Deleuze denies the primacy of identity over difference; identity is rather a particular composite of an open-ended series of differences (Deleuze, 2002, pp. 332–33). Serres formulates this abyss of endless differences as Urnoise ('bruit de fond') and builds on this "non-concept" the stories of *Genèse*. Deleuze spurns opinion as a crutch we use to feel secure, thereby closing off all variabilities and possibilities for creative action (Deleuze and Guattari, 1991, pp. 194–95). In Serresean texts, particularly in *Genèse* and *Les cinq sens*, opinion appears as noise or murmur that constructs history as a movement of repetitive, linear actions that restrict possibilities for inventive thought. In later works, Serres demonstrates how opinion becomes dominant as a culture of death culminating in Evil per se. Sharing a distrust of dialectical thinking, both philosophers consider the excluded middle (le tiers exclu) emblematic for their resistance to traditional thought systems. In Deleuzian writings, it refers variously to difference as preceding identity, to the fold, transversal relations, or the undecidable inside-outside. For Serres, the excluded middle becomes the third (tiers) element that dialectics forgets or deliberately suppresses as rationally absurd. It is his "quasi-object" growing into the multiple, iterating into the chaotic and the topological space-time in which the human becomes the middle-instructed (le tiers-instruit) who invents and creates topological trajectories for a non-linear history of life (*Le Tiers-Instruit*).

The expression "excluded middle" is rendered in French by the "excluded third", a linguistic advantage for Serres, who develops his stories of the "multiple" out of the explosive force of an ever more dominant parasitic third who is the ultimate threat for any static, dialectic system. In Serresean texts, the "third" is therefore not only a logical exclusion to be unearthed from the simple dictum of 'tertium non datur'; it also appears in the form of material, concrete entities, be they humans, any living being, an inanimate object or the world, in short, any entity deemed irrational by the norms of traditional logic. It is Deleuze's inside-outside twisting in an in-between fold. In *Le Parasite*, the third appears as a parasite of triple meaning (in French): a bacterium or annoying insect, a sycophant and static background noise in information theory. Through stories and fables, Serres demonstrates the tenacious efforts of the parasite/excluded third to become included, to gain entry into a given system, eventually overwhelming it by becoming him/itself the system and renewing and enriching it creatively, or attacking it in case of systemic resistance to the intruder. In this way *Le Parasite* demonstrates 'an epistemology of human relations' (Harari et al., 1982, p. xxxix) that addresses the dilemma of the excluded middle: For any philosophical inquiry into the nature of the relationship between subject and object, it is not 'a problem of the Other who is only a variety - or a variation - of the Same, it is the problem of the third man' (Serres, 1968, p. 41).[3]

The fascinating aspect of *Le Parasite* is the steady and inexorable narrative evolution of this pesky bug into a 'cataclysmic inundation of infernal proportions' (Assad, 2000, p. 275), because the little irritation grows and multiplies into a monumental Evil. In order not to judge this narrative as slightly exaggerated or quirky, the irreversible parasitic process necessitates an understanding on the part of the reader that the French "mal" expresses "bad" as well as "evil", and that this signifier has an extended chain of signifieds, from the formulaic cliché "pas mal" ("not bad") in response to a conventional greeting, to the ethical problem of evil. The initial slight inconveniences caused by the parasitic excluded third swell into a diabolical "Mal" (Serres, 1980, p. 341), which reigns over a battle field of Death, as Serres reads it in Homer's 'Odyssey' where the final scene plays out 'in the midst of corpses' (Serres, 1980, p. 339). As the story of a process, *Le Parasite* informs a theory of human relations, where Evil and History become partners, bearing violence and death. The theme of a culture of death remains throughout Serres' later writings, gives birth to a description of deliverance from this curse in *Le Tiers-Instruit* and returns in a contemporary form 30 years later in *Le Mal propre*.

This bleak view of historical processes is offset by a second, more peaceful aspect of the excluded third, also demonstrated in *Le Parasite*, of which one fable serves as a poignant example of Serres non-linear logic. After a discussion of history as a flow of circumstances instead of the traditional dualistic arena of conflicts, Serres re-tells La Fontaine's fable 'The Countryman and the serpent' (L'homme et la couleuvre) in such a fashion that the "third" can be understood as a desirable alternative to the "Mal" of its diabolic cousins (Serres, 1980, pp. 35–8).

On a cold wintry day, a farmer finds a snake in his field, chilled and frozen, and decides to carry it home so the beast can warm up by the fireplace. Arising from its stupor, the snake returns to its usual hostility, coils up, raises its head and lunges at its benefactor. He, in turn, calls the viper an "ungrateful wretch", grabs an ax and cuts it up. As is his custom, La Fontaine adds an exhortation, that charity is good but should always be given wisely. He reads this scene from the standpoint of the farmer who can at least expect a thank-you as a sort of minimal rent for an overnight stay in his house. Both, the farmer and the fabulist, judge the event by dualistic standards: here the charitable man, there the ungrateful snake, pitted against each other in a deadly struggle, says Serres. Reflecting an unwavering binary logic, bad reckoning on the part of the farmer has brought about this violent state. Retold in the early pages of *Le Parasite*, this fable foreshadows the evil described in its last pages, where the infernal swarms of competing parasites, locked in repetitive rivalries, fill 'a book of history, a book of Evil' (Serres, 1980, p. 342).

Serres, however, uncovers the underlying story of an excluded middle. In contrast to La Fontaine and traditional interpretations, he reads the fable from the viewpoint of the snake: it/he was removed from his space, albeit frozen, was never asked for his consent, lost his freedom, and instead is suddenly obligated to someone. His space (nest or den) was invaded and taken from him by the farmer. An outsider intrudes and becomes an insider, the inside (the snake in his space of hibernation) is ousted, becomes an outsider, and is unwittingly forced to become a beggar for warmth. He protests; against the farmer's demand for a thank-you, he demands – expressed by his attack – retribution for the loss of his niche. So Serres asks: Who must pay? The snake for hospitality received, or the man for taking what belongs to the animal? Since either side is right and wrong, the communication between them veers towards violence. Serres rejects this outcome as the only one possible, because it is based on a binary concept of Same and Other, what he calls the 'hard logic of exchange' that ignores, or excludes as illogical, the betweenness of any communication. This between is the undecidable question 'who pays?' that fills the space of a Third who is equally same and other, being and non-being (Serres, 1980, p. 37). The point of view of the snake is presented here as a Deleuzian inside-outside, inverted like a glove, or similar to a Moebius strip where inside is outside but remains equally inside, the outside being the inside and equally remaining outside (Deleuze, 1988b, p. 97). Remarkably, the Deleuzian triple inside/outside/in-out-side is clearly accounted for in La Fontaine's fable: The farmer cuts the snake into three pieces, specifically spelled out in the poem as head, tail and trunk. For Serres, this gesture is the mirror image of the same (the head), the other (the tail) and the trunk referred to as the 'at-the-same time same/other, [or] being/non-being' (Serres, 1980, p. 37). Cutting off the head of the snake would have sufficed to eradicate the danger. Yet, no doubt unbeknown to himself, by describing this triple cut La Fontaine gives credit to a 'logic of three values' that could have led to a more peaceful resolution, if heeded (Serres, 1980, pp. 36–7).

The undecidable and seemingly contradictory nature of the excluded middle, as it reveals itself in the fable, is for Serres, however, a significant passage to connect with the sciences, fluid mechanics, thermodynamics, information theory and in particular with contemporary developments in physics and mathematics concerning non-linear dynamical systems theory (chaos theory) and complexity theory. In a series of texts published between 1982 and 1991, Serres develops the notion of complex time, whereas tradition expresses time in terms of an irreversible and regular flow. For Serres, time is percolating, non-linear, with unpredictable deviations and variations in speed; in short, time is chaotic, similar to the manifestations of the excluded middle. His argument for such reflections is given strength by the fact that in his native tongue weather and time are expressed by one and the same noun, "temps", so that unpredictable characteristics of evolving weather systems can more easily be transposed to time itself, especially since time is recognized as a key factor in dynamical systems.

The excluded third can no longer be thought of as a third; the numerical reference still harks back to the dualism of same and other, and the principle of identity. In the undecidable space of the middle/third, Serres sees instead the "multiple" in the qualitative sense that Henri Bergson ascribes to continuous multiplicities. The swarms of parasitic insects are merely a numerical multiple, or a difference in degree. *Genèse* is the first essay to express the multiple as a difference in kind, as fusion, as continuously different in the Deleuzian sense and as duration in the Bergsonian sense. This leads to a theory of non-linear time that Serres develops in an empirical, immanent fashion in discourses on the multiple, the métis, and on mixed bodies ("corps mêlés"). The objective of his arguments is the multiple as a new object in philosophy, and 'history is the ultimate goal' (Serres, 1982, p. 15).

Détachement continues the story of the multiple in terms of non-linear trajectories of time and history. *Les cinq sens* circumscribes the possibility of an immanent experience of the world by the subject who divests himself of the "language screen" summarily called culture that humans have erected between themselves and reality. In this remarkable text, Serres suggests that a truly new knowledge is understanding that the binary systems on which Western thinking has been built do not correctly model reality and that most systems fall between the poles of dualistic structuring. It is a philosophy of circumstances uniting the circum- to the linear -stance, and thereby expresses a 'topology of mappings' as the true picture of reality in process. Like the grazing goats, this understanding leaves the straight Cartesian path of rationality, and opts for a method of the unpredictable that Serres finds in the Homeric 'Ulyssean trajectories'.[4]

The Serresean understanding of history is detailed in *Statues*, a text that brings together order and chaos in fuzzy boundaries where the dynamics of subject and object are no longer distinct and where time plays its operating role in the notion of generative death. In a later text, Serres clearly rejects traditional historiography and maintains that the development of history resembles what is understood today as chaos theory (Serres et al., 1995, p. 57). *Le Tiers-Instruit* is an educational manual – in the Serresean style – for the instruction of the excluded third into the new knowledge of which death as a creative force is a major part. Very Deleuzian in its pursuit of images that display the middle-ground or middle-fold in which the middle-instructed (le tiers-instruit) learns to become manifold and bifurcate into an inventive reality, he enters a time of "pure passing" but does not dwell in time (Serres, 1987, p. 34). The trajectory of his life goes towards a region of invention but never comes to rest there. The middle-instructed will always tend towards the unpredictable and thereby is the guarantor of creativity, which for Serres is the equivalent of a History of Life. How the historical activities of a middle-instructed interact with the material world in which he lives and invents is the topic of *Le Contrat naturel*, where time, in the form of prescription, is the founding operator for arguments concerning the question of right.

· · ·

The tale of the giant sequoia tree (Serres, 1983, pp. 99–107) is an example of Serres' notion of the new time in its topological manifestations. He chooses a tree, since trees have symbolic significance for early Western rituals, although he makes only an oblique reference to the Edenic Tree of Knowledge as an Ur-symbol. Disillusioned by the excesses of contentious human knowledge, Serres searches for signs of a tree of life. We commonly forget that God did not exile Adam and Eve from Paradise for having partaken of knowledge. The Bible speaks of a second tree, the Tree of Life, equally off limits for finite human hands, because, once picked and tasted, its fruit would bestow immortality. In a pre-emptive move, God exiles the couple from his garden so that, already having disobeyed his law in order to gain knowledge of good and evil, they would not attain immortality as well and become God-like (Gen. 3:22). The difference between this Edenic story, never mentioned by Serres, and his tale of the sequoia underscores the moral of his fable, for he discovers the work of immortality within the finite human sphere, through an immanent experience of nature, without once transgressing into the transcendent sphere of the divine.

On a visit to the redwood groves of Northern California, one particular tree catches Serres' attention, for its "colossal, monstrous" majesty fills him with awe and terror. The other trees form a forest, but this one is a "temple". Serres knows he is in the presence of something sacred that has nothing to do with a transcendent experience. Rather, the immediate signs of life, the green foliage high up on this 4000-year-old tree, make him aware of the immanence of pure nature, which human cultural and technological activity has obfuscated over millennia. A museum details the history of these endangered trees, but Serres concentrates exclusively on the dynamics of this living creature, which is so majestic and so old that it seems to defy death. He muses that our prehistoric ancestors adopted this tree so that it might become their messenger to the gods, with its mighty spire stretching upwards to the heavens. It is their orant that will prolong their prayers in perpetuity. Making the ageless tree the focus of their sacred rituals, the ancients learnt how to triumph over death and invented their own immortality. Central to this fable is Serres' temporal perspective. Neither growth-rings nor girth or height as spatial measurements are important, but the idea of a quest for a long-lived species. Recognizing time as a giver of life, not of destruction and death, the ancients planted a visible, living promise of their own immortality. They did taste of the tree of life, in blissful ignorance of a divine injunction; they perceived a 'being of nature' in its full immanence.

Serres participates in their celebration of immortal life within the finitude of human existence. He adds other examples of perpetuity: The domestication of animals and the cultivation of grasses into crop-producing plants, the invention of writing, the development of logic, arithmetic and geometry, are all signs of our immortality that our ancestors invented as their legacy to us. Once invented, these sciences never disappeared but over time flourished into multiple cultural expressions. We consider only their utility, which is a static perspective, and forget that in these inventions and their enduring longevity the genius of the ancients has preserved the gift of their and our immortality. The fable of the sacred sequoia and its visible majestic life-force suggests time as a dynamical, inventive process, not as a string of static facts or events that are counted out to create History, a process that Serres marks as a faulty historicism, parallel to the "cinematographic method" of the sciences that Henri Bergson rejects in favour of the 'flux de la durée' (the flow of duration) as a time of invention (Bergson, 1963, IV, p. 784).

For Serres, the "new time" of inventive immortality is the necessary antidote to combat parasitic Evil and our culture of strife and death. It is the life-force, Bergson's much celebrated "élan vital", here expressed in mythical form. For Serres, mythology shares with the sciences and philosophy the passages on the road to what it means to know. Time – and human history – expressed in the sequoia fable is thus a valid topological construct that follows its own non-linear evolution.

The introductory chapter of *Hominescence* recalls the ancients of that story, who lived life in all its natural force and claimed immortality in the form of concrete inventions that fashioned the culture we take for granted today. What makes for a very different reading in *Hominescence* is a sustained effort to describe an irrevocable evolutionary leap, from the immortality evoked in the sequoia myth to "a new immortality" (Serres, 2001, pp. 8–9). It is a text on history-in-the-making that is neither total absence of historical conscious nor full, mature History. It is "historescence", a "third-position" reality for the excluded middle reared to become the 'middle-instructed', now sent out to learn to live in a third space of global proportions. It is no longer the past but not yet the future, and its present is unstable, as passing and moving as the state of adolescence or luminescence. The suffix -escence, 'in the process of becoming', promises a portrait of humanity that lives on an evolutionary cusp. Indeed, in this text, Serres favours the term evolution, as it concerns the human individual, the Earth we all inhabit and the communication revolution. His argument takes into account the double effect of evolution, selection and mutation. Selection was and is a slow but steady adaptation to changing natural conditions. It was selection that empowered the "ancients" to invent systems we still live by today. Mutation, on the other hand, creates something new, haphazardly. Today, however, biochemistry and genetics have solved the mystery of random, chance mutation; science has learnt to manipulate it:

We intervene in mutation, minimize chance, accelerate [evolutionary] time and invent GMO's and, perhaps, whole species; here then 'immortality' enters again, for without fail, the new genome will become part of the chain of life (Serres, 2001, p. 9).

An immediate result is contingence instead of evolutionary necessity. "Hominescence" is therefore not the birth of a new human in the sense of a "new Adam", but a coming-up, a beginning-to-develop of a human who is 'a mixture of unpredictability and rationality that cannot be analyzed, a chaotic and contingent adventure' (Serres, 2001, p. 11). Contingence becomes one of the key notions of this text, as are prescription, percolating time, possibilities, feedback loops, relations and communications, folds, the theme of "never before" and "totipotency", the latter a Serresean neologism that expresses the limitless and all-encompassing possibilities of the hominescent human. They concern his body mutations (longevity, health options, genetic enhancements, etc.), the changing relationship with the Earth through global feedback actions on his part that mutate the Earth as well as its inhabitants, or the virtual realm of communications and information data banks that allows him and his conversation partners to be everywhere and nowhere in particular.

For Serres, today's technologies unlock a new time, create new living beings, change our world and globalize virtual communication networks. We live a radical 'bifurcation where evolution reappears in order to throw itself again into history, whereas until now history lifted us out of [evolution]' (Serres, 2001, p. 11). *Hominescence* sketches the astonishing successes of science, while at the same time lamenting the stagnation of traditional philosophies. J.T. Fraser, internationally known scholar of interdisciplinary studies on time, calls this split between the unimaginable swiftness of technological advances, on one hand, and the faltering efforts of traditional philosophical systems to account for corresponding changes in human values, on the other, an 'identity crisis of mankind' living the reality of a 'time-compact globe' (Fraser, 2007, p. 392).

In this light, *Hominescence* is Serres' follow-up of his own scathing critique of epistemology, detailed in the *Hermès* series. Reminiscent of the "where?" in *Atlas*, it opens new ways to ask the "why" of things while steering clear of theoretical speculation. Sketching the portrait of a new emerging human, a newly globalized world, and the virtual communication arena of relationships that change our sense of space and time, *Hominescence* is the most expansive essay on Serresean philosophy, to date. Not as pessimistic as Fraser, for whom the rapid developments of our era change our awareness of time to an "experiential instant" (Fraser, 2007, p. 366), it is a philosophy of contingence and possibilities: Today '[we] discover the horror of all ontologies . . . What is this human? Answer: A 'possible' in a pleated fan (éventail) of possible powers, potencies, yes, omnipotency, since he can become everything' (Serres, 2001, p. 63). Implied in the notion of immortality, Serres even speaks of a philosophy of non-knowledge ("non-savoir"), in the sense that the hominescent remains open to all "possibles" and avoids restrictive speculations on finitude, determination and the straightjacket of rational philosophical systems.

Thematically, Serres demonstrates this new way to knowledge with a threefold approach: First, the physical body is being overhauled thanks to medical, nutritional and technological advances, to live longer, better and more perfect. 'Homo universalis begins to live in the heady air of relative infinitude' (Serres, 2001, p. 68). Second, with a shift away from traditional agriculture and animal husbandry, which since the early twentieth century rapidly lost their central and constituent position in the formation of Western culture and civilization, agro-business and industrial and technological developments have changed our world on a global scale. Serres emphasizes two situations never before encountered: Human global action affects and alters our planet and *Lebenswelt* to a degree that forces humans, in turn, to adapt and change in order to live in, under and by these altered conditions. What one should understand as manipulated mutations on a global scale is expressed as global feedback loops ("boucles") that inexorably wed the Earth and the human in a never before envisioned union, for better or worse. Earth is becoming a political subject: 'Born of the concrete hard sciences, the Earth enters into History. That is also what I mean when I speak of hominescence' (Serres, 2001, p. 185).

Third, the new technologies allow global communication networks to become virtual powers that shape the lives of individuals as well as social groups. Serres understands this very concretely as a stage for fundamental changes in the relationships "among ourselves". The Web and 3G (and future nG?) gadgets allow us to be anywhere at any time. As individuals, we no longer identify with a place and a moment in time, with a here and now, as we have done for millennia:

> The universality of the new humanism is the result of the extensions we inhabit from now on. Space without distance implies an 'I' without space. We no longer live with geometry, the Earth, and measurements; we inhabit instead a topology without metrics nor distance, a qualitative space (Serres, 2001, p. 198).

Extensions imply stretching, twisting, enlarging; they imply movement. Serres creates here a topological sketch of a future hominescent history that is foreshadowed by Henri Bergson's non-numerical qualitative multiplicities.

Serres describes the past not as a historiographer but as an archeologist in order to find the material, concrete sources of our "exo-Darwinean" evolution into hominescent beings: 'That is why this book often burrows below History before rejoining it, sometimes' (Serres, 2001, pp. 206–207). Disavowing ontological or historicist terms, he portrays the hominescent as a dynamical being whose body, medically, nutritionally and technologically enhanced to near totipotency supports all contingencies for a non-linear creative life blessed with an invincible spirit: the hominescent who can become everything. Left unanswered is the question whether his creative trajectories will tend towards good or evil. However, Serres hints at a possible answer, when he contrasts the nature of traditional philosophy to iconoclastic non-linear thought worthy of a hominescent:

> The human is horrified of the notion of being. I even begin to doubt that, circling around in vague generalities of its own language, ontology will ever know how to discourse on pebbles, backwaters, crocodiles, or sequoias. [. . .] It only knows dead corpses (Serres, 2001, p. 65).

The ethical question returns in *Le Mal propre*, a provocative little text on first perusal. In 'Revisiting The Natural Contract', Serres had already outlined a global situation of "never before" forcing us to accept that 'any change of scale requires an adjustment of concepts' (Serres, 2006, p. 10). He does this in *Le Mal propre* in a most elementary, often shocking, on occasion brutal manner.[5] It is a "tough-love" text revealing a passionate concern for the hominescent generation, himself included. In this "graffiti of rage" (Serres, 2008, p. 59) he appeals to our moral duty to rethink the right to property born of the human drive to appropriate a place called one's own and defended with one's life. This elemental urge is affirmed not by legal or social agreements, but by actions of the body that go back to behaviours common to animals and shared by humans in their evolutionary development (Serres, 2008, p. 15).

The right to ownership is originally a natural impulse and precedes any contractual law. Animals indicate territorial rights with their droppings and markings. Ancient rites and ancestor cults show that humans did likewise, their "markings" were primarily the burial sites of their family or clan members. The corpses of their dead marked the territory, it became their "pagus", field, farm and dwelling. Serres cites the example of Romulus who killed his rival brother Remus, buried him, and above his grave founded the city of Rome, thus becoming its proprietor and master. 'Romulus remained true to the wolves who had raised him' (Serres, 2008, p. 16). Serres underlines this statement to reiterate the importance of our original animal actions, when it comes to our sense of right to property. The title of the first half of the text, 'Urine, manure, blood, sperm', refers not only to the behaviour of animals but also to rudimentary customs of our farming ancestors, repeated in various forms throughout human history.

The title "Le Mal propre" carries multiple meanings. "Propre" refers equally to ownership, cleanliness and intrinsic quality. Serres collapses the three meanings: Property is established by the action of marking, which is basically a process of soiling a clean object for all but the one who marks and becomes by that fact its owner. Whether using a hotel bed, spitting in a bowl of soup, or Serres' name on this book, each gesture declares the owner of the object. The etymological connection allows Serres to underscore the fundamental theory for this text, that there is 'a behavior shared by all living species: one's own is acquired and retained by the dirty [gesture]. Better yet: one's own is dirty' (Serres, 2008, p. 7). A second translation is equally valid: 'What is clean is acquired and retained by what is dirty. Better yet: what is clean is what is dirty.'

Topologically speaking, this contradiction is non-contradictory and presents a fundamental dilemma for human relations. It is the "intrinsic Evil", le "Mal propre", that is, the onset of what Serres understands as the 'nightmare we call History' (Serres, 2008, p. 24).

With this dynamical premise, Serres recalls what can only be characterized as a History of Pollution. Polluting by markings becomes polluting with garbage, becomes 'global excrements of our species' (Serres, 2008, p. 54). Physical hard ("dur") garbage is soon joined by soft ("doux") garbage that is noise pollution, advertising, commercials and billboards that get ever larger and cover the countryside with their screaming messages. The problem of pollution is of course recognized as a primary concern and tackled by many scientists. But Serres maintains that their work addresses the how of pollution. The task he sets for himself is to uncover and understand the why of this scourge and to uproot and eradicate it.

The Serresean history of pollution develops from the marked boundaries of the animal lair to the pagus or plot of land of the ancestral peasant, to acquisition of territories by conquest, to industrial production of goods, to appropriating radio frequencies for beaming out one's noisy messages – Serres' list is too numerous to complete here. What crystallizes out of his discourse is the human need and desire for a place of one's own, a private space proper to oneself. We pollute because we strive for a niche, our proprietary lair. As our culture and civilization evolved, the desire for property grew ever more rapidly into a desire for domination, with the resultant wars, violence, colonization of other countries, massive publicity and advertising that seeks to channel human desire for more goods and conveniences, and the total subjugation of the physical planet itself that is slowly turning into a global garbage heap.

The clean, the dirty and the evil, these three notions come together when one considers contemporary globalization. The human has become a being-in-the-world, who has seen the Earth photographed from afar and who has fabricated world-objects of world dimensions. The atomic bomb, satellites, the internet, nuclear waste, etc., have worldwide consequences. The relationship between subject and object, which was the foundation of philosophical thought and knowledge for centuries, is now radically changing. 'We ourselves suddenly depend, and increasingly so, on things that depend on actions that we undertake' (Serres, 2006, p. 5). We have to think knowledge and action differently because world subjects and world objects, and their interactions, are marked from now on by the "never-before" (Serres, 2006, p. 8).

The history of pollution and the history of appropriation are one and the same. Today we face the overwhelming reality of pollution/appropriation that needs to be continuously augmented to satisfy the desires of the world-subject. He becomes a world proprietor, but leaves the world covered in growing layers of garbage, hard and soft.[6] The future is one of contentious masters and owners of all of nature, no longer one of humans marking or staking out local plots of land or a niche. 'Globalized, present-day pollution results from the battle to possess space in its totality. Do they give a thought to the possibility that the loss of limits may suppress the frontiers of property as such?' (Serres, 2008, p. 1).

Serres offers a solution to this march into disaster for both humans and nature. To be human, he maintains, means to have a place that offers protection, food and a space for action. However, he suggests that we entertain the idea of "de-possessing" the world, by uncovering and lifting the multiple layers of dirt and garbage, hard and soft, that choke the Earth and cover nature's beauty (Serres, 2008, p. 74). De-appropriation is the key to all future action. De-possessing starts therefore at the basic level of one's niche. Serres proposes that instead of a proprietor the human become a "locataire", a tenant of a niche, a place, the world and nature. The English "tenant" is not quite as helpful to Serres' argument, while the French "locataire" derives directly from locus, place; it emphasizes the place in a neutral mode, without any link to possession, whereas "tenant" implies a contractual relationship with a proprietor. The beauty of the real world, of the Object as such – so ardently pursued in *Les cinq sens* – will reappear, once we cease to mark property, and the crust of pollution is lifted. Serres promises a state of ecstasy when that future moment of beauty and peace arrives.

Although not mentioned directly, Rousseau's hypothetical founder of civilization plays a major role in Serres' deliberations in *Le Contrat naturel*.

In *Le Mal propre*, Serres squares off with his compatriot's conjecture and does so in a way that lightens the harsh and often apocalyptic tone of this text. Having quoted Rousseau's well-known passage and finding fault with the conventional premise of a contractual right to property (Serres, 2008, p. 16), Serres backs up his own meditations on the Evil, the "propre" and the dirty, with deconstructive reiterations of Rousseau's words. Throughout this text, we read Rousseau in multiple versions: of a farmer discovering the fruitful use of manure (p. 10), of Livy (p. 16), of Latin explanations (pp. 18–19), of blood sacrifices (p. 19), of sexual conquest (p. 32), of financial expansions (p. 52), of a Jean-Jacques website (p. 52) and of ecological considerations (p. 64). The intent of this spirited quid pro quo is to convey the argument that Rousseau's assumption of a legal contract as the origin of civilization is erroneous, whereas Serres posits a natural one, having studied ethological and anthropological sources.

Globalization has breached the frontiers set by local appropriation; the motto 'everything is ours' erases borders and lines. We occupy a space without limits and claim proprietary rights to a virtual world (the Web, UMTS, etc.). But we have to recognize that the topological space we move in must be a space for a new history, that of the good "locataire" who lives in a place or locus, with reserve, modesty, discernment, responsibility and a degree of detachment, all attitudes that express the tenant's moral obligation to save the reserves of the physical world around him (Serres, 2008, p. 86). Yet, no matter how frail and miserable we are in an ontological sense, it is the 'propre de l'Homme', our characteristic as humans, to have a vital and natural right to a place. How we manage this right in the light of an ethical reserve we have to adopt for the sake of the planet, our ultimate niche, is outlined by one last deconstructive rendition of Rousseau's words: "'The first who enclosed a garden and dared to say 'This is enough for me', and never drooled over more space than needed for himself ('égonome'), made peace with his neighbors, and defended the peaceful right to sleep, to warm himself, and above all the divine right to love." This is Jean-Jacques in a version by Michel Serres' (Serres, 2008, p. 87).

When Serres calls upon Montaigne to help him hold on to the sweetness of his mother tongue or the subtle music of his soul, in the middle of the overwhelming din of our high-wired world (Serres, 2008, pp. 60–61), the reader understands that Serres has a reservoir that will sustain the "locataire" on the ever non-linear road to peace, peace with himself, with his neighbour "locataires" and with the Earth. 'It suffices for me!' is Serres' version of Montaigne's 'vivre à propos' (Montaigne, III, 13). Living with discernment, with good judgement is living in a topological space that is sweet, volatile, unrestricted by fences, peaceful, sufficient and undemanding. Montaigne's 'art de vivre' is here given a modern future face. The hominescent arising from the last paragraphs of *Le Mal propre* lives and respects the real world around him. We read here a feedback loop to the *Hermès* essays and their search for a perfect union between subject and object. Leaving theory behind, digging deep below History, Serres finds it in the immanent conditions for a natural contract between the guardian tenant, the "locataire", and the Earth, our singular locus.

Notes

1 As quoted by Philippe Sollers in *Le Nouvel Observateur*, Nov. 5–11, 2009, p. 54. This and subsequent translations of French sources are mine, unless indicated otherwise.
2 Except for occasional critical remarks in early works, Serres is silent on contemporary philosophical and epistemological works. The reference to Deleuze is thus the more significant and testifies to Serres's deeply felt kinship with Deleuzian thought.
3 Translation by Harari et al., 1982, p. xxvi.
4 Serres's rendition of Ulysses' torturous sea voyage is a veiled description of a nonlinear dynamical system with its tell-tale trajectories tending towards a basin of attraction (Serres, 1985, p. 287).
5 An example is a highly critical commentary on a text by Immanuel Kant (Serres, 2008, pp. 33–34).
6 The catastrophic oil spill in the Gulf of Mexico, at the time of this writing, is a stark confirmation of Serres's theory of pollution/appropriation.

Bibliography

Assad, M. (2000), 'Language, nonlinearity, and the problem of Evil'. *Configurations*, 8(2), pp. 271–83.
Bergson, H. (1963), *L'Évolution créatrice*. Paris: Presses Universitaires de France.
Deleuze, G. (1988a), *Le Pli. Leibniz et le baroque*. Paris: Éditions de Minuit.
—(1988b), *Foucault*. Translated by S. Hand. Minneapolis: University of Minnesota Press.
—(2002), *L'île déserte et autres textes*. Paris: Éditions de Minuit.
Deleuze, G. and Guattari, F. (1991), *Qu'est-ce que la philosophie?*. Paris: Éditions de Minuit.
Fraser, J. T. (2007), *Time and Time Again: Reports from a Boundary of the Universe*. Leiden, The Netherlands: Brill NV.
'Genesis'. The Jerusalem Bible (1966). Garden City, New York: Doubleday and Co.
Harari, J. and Bell, D. (1982), *Hermes: Literature, Science, Philosophy*. Baltimore: Johns Hopkins University Press.
Montaigne, M. (1980), *Essais*. Paris: Bordas.

Serres, M. (1968), *Hermès I, La communication*. Paris: Éditions de Minuit.
—(1972), *Hermès II, L'interférence*. Paris: Éditions de Minuit.
—(1974), Hermès III, La traduction. Paris: Éditions de Minuit.
—(1977), *Hermès IV, La distribution*. Paris: Éditions de Minuit.
—(1980a), *Hermès V, Le passage du Nord-Ouest*. Paris: Éditions de Minuit.
—(1980b), *Le Parasite*. Paris: Grasset.
—(1982), *Genèse*. Paris: Grasset et Fasquelle.
—(1983), *Détachement*. Paris: Flammarion.
—(1985), *Les cinq sens*. Paris: Grasset.
—(1987) *Statues*. Paris: François Bourin.
—(1990), *Le Contrat naturel*. Paris: François Bourin.
—(1991), *Le Tiers-Instruit*. Paris: François Bourin.
—(1994), *Atlas*. Paris: Éditions Julliard.
—(2001), *Hominescence*. Paris: Éditions Le Pommier.
—(2006), 'Revisiting The Natural Contract'. Translated by A. Feenberg-Dibon. Edited by Arthur and M. Kroker. *1000 Days of Theory*. www.ctheory.net, td039.
—(2008), *Le Mal propre*. Paris: Éditions Le Pommier.
Serres, M. and Latour, B. (1995), *Conversations on Science, Culture, and Time*. Translated by R. Lapidus. Ann Arbor: The University of Michigan Press.

Chapter 6

Post-Human Humanities

Claire Colebrook

Suddenly a local object, nature, on which a merely partial subject could act, becomes a global objective, Planet Earth, on which a new, total subject, humanity, is toiling away (Serres, 1995, 5).

There was something odd about Stanley Fish's speedy intervention in the "debate" about the closure of certain humanities departments:

But keeping something you value alive by artificial, and even coercive, means (and distribution requirements are a form of coercion) is better than allowing them to die, if only because you may now die (get fired) with them, a fate that some visionary faculty members may now be suffering. I have always had trouble believing in the high-minded case for a core curriculum — that it preserves and transmits the best that has been thought and said — but I believe fully in the core curriculum as a device of employment for me and my fellow humanists. But the point seems to be moot. It's too late to turn back the clock (Fish, 2010).

In the general milieu of non-debate that pitched economic rationalism against an unquestioning right for the humanities to continue existing in its current form, Fish admitted that certain nineteenth-century "pieties" would not be believed. Fish himself did not disclose whether he believed these pieties or whether they ought to be believed; he went on to admit that keeping the valued humanities alive would require possibly coercive means. These means would not be a justification of the humanities but "aggressive explanation" of the "core enterprise". Along the way Fish laments that it would be the French departments – French, the once hot-bed of real ideas – that seem to be expendable in the way that Spanish is not. Now, such a paean is odd, given that one might have thought that if one really valued and wanted to sustain what "we" learned from the French in their high theory heyday it might have been that education as a "core enterprise" might be worth questioning (both for reasons of politics in Foucault's sense, or the way disciplines constitute illusions of "the" polity, and for reasons of good thinking, such that 'keeping something you value alive' might best be achieved not by clinging to survival but by a joyously destructive and active nihilism). Fish already suggests in his title – 'The Crisis of the Humanities Officially Arrives' – that the crisis was implicit up until now. Indeed the humanities have been in crisis, and for good reason. If, as Husserl already noted very early in the last century, the "sciences" were in crisis because of a certain notion of "man" as a natural animal blessed with technical reasoning capacities, then such a crisis could not but affect the humanities. Even Husserl accepted the impossibility of grounding any new knowledge or future-oriented discipline on man as he actually is and suggested that dealing with the crisis would entail opening a new line of thought beyond natural "man".

Today, in a century that can begin to sense, if not articulate, humanity's capacity to destroy its own species-being, along with the milieu that it has constitutively polluted to the point of annihilation, what sort of defence might one make for the future of humanities disciplines? Should one not, rather, say "no" to everything that has defended and saved man and his future, especially to the concept of life and potentiality of which man would be the utmost expression? Do we not require a new discipline? This would need to take the form not of the humanities, especially if the humanities were to take on a certain motif of the post-human. That is, if the humanities were to live on by consuming, appropriating and claiming as its own the life of animals, digital technologies, inter-disciplinarity (or the rendering of science as human), then there would merely be a continuation of a reactive nihilism.

Post-humanism, as I will define it here, is not an overcoming of the human but takes a similar form to the structure of nihilism. If belief in a transcendent redemption negated the force of this world for a higher world, then a reactive nihilism responded to the loss of transcendence with despair, the horror that there might be nothing more than this world. In this respect, the retreat to a world in which there is only man, not God, remains theological – for God has been subtracted but the world as God-less (abandoned to man) remains. The post-human, similarly, renounces human privilege or speciesism but then fetishises the post-human world as man-less; "we" are no longer elevated, separated, enclosed, detached from a man-less world, for there is a direct interface and interconnection – a mesh or network, a living system – that allows for one world of computers, digital media, animals, things and systems. There is a continuation of the humanities, which had always refused that man had any end other than that which he gave to himself, in the post-human notion that man is nothing but a point of relative stability, connected to one living system that he can feel affectively and read. Not only have motifs such as "affect", "post-human", living systems and digital media been explicit topics – giving the impression that "the" humanities can survive criticisms of the illusions of a once-dominant (supposedly) Cartesian rationalism, these motifs have intensified and entrenched the strategies that have always marked the humanities. They allow for business as usual – in the same manner that nihilism allowed for a continued theologism – at the same time as this business is conducted in a reactive and resentful mode. For what have "the post-human", "affective" or "ethical" turns licensed? There has been an avowed reaction against a supposed linguisticism or textual narcissism (also referred to as linguistic idealism), so that the God of language is dead, and we no longer believe that this world of ours is given order from without, by "a" system of language or structure, which it would be the job of literary critics or cultural studies to decode.

The humanities would, through all its demarcation disputes, attacks, defences and mutations, be defined not by a normative notion of the human but by an anti-normative insistence that man is not, for he has no positive being other than that which is given to him by virtue of his historical and living becoming. The humanities would be primarily critical and interpretive, and would be entwined with a logic of negation and refusal. The sciences would be procedural, operating from within paradigms (however sophisticated, reflected upon or provisional) while the humanities would occur through self-distancing or reading: whatever life or system is given, it is the task of the humanities – because there is no such thing as the human – to open a space of conversation, legitimation, questioning or critique. Without such a space, one would be reduced to the ruthless actuality of metrics or utilitarianism. "Man", as given in the humanities, is not the man of science (subjecting the world to so many repeatable, efficient and quantifiable functions). Nor is the humanity of the humanities the "man" of the human sciences (whereby man's social and political being can be read as an expression of what Foucault refers to as his "empirical density": man speaks and labours because of the needs of life, and it is this emergence from life that allows man to read himself in today's anthropology, social linguistics, evolutionary psychology and cognitive archaeology). The man of the humanities was already post-human, possessing no being other than his reflexive capacity to read his own ungrounded and utterly flexible becoming. 'At the very moment that we are acting physically for the first time on the global Earth, and when it in turn is doubtless reacting on global humanity, we are tragically neglecting it'

(Serres, 1995, 29). For Serres, then, humanity is not a concept that grounds the humanities, nor is "man" a concept expressed by the various disciplines that comprise the humanities. Rather, "humanity" is a meteorological imperative, a concept that needs to be created today in order to confront the change in techno-geological climates. Serres' work, despite its manifest humanism in *The Natural Contract*, does not take the form of a resistance to the technical reduction of man to systems. (What his work requires, like that of Deleuze, is not a resistance to calculation but a more subtle differential calculation: a reckoning of the quantities and systems produced by the relations among the bodies of the human species and the other forces upon which it is parasitic.) His is not a post-humanism that would happily conflate human existence with life in general. Such post-humanisms are really ultra-humanisms insofar as they attribute all the qualities once assigned to man – qualities such as mindfulness, connectedness, self-organizing dynamism – to some supposedly benevolent life in general that needs to be saved from the death of merely calculative systems.

This is, supposedly, the value of the humanities today, both in its ideal resistance to a culture of economic rationalism and narrow utilitarianism and in its less pious claim to educate students with transferable skills or critical reasoning or rhetorical flexibility. The humanities of post-humanism has happily abandoned speciesism and exceptionalism – man is no longer adjudicator or hermeneutic arbiter outside the web of life – for there is one de-centred, mutually imbricated, constantly creative mesh, system or network of life:

> The ecological thought imagines interconnectedness, which I call the mesh. Who or what is interconnected with what or whom? The mesh of interconnected things is vast, perhaps immeasurably so. Each entity in the mesh looks strange. Nothing exists all by itself, and so nothing is fully 'itself.' There is curiously 'less' of the Universe at the same time, and for the same reasons, as we see 'more' of it. Our encounter with other beings becomes profound. They are strange, even intrinsically strange. Getting to know them makes them stranger. When we talk about life forms, we're talking about strange strangers. The ecological thought imagines a multitude of strange strangers (Morton, 2010, 15).

But it is the sacrifice of man as Cartesian subject in favour of the post-human ecology of systems that allows the humanities to live on. If the human is assumed to be nothing more than an interface, already at one with a world that is one living system, then post-humanism is nothing more than the negation of a humanism that never was. It is an ultra-humanism precisely because once man is abandoned as a distinct system or inflection he returns to characterize nature or life in general, just as the death of God left an implicit and widespread theologism that no longer had a distinct or explicit logic. Post-humanism is an ultra-humanism and partakes of the same metaleptic logic of reactive nihilism. In nihilism, a higher world is posited to justify or grant worth to this world. This higher world is posited from a reaction against the force of this world. When that supposed transcendence is no longer affirmed, this world becomes a world minus transcendence, godless, worthless, void and negated. Humanism posits an elevated or exceptional "man" to grant sense to existence, then when "man" is negated or removed, what is left is the all too human tendency to see the world as one giant anthropomorphic self-organizing living body. Not surprisingly, there become increasingly shrill calls for human meaning (including a pragmatic or humanized religion, and a certain substitution of literature for God as the ground of human sense-making). "Man" is effected as that animal who would be especially poised to read the logic of life, and this is because of his capacities for speech and sociality; it is the creation of man that enables a certain concept of life. When man is destroyed to yield a post-human world, it is the same world minus humans, a world of meaning, sociality and readability yet without any sense of the disjunction, gap or limits of the human. Like nihilism, the logic is metaleptic: the figure of man is originally posited in order to yield a sense or meaning of life, and yet when man is done away with as an external power what is left is an anthropomorphic life of meaning and readability. A certain idea of man – Foucault notes – was intertwined with the possibility of the human sciences and of a concomitant notion of life. If, for Foucault, both "man" and "life" emerge in the eighteenth century, this is because there is a new distribution in the table of knowledge, a new fold between inside and outside. Rather than examining the forms of living being in a world of analogies – with humanity being an expression of a broader cosmology – there is now something like life as such with its specific temporality and imperatives. Whereas humans had been privileged beings (blessed with reason), it is now man who is at once empirically constituted by life (required to speak, labour and constitute polities because of the needs of his species being) and yet also capable of reading that logic of life as transcendental: psychoanalysis, Marxism, ethnography, structuralism and (today's) evolutionary psychology or cognitive archaeology all account for the modus of the human organism according to a certain logic of life.

The end of metaphysics is only the negative side of a much more complex event in Western thought. This event is the appearance of man.
However, it must not be supposed that he suddenly appeared on our
horizon, imposing the brutal fact of his body, his labour and his language
in a manner so irruptive as to be absolutely baffling as to our reflection.
It is not man's lack of positivity that reduced the space of metaphysics so
violently. No doubt, on the level of appearances, modernity begins when
the human being begins to exist within his organism, inside the shell of
his head, inside the armature of his limbs, and in the whole structure of
his physiology; when he begins to exist at the centre of labour by whose
principles he is governed and whose logic eludes him; when he lodges
his thought in the folds of a language so much older than himself that
he cannot master its significations, even though they have been called
back to life by the insistence of his words. But, more fundamentally, our
culture crossed the threshold beyond which we recognize our modernity when finitude was conceived with an interminable cross-reference
with itself. Though it is true, at the level of the various branches of
knowledge, that finitude is always designated on the basis of man as a
concrete being and on the basis of the empirical forms that can be tied
to his existence, nevertheless, at the archaeological level, which reveals
the general, historical a priori of each of these branches of knowledge,
modern man – that man assignable in his corporeal, labouring, speaking
existence is possible only as a figuration of finitude. Modern culture can
conceive of man because it conceives of the finite on the basis of itself
(Foucault, 2003, p. 346).

Today, even though man as a privileged being has been incorporated into a
post-human plane of interacting living systems, what remains is the reactive
and ultra-human logic of finitude: it is because there is life or a being's relationship with an ecology that one can only know the world as it is given
through organic conditions. A being is alive insofar as it maintains itself and
does so in relation to a milieu that it perceives according to its own capacities; humans and animals have worlds, and the world is neither so much
data to be represented by an imposed order nor a book of life, but an inter-
active and dynamic mesh of living systems. One can account for language,
labour and life according to a single logic of man: a being emerges from the
needs of self-maintenance (which in the case of man requires language, the
polity and labour), but it is man who has the capacity to read the enigmatic
density of life. His empirical being is the sign of a broader logic (a transcendental logic of life).

If the humanities – for Foucault – had any value, it would not be as an extension of this logic – such that we might see literature as emerging from evolving and self-furthering life, or as somehow the means by which the empirical being of man might be awakened to his proto-transcendental powers of critique. Rather what Foucault referred to as literature would evidence something like a force beyond life, a machinic power that could not be referred back to the self-furthering human organism (Deleuze, 2006, p. 110). Language would not be the system through which we could read man's emergence from a general order of life as self-maintenance; it would not be world-disclosive, nor an extension of organic and organizing imperatives of life.

Now if it is this man (of finitude) that has been removed from exceptionalism in the post-human landscape, and if the humanities disciplines have abandoned poetic assumptions of human speech as a special or privileged domain for revelation, what remains is a negative or reactive continuation of anthropomorphic projection by other means. Self-maintaining organicism and auto-poeisis are everywhere. In terms of theory, this has led to a post-human landscape in which there is one general dynamic system with animals, machines and digital codes all woven to constitute a single ecology; the knowledge procedures are generally extensive, subsuming more events within the domain of one evolving and efficient life. (What is not considered are radically differing intensities, or intensive multiplicities, in which different speeds and economies open different and incompossible systems.) Not only have explicit versions of literary Darwinism led to a rejection of high theory (a high theory that had supposedly imprisoned thought in language [Carroll 2004, 29]), there has also been a more general proclaimed post-humanism that considers the absence of man to be a license for a new literalism, with direct talk of life, affect, bodies and ethics/politics.

The ethical turn, like the affective turn, is a turn back away from a supposed human centredness on language to the real and collective conditions of existence. One might cite, as an example, Eva Ziarek's critique of Agamben. Agamben had already attacked the deconstructive attention to limits in order to retrieve the event of saying or opening of the political (Agamben, 1999, 209). Ziarek, in turn, wants to take Agamben's general concept of potentiality, from which the polity would open, and locate this force in inter-subjective communality: 'potentiality cannot be understood, as Agamben seems to suggest, in terms of the isolated subject and what "he can or can not do," because it is fundamentally a relational concept, emerging from the encounter with another "you"' (Ziarek, 2010).

In a similar manner, Hardt and Negri also want to turn away from the locatedness of centering points of view, and therefore from language and other constituting, inhuman and transcendent (to human life) systems, to the commons, the multitude – immanent political bodies that would have nothing outside or beyond themselves (and certainly not any imposed norm of humanity): 'The primary decision made by the multitude is really the decision to create a new race or, rather, a new humanity. When love is conceived politically, then, this creation of a new humanity is the ultimate act of love' (Hardt et al., 2005, p. 26).

In addition to these general affirmations from theory that would now return man to the one common life of which he is a political and benevolent, ultimately productive, expression, new "post-human" objects of interest also return differential structures to purposive, self-maintaining, fruitful and generative life.

Digital media studies and animal studies affirm a continuous milieu of exchange in which there is neither a radical outside nor any limit to human comprehension. There has emerged in addition to a post-humanism that affirms a simple, continuous interface, a critical post-humanism that affirms embodiment. In reaction to those who feel that humanity may extend or overcome itself through technology, there have been those who stress the resistance and significance of the embodied substrate, directly rejecting the "substrate neutral" claims of those who stress computation (Dougherty, 2001). Critical post-humanism reacts against the idea that the body is a contingent hardware or means for an intelligence or humanity that is primarily informational, and in doing so is more critical of the humanist (or Cartesian, or rationalist) assumptions that "we" have now arrived at a point in history where technology might overcome the body. Critical post-humanism is, I would suggest – like other affective, ethical, corporeal or post-linguistic "turns" – a retrieval of the lived body that follows the same logic of reactive nihilism.

Both Serres and Deleuze, by contrast, focus on the inhuman multiplicities of systems: Serres' concepts of parasitism and pollution allow for an examination of what Deleuze and Guattari refer to as stratification (Deleuze and Guattari, 2004, p. 176). While systems are relational, it is also the case that appropriations, overcodings and disturbances produce distinct registers. The human, as a concept, would be one way of thinking technological, meteorological or disciplinary thresholds that create intense ruptures. Humanity would be a disturbing outcome of systemic events, not an origin. Given that both Serres and Deleuze's concepts of humanity or "the people" are futural – gestures towards how we might think the ways in which the human-sensory motor apparatus has intersected with and created new speeds for other systems – it is not surprising that Serres and Deleuze and Guattari have a counter-interdisciplinary mode of linking discourses without commensurability. What occurs is cross-contamination or discursive germinal warfare rather than communication and a common life world.

It was the genius of Foucault to take a logic of life and show its direct consequences for human disciplines. It is the turn to life – the idea that social historical man can be explained by a more general process of species being (or man as a labouring political animal) – that enables social sciences. These disciplines are reactive because they no longer present norms as direct imperatives but as following on from the needs of life; there can only be biopolitical management of populations if there are human sciences that enable an ethics of knowledge, an organization of the human species according to broader requirements of existence. The humanities, if they react against this reduction of man to a material body and affirm either the capacity of man as a speaking, labouring being not to speak or work (Agamben's impotentiality), or more standard humanist affirmations of that which is not quantifiable because embodied, affective and lived, do nothing more than maintain the normative logic of life that would entail their redundancy. That is: let us say that the human sciences and biopolitics reduce "man" to bare life, to being manipulable and manageable data. It follows that either the humanities become a supplement to this model – business ethics, bio-ethics, the production of transferable skills or critical reasoning – or, it argues that "humanity" is never simply data, information, animality or bare life, but has an excess of potentiality that remains unactualized. This would allow certain versions of post-humanism – those that argue for the ways in which animals or digital media complicate any simple Cartesian or rationalist model of the human – to keep the humanities alive. Man would not be mere biological mass, nor an information machine, and for this reason his "rights" could neither be saved in themselves nor extended to animals and humans: on the contrary, the embodied interactions of humans, machines and animals would evidence a richness of the vital, of the affectivity or the suffering, of the lived body. So if man as a particular and exceptional being has been vanquished, what is saved is nevertheless a highly normative (theological-organic) logic of life in which the bounded and self-separating body with a world of its own is affirmed against various calculative reductivisms.

Stanley Fish's objection to the closing of humanities departments never makes quite clear just what mode of humanities he wishes to save, or why such survival would truly be worthy. He does refer to the horror of closing French departments when it was precisely the French culture that was the breath of life for humanities departments in the 1980s. Leaving aside what

French might contribute to the twenty-first century, one needs to ask what aspect or consumed fragment of French theory yields a properly viable mode of humanities study. A certain strand of French thought – one highly suspicious not only of "man" but of certain structures of knowledge in which the emergence of systems and idealities might always be returned to the lived – is precisely what has been occluded in the so-called post-humanism of today. Indeed, the humanism that has been rejected is Cartesian computational or cognitive rationalism in favour of embodied, affective, distributed, emotional or subjective life. The humanities would somehow return disengaged logics and structures to the properly living or embodied plane of life from which they emerge. It is not only Habermas (1987), then, with his insistence that sciences always emerge from a lifeworld, who domesticates and anthropomorphizes knowledge systems, it is what currently passes for French-inflected theory that celebrates the primacy of the lived. N. Katherine Hayles, one of the key figures of contemporary post-humanism, proclaims her distinction and theoretical sophistication from a naïve computationalism in a return to embodiment, and the lived. For Hayles:

> The computational universe becomes dangerous when it goes from being a useful heuristic device to an ideology that privileges information over everything else. As we have seen, information is a socially constructed concept; in addition to its currently accepted definition, it could have been, and was, given different definitions. Just because information has lost its body does not mean that humans and the world have lost theirs.
>
> Fortunately, not all theorists agree that it makes sense to think about information as an entity apart from the medium that embodies it. Let us revisit some of the sites of the computational universe, this time to locate those places where the resistance of materiality does useful work within the theories. From this perspective, fracture lines appear that demystify the programme(s) and make it possible to envision other futures, futures in which human beings feel at home in the universe because they are embodied creatures living in an embodied world (Hayles, 1999, p. 244).

This post-humanism is reactive in two inextricable senses, morally/politically and epistemologically. As Nietzsche described the logic of ressentiment: one posits a value outside life (humanity) that would render life meaningful or worthy, and when that value is no longer affirmed or believed in one lives on in a state of weak, mournful and enslaved subjection. Various calls to save the humanities rely upon an asserted "something" that must be irreducible to the quantitative materialism of economic rationalism.

Methodologically or epistemologically this mystical "x" can either be the return of the subject as event (Badiou), the human as bare potentiality witnessed in its impotentiality (Agamben), the affective or lived experienced that is manifest precisely in its alienation. Just as Foucault (1978) argued that the subject would be maintained by a process of enquiring into his hidden sexuality that must be the cause of his being, so the human and humanities survive by continually searching for that ultimate cause from which calculative and scientific reasoning must have emerged. Here are two further examples: first, Mark Hansen, self-proclaimed new philosopher of new media, insists that it is precisely when digital media produces images with which I strive (but fail) to identify or empathize that "my" lived and affective embodiment is, by default, re-affirmed:

> ... the shift of affective power here explored – from image to body – goes hand-in-hand, and indeed exemplifies, a larger shift currently underway in our incipient digital culture: from the preformed technical image to the embodied process of framing information that produces images. What this means, ultimately, is that we can no longer be content with the notion that we live in a culture of already articulated images, as philosophers and cultural theorists from at least Bergson to Baudrillard have maintained.... Bluntly put, the processes governing embodied life in the contemporary infosphere are disjunctive from those governing digital information. Accordingly, in our effort to reconfigure visual culture for the information age, we must take stock of the supplementary sensorimotor dimension of embodied life that this heterogeneity makes necessary. Since there is no preformed analogy between embodiment and information, the bodily response to information – that is to say, affectivity – must step in to forge a supplementary one. In order for us to experience digital information, we must filter it through our embodied being, in the process transforming it from heterogeneous data flux into information units – images – that have meaning for us to the precise extent that they catalyze our affective response (Hansen, 2003, p. 225).

That is, the more inhuman, dehumanizing, replicating, alienating or simulating the image – the more the human appears as nothing more than appearance susceptible to inauthentic doubling – the more my alienated and impossible human feeling persists. It is as though the intensity of the despair I feel at your claims that God does not exist simply proves – through my very sense of loss and sadness – that really there must be a God or spirituality after all, known in His retreat or in my mourning. I feel a loss of meaning, ergo it is.

The second comes from Zizek, who draws upon Ranciere and Badiou to criticize a postmodern politics of a single domain of circulating opinions and tolerated identities in order to affirm the event of the subject. In a mode akin to St. Paul's universal Christianity in opposition to Greek sophistry or 'the Jewish discourse of obscurantist prophetism', the subject is not an affirmed substance within the world, nor a messianic visitation from another world, but is given only in its act of break or disorder – again known only in its not being known:

> ... the way to counteract this remerging ultra-politics is not more tolerance, more compassion and multicultural understanding but the return of the political proper, that is, the reassertion of the dimension of antagonism that, far from denying universality, is consubstantial with it. Therein lies the key component of the proper leftist stance, as opposed to the rightest assertion of particular identity: in the equation of universalism with the militant, divisive position of engagement in struggle. True universalists are not those who preach global tolerances of differences and all-encompassing unity but those who engage in a passionate fight for the assertion of truth that engages them (Zizek, 1998, p. 102).

The problem with humanism, so it seems, is that it is deemed to be rather inhuman. The Cartesian subject of calculative reason, along with computational theories of mind or representation, including both older humanisms of man as supreme moral animal and post-humanisms envisioning a disembodied world of absolute mastery, cannot cope with the complexity and dynamism of affective life. The humanities should, then, be post-human in this quite specific sense: the destruction of man – the being who represents a world to be known – would give way to one single domain of life as living system. There would no longer be a privileged centre of knowing, nor "a" world in general, just a web, network or mesh of multiple worlds. This would either yield a macro-organicism of Gaia and deep ecology along with a humanities oriented towards care, concern and eco-criticism or deep ecology, or – and these two paths are not mutually exclusive – a highly interdisciplinary mode of humanities in which words and texts are part of the same circulating web of things, bodies, technologies, images or any other event. It is not surprising then that philosophy has argued for connecting the mind back to the world (Clark, 1997) or putting mind into life (Thompson, 1997), and for thinking of societies and living bodies, as well as political systems and languages as assemblages of inter-connected and immanent, but always realist and material, registers (De Landa, 2006;

Protevi, 2009; Latour, 2005). But if systems theory, assemblages and living systems approaches allow the humanities to live on, no longer as privileged decoders of culture but just as readers of systems alongside other (possibly more scientific) readers, then perhaps the most valiant post-human ultra-humanist modes of humanities have been those that appeal to science for a grounding of their modes of reading; no longer are they seduced by the specialness of literary objects. It is in this manner that Brian Boyd neatly points out Derrida's ignorance of the scientific findings for language's emergence from life, a point that then allows Boyd to pursue a science-based literary Darwinism that, like the work of Joseph Carroll, corrects the "high theory" notion of linguistic construction:

> If they had been less parochial, the literary scholars awed by Derrida's assault on the whole edifice of Western thought would have seen beyond the provincialism of this claim. They would have known that science, the most successful branch of human knowledge, had for decades accepted anti-foundationalism, after Karl Popper's *Logik der Forschung* (*The Logic of Scientific Discovery*, 1934) and especially after Popper's 1945 move to England, where he was influential among leading scientists. They should have known that a century before Derrida, Darwin's theory of evolution by natural selection—hardly an obscure corner of Western thought—had made anti-foundationalism almost an inevitable consequence. I say "parochial" because Derrida and his disciples think only in terms of humans, of language, and of a small pantheon of French philosophers and their approved forebears, especially the linguist Ferdinand de Saussure. There was some excuse for Derrida in 1966, but there is none for the disciples in 2006, after decades of scientific work on infant and animal cognition (Boyd, 2006).[1]

Like all the other turns, returns or reassemblings, Boyd's argument takes the form of a redemption narrative: we used to be Cartesian, computational, humanist, linguistically enclosed, but now we have discovered life. The humanities now takes everything in and in abandoning the closure of the literary object regains the world, the living, dynamic and inter-disciplinary world. De Landa also writes about materialism's capacity to save us from linguistic narcissism or idealism, while Andy Clark specifically refers to putting the world back together again (although his culprit, as with Evan Thompson, is not French theory but Cartesianism and computationalism).

Would the humanities be worth saving in such a world? Would not humanities scholars be better replaced by journalists – reporting and disseminating findings from the sciences – or by scientists themselves? If, as Boyd claims, understanding literature really requires understanding evolution, would you not rather trust someone with a rigourous training in that area? And if the body and its neural responses were really the basis for what goes on in digital media, who would you save, a critic who can correct Deleuze by looking back to Bergson or someone who just received an NSF grant for a new fMRI machine?

There is a definite historical sense and teleology here: language, literature and the objects of the humanities – including "man" – emerge from life. Man, unfortunately, made the mistake of regarding himself as distinct from life, leading to Cartesianism and linguisticism, but science has redeemed us. Neuroscience has returned the brain to affective emotional life, and evolutionary theory has returned that living affective life to a broader narrative of the organism's efficiency. Inter-disciplinarity will save the humanities as will a sense of historical emergence or genesis. We will become post-human via consumption – absorbing information and methods from the sciences – and extension: no longer limiting human predicates such as thought, affect, pathos and signification to humans.

It might seem to follow, then, that a combination of the work of Gilles Deleuze and Michel Serres would finally be in order. Consider the key motifs of their works: an inter-weaving of different disciplinary registers (mathematics and poetry), a refusal to isolate the human animal from life, a sense of life as a multiplicity, a complex historical sense that would destroy the history of man in favour of a history of bodies (where bodies would include technological objects, words, languages, animals, polities, cities and images) and an emphasis on sense. The latter term would not be meaning the way in which the world is for "us" but would open out onto a broader domain of interaction and relations. What I would suggest, though, is that there is an inhuman (rather than post-human) approach to knowledge offered by the ways in which Deleuze and Serres approach the problems of history and sense, and that such an approach would not extend the life of the humanities by melding it with a single inter-disciplinary domain of which the sciences would also be a part, but would intensify certain dimensions of the humanities only by destroying certain majoritarian, anthropomorphic or dominant components.

It is true that Deleuze and Guattari weave together insights from science linguistics, art, philosophy and the social sciences, not only in *A Thousand Plateaus* but also in *What is Philosophy?*, which specifies the economic, imaginary, geographical and historical conditions for something like the philosophical practice for creating concepts. They also locate art, not in human practice, but in animal life. However, it is precisely through the expansion of a disciplinary tendency beyond its human form that Deleuze and Guattari destroy a certain model of inter-disciplinarity. If one could think of concepts, affects and functions not as practices grounded in a self-maintaining human life, then one would not only have to rethink the supposed self-evident good of inter-disciplinarity and the unity of the humanities, but also the future and survival of disciplines and the dominant image of the (now highly humanized) humanities. Such a future would not assume the value of living on in its current form, either of humanity or of the humanities, and it would abandon such assumed values precisely because of what we might refer to – after Serres – as climate change. If we could imagine the radical sense of climate, from clima and inclination, or the inflection that yields a certain patterning of what surrounds us, then we might say that it is now the time to question the human and post-human basis of thinking, especially when the post-human has been a return of the human into one single life with one single inclination: that of ongoing self-maintenance. To conclude with a more positive – which is to say, destructive – approach to thinking beyond the inter-disciplinarity of the humanities, I will conclude with drawing upon two concepts from Serres – parasitism and pollution – and two concepts from Deleuze and Guattari: concepts/affects and higher deterritorialization. Assembled together, these concepts can yield a new sense of sense and a new sense of history.

At its broadest, the concept of parasitism would at first seem to place Serres' approach within a single and unified field of knowledge, as it yields a model not just for relations among living bodies, but for information systems and – one might say – life in general. But if the relation of parasitism, and its capacity to displace the illusion of predator-prey relationships, is general , then what parasitism discloses are irreducible differences and singularities that require highly discerned cuts and judgments. Whereas a predator would be a vaguely self-sufficient body, capable of maintaining itself and using some other body as means of sustenance, the parasite would have no existence other than that of supplementarity: 'And that is the meaning of the prefix para- in the word parasite: it is on the side, next to, shifted; it is not on the thing, but on its relation. It has relations, as they say, and makes a system of them. It is always mediate and never immediate' (Serres, 2007, pp. 38–9).

To claim that man is parasitic, rather than a predator, and that this occurs in a life of parasitism in general, entails several consequences for humanism, post-humanism and the "disciplines" that might be adequate to thinking the inhuman. If one abandons the concept of predator, then one also abandons the concept of the good and just relation: it would not be the case that a proper humanity would use "its" natural milieu according to reasonable or ecological needs, maintaining a balance with a world he uses but towards which he could also contribute (by cultivating, re-planting, mitigating, adapting, capping, trading and offsetting). There would be no good humanity of reasonable predatory use that might be morally distinguished from a parasitic humanity, which would be nothing more than a consumer or digester of energies not its own. For that is the nature of distinction and being: one is not a unified body that then might produce good (self-sustaining) or evil (ultimately short-term and destructive) relations to one's milieu.

Let us accept that humanity is and must be parasitic: it lives only in its robbing and destruction of a life that is not its own. Our current predicament of climate change, whereby we have consumed and ingested blindly – bloating and glutting our body politic through the constant destruction of resources without recompense – would not be a late accident, nor a misjudgement of a post-industrial age. To be a body is to be a consuming body, to be in a relation of destructive consumption with what is effected as other, as resource, through consumption. Climate change would be the condition of human organicism in general: for there would be no climate, only clinamen, an inclination, deviancy or parasitism that creates a supplemental body (of man), who would then retroactively imagine that he has an environment, a *clima*, for which he ought to have been more mindful. But if this places humanity as an illusion of a general parasitism, then it is also the case that "man" occurs as a specific inclination or deviation, and it would be the task of thinking to examine each parasitic swerve according to its own differential. The deviation that enables mathematical systems, for example, would occur when the counting procedure deflects from living praxis and becomes a formalized supplemental system. From here one could then examine the geneses of formalization and ideality. Similarly, one could see poetry as a specific parasite, taking the language of speech and action and developing a relation among sounds and rhythms of the voice and script, but with no benefit to the organic or living bodies and practices from which it emerged.

Attempts to return systems to the sense of their origin – to see literature as benefiting the bodies from which it emerged, to see digital media as grounded in affect and embodiment or to see disciplines as aspects of one self-maintaining lifeworld would be to suffer from the illusion that parasitism goes in two directions. Not only does Serres insist that it does not; this irreversibility can be evidenced by any semi-autonomous or parasitic system. A system develops its own laws of survival irrespective of its host, and this is so even if the complexity of relations often confuses – for observers – who is host and who is parasite. Not only could there be no general inter-disciplinary humanities, whereby each discipline recognized its place in the ongoing self-understanding of man; each declination or parasitism would have its own inflection. As parasitic, it could not be grounded in "the" body of a single life.

This leads to pollution, which cannot be seen as some late-industrial nor specifically human inclination. It would not be the deviation from proper inhabitation, for inhabitation as such involves not just added markers or territorial inscriptions, but contributing something like waste or matter that elicits disgust or revulsion to an approaching outsider (Serres, 2008, p. 29). There is a connection here with parasitism that further debilitates (or ought to debilitate) "our" usual notions of ecology, environment and symbiotic inter-connectedness. Pollution is not simply making a niche, having a world that would, in turn, contribute to other worlds; to pollute or mark a space as one's own habitus is to subtract, diminish and defile the origin's integrity. But if there is only pollution, and if there is no clean or ethical living, or if ethos is entwined with abjection, then one could not attribute climate change to man alone. That is another way of saying that climate change would not be recognizable as long as one remained in a human or post-human mode of thinking: for such a mode would begin with man destroying his milieu (anthropogenic climate change would then require man to mitigate, adapt or trade in order to live on). And post-human celebrations of a single ecology would not be able to face a condition of climate change in general. To live and inhabit is to be parasitic, to pollute, to alter the clima, to effect an inclination that cannot be remedied or mitigated by some return or retrieval of the proper.

This suggests several critical and positive conclusions. Critically, one could no longer ground ethics on an understanding of a proper humanity: not only humanity in general but any living form – any being that marks or territorializes itself – must distinguish itself from its milieu. In the beginning would be neither mutual exchange nor symbiosis but theft (Deleuze and Guattari, 2004a, p. 203). Survival and self-maintenance, or the creation of a specificity or identity, require deviation and distortion.

Where does this leave notions of ecology, symbiosis and Gaia? On the one hand, Serres' focus on the clinamen reinforces the relational aspect of all being: there are not identities or terms that then enter into relation, nor a world of individuals or beings who must then somehow contract with or contact each other. But this is not to suggest either that there is one harmonious world, expressed each in its own way by each living form. On the contrary, as in Deleuze's monadology, Serres' Leibnizian world is one of incompossibility. Not only is each inclination or deviation an opening and disruption of a quite specific or singular differential – a quite singular creation of a field – it occurs always as disruption of other differentials and relations. The emphasis on parasitism and pollution precludes any nostalgia or restoration. This then yields a far more positive conception of a natural contract, which would not be man becoming one with nature as one living and symbiotic whole. Rather, it is precisely that position of man as an inter-disciplinary animal – man as assembler and negotiator of a single field of knowledge – that would give way to a natural contract that is a multiplicity, with divergent rather than harmonious lines of inflection. Climate change in a positive sense, following on from this parasitism and pollution, would occur as a negotiation or natural contract of the infinitely multiple. The contract is at once epistemological and legal, for it requires not only that man recognize his natural milieu, but that the very concepts of milieu, environment and climate in their singular sense would have to be rendered obsolete if nature also "contracts". Nature also has its inflections, worlds, multiplicities and differentials. There has always been globalization; each event in the world is a disturbance or distortion that enables something like an inflection or inclination to occur from chaos. (A new threshold occurs with modern post-industrial humanity precisely because its inflections do not just radiate outward and create local distortions but deterritorialize or become inflections of the whole, capable of infecting or polluting every other line of system or parasitism.) The "contract" of the natural contract is therefore not a signature (an act of the hand, inscribing a blank surface) but a contraction (the introduction of a noise or pollutant that ramifies throughout the open whole). Here is where Serres' work connects with Deleuze's similarly divergent Leibnizism. The world is a monadology, an infinitely divisible chaos in which smaller differentials will enable subtler relations and encounters – so that there is no nature in general outside or beyond the multiplicity of contractions: 'organs fully belong to matter because they are merely the contraction of several waves or rays: the nature of a receptive organ is to contract' (Deleuze, 2006b, p. 111). If, today, networks of technology and techno-science have, in their parasitism, effected something like a totality of nature in general, this is not as an object of scientific knowledge so much as a field of implication:

Classical Western philosophy never calculated the cost of knowledge or action but considered them to be free of charge. However, as soon as work appears, everything is subject to the martial law of price. The yield of work is never one on one; there are always residues and garbage. As long as work remains cold and local, price is calculated in terms of profit and loss. As soon as heat enters work, the productivity of the thermic machine is calculated. When world-objects are in operation, the cost becomes commensurable with a world dimension. Local, negligible waste is succeeded by global pollution of the world (Serres, 2006).

In a manner that seems close to Hardt and Negri's positing of a new global humanity effected through the immaterial networks of technology, Serres suggests that a global "we" has emerged, requiring a reflexive discipline concerned with humanity's total polluting power. Here is where one might note a disjunction between the affirmation of the people as "missing" in Deleuze and Guattari (1994, p. 176) and Serres' almost mournful lament of this new "we" with unforeseen destructive powers that finally produces nature as a totality (not so much as on object of knowledge but as a consequence of destruction).

For Serres, something like humanity has been rendered possible and effective not because of knowledge as recognition but because of a general polluting and parasitic power that has overtaken the locality of systems and relative disturbances. If we align this new "subject" with Deleuze and Guattari's recognition of capitalism as an axiomatic, then this provides us with a new way of thinking about a positively destructive "humanities". This would be inhuman, rather than post-human, precisely because the creation of the single system or axiom where work and production overcode all other relations, including supposedly environmental or ecological imperatives of survival and adaptation, would need to be annihilated to give way to differentials along a different axis.

Consider, here, Deleuze and Guattari's created concepts, in *What is Philosophy?*, which are not extensive insofar as they do not name or generalize actually existing disciplines but are intensive: they create or mark out speeds and rhythms for thinking. Consider concepts: although it is possible in a weak and general sense to locate concepts as one part of everyday speech, Deleuze and Guattari create a concept of concepts. A concept, considered philosophically, possesses a unique speed and rhythm. The concept of the cogito, for example, did not label an already existing entity, nor did it perform a move in an already practiced language game. Rather, when Descartes creates the concept of the cogito he slows thought down, retreats from action and efficiency, and from practical communication and institutes, a thoroughly new, virtual and philosophic terrain. Doubt is oriented to a perception of the world as calculable, of "a" subject as self-present, of philosophy as a mode of questioning and of bodies as suspended or placed in parentheses. Similarly, Deleuze and Guattari also create the concept of affects/percepts and functions. The former do not describe already existing art practices, nor what art always is. Like the concept of philosophy and its capacity to create concepts, the concept of art (as the production of affects/percepts) intuits a potentiality that may exist in a mixed or impure form in thinking as it currently is, but that can be intimated and gestured to futurally in what thought might be. What would it be to create a percept that would not be the perception of some observer, or an affect that would not be the affection of an author nor an affection produced in the reader/viewer?

By creating the concept of the concept, Deleuze and Guattari allow for a new mode of philosophy: if democracy is a concept, then the problem of democracy is not so much what it is (what social systems are really democratic), but the orientation it creates in thinking. What would it be to develop a socius with no other power than its own capacity for decision? Similarly, by creating the concept of affects and percepts, they enable a new mode of art theory: how might we imagine a work, not as the communication of an author, nor as the representation of a world, nor as the meaning it yields for its readers, but as a "stand alone" or monumental detachment of percepts and affects from the lived? The affect or percept would yield colour as such, melancholy as such: one might think here of the attempt to capture light in paint, to capture the sounds of the earth in synthesizers, or the striving to sculpt courage in stone. Deleuze and Guattari's concepts – the concept of philosophy as the creation of concepts, of art as the production of affects – allow us to think beyond "the humanities", beyond "inter-disciplinarity", and they do so in ways that intersect fruitfully with Serres' concepts of parasitism, pollution and a new humanity.

For Serres, a threshold is reached with current extensions of pollution that create a difference in kind. Humanity is no longer one pollutant or polluter among others, creating a territory, milieu or inclination. Humanity effects a climate change of climates; there are no longer multiplicities of inclinations, but an inclination or clima that has extended to such a degree that it constitutes a difference in kind – a pollution of such intensity that it now precludes the dynamisms, systems and disturbances of anything outside its own terrain. Serres argues that this calls for a concept of humanity. Such a concept would not be a reflection upon man as he is or has been, would not be a critical uncovering of the specific life of man. As a futural concept it would, like Deleuze and Guattari's created concepts of philosophy, art and science, require and enable an interrogation into humanity as inclination. How is it possible that in a life or earth that is nothing other than a multiplicity of inclinations and parasitisms, one specific line or disturbance has taken over the whole, at the very expense of its own tendency? If all life is improper, noisy, disturbing and deprived of any grounding or proper form – if, in the beginning, is the swerve – then how might one account for both the overtaking of the plane of disturbances and the emerging desire for a survival not of man as he is – a humanity that would manage its polluting tendencies – but that might create a new concept of itself?

The very concept of the humanities in its dominant form – as critical and inter-disciplinary – would need to be destroyed in a productive manner. This is because the idea of man that underpins the humanities as an interdisciplinary problem has been extensive: disciplines are activities, achieved by a division of labour, with man examining himself as a historical animal whose life creates him as a social and linguistic being capable of self-reflection and communication. It is not surprising that this man of reflexive knowledge and moral self-management confronts climate change as an extensive and managerial problem: How might we use less in order to live longer, how might we act more frugally in order to survive? But if we accept that there are capacities or potentialities that are not those of managerial man – either Serres' future humanity or Deleuze and Guattari's 'still-missing people' – then we would have to abandon the idea of earth as environment to which we might bear our proper and restorative relation, along with the humanities as some domain of communication that might return us to our better selves. A futural approach to disciplines would embrace and intensify the distinct inclinations of thinking – the differences of thinking in concepts, colours, sounds, affects – and would not assume precisely what climate change forces us to question: Why, if information regarding our polluting and parasitic existence is so extensive, are we so incapable of thinking intensively, of imagining a different inclination beyond that of the adaptation and survival of man?

Notes

¹ See also Boyd, B. (1998, p. 1): 'In the social sciences since the 1900s and the humanities since the 1960s, the world and the mind have increasingly been seen as socially, culturally, or linguistically constructed. Culture, not biology, shapes what we are; language, not the world, determines what we think. If we are what culture, convention, discourse, or ideology make of us, then there is no such thing as a universal human nature, and to believe in such a thing would be to commit the naive error, or the reactionary crime, of "essentialism".'

When the sociologist Emile Durkheim at the end of last century and the anthropologist Franz Boas at the start of this one tried to sever the study of humanity from biology, they had good intellectual and social reasons for doing so in a world where the muddled and heartless doctrines of Social Darwinism and eugenics held popular and even "scientific" sway. 1: But there was no such excuse when literature departments around the world became mesmerized by the way Roland Barthes, Jacques Derrida, Michel Foucault and Jacques Lacan drew on the limited linguistics of Ferdinand de Saussure to concur that 'Man does not exist prior to language, either as a species or as an individual.' 2: The new gospel of Theory, propelled by the messianic self-assurance of its prophets, spread through the humanities and the social sciences. What their converts failed to realize was that to follow parochial Paris intellectual fashion meant not only to exclude the world outside language but to ignore some of the major intellectual developments of our time in the understanding of human nature.

Bibliography

Agamben, G. (1999), *Potentialities: Collected Essays in Philosophy*. Translated by D. Heller-Roazen. Stanford: Stanford University Press.

Boyd, B. (1998), 'Jane, Meet Charles: Literature, Evolution, and Human Nature.' *Philosophy and Literature*, 22:1, pp. 1–30.

—(2006), 'Getting it All Wrong,' *The American Scholar*. http://www.theamericanscholar. org/getting-it-all-wrong/

Carroll, J. (2004), *Literary Darwinism: Evolution, Human Nature, and Literature*. London: Routledge.

Clark, A. (1997), *Being There: Putting Brain, Body, and World Together Again*. Cambridge, Massachusetts: MIT Press.

De Landa, M. (2006), *A New Philosophy of Society: Assemblage Theory and Social Complexity*. London: Continuum.

Deleuze, G. (2006a), *Foucault*. Translated by S. Hand. London: Continuum.

—(2006b), *The Fold: Leibniz and the Baroque*. Translated by T. Conley. London: Continuum.

Deleuze, G. and Guattari, F. (1994), *What is Philosophy?*. Translated by H. Tomlinson and G. Burchell. London: Verso.

—(2004a), *Anti-Oedipus*. Translated by R. Hurley, M. Seem, and H. R. Lane. London: Continuum.

—(2004b), *A Thousand Plateaus: Capitalism and Schizophrenia*. Translated by B. Massumi. London: Continuum.

Dougherty, S. (2010), 'Culture in the Disk Drive: Computationalism, Memetics, and the Rise of Posthumanism.' *Diacritics*, 31:4 (Winter 2001), pp. 85–102.

Fish, S. (2010), 'The Crisis of the Humanities Officially Arrives.' *New York Times*, October 11, http://opinionator.blogs.nytimes.com/2010/10/11/the-crisis-of-the-humanities-officially-arrives/?emc = eta1

Foucault, M. (1978), *The History of Sexuality: Volume One*. Translated by R. Hurley. New York: Pantheon Books.

—(2003), *The Order of Things: An Archaeology of the Human Sciences*. London: Routledge.

Habermas, J. (1987), *The Philosophical Discourse of Modernity: Twelve Lectures*. Translated by F. Lawrence. Cambridge, Massachusetts: MIT Press.

Hansen, M. (2003), 'Affect as Medium, or the Digital-Facial-Image.' *Journal of Visual Culture*, 2:2 (August 2003), pp. 205–28.

Hardt, M. and Negri, A. (2004), *Mutltitude*. New York: Penguin.

Hayles, N. K. (1999), *How We Became Posthuman: Virtual Bodies in Cybernetics, Literature, and Informatics*. Chicago: University of Chicago Press.

Latour, B. (2005), *Reassembling the Social: An Introduction to Actor-Network-Theory*. Oxford: Oxford University Press.

Morton, T. (2010), *The Ecological Thought*. Harvard University Press.

Protevi, J. (2009), Political Affect: *Connecting the Social and the Somatic*. Minneapolis: University of Minnesota Press.

Serres, M. (1995), *The Natural Contract*. Translated by E. MacArthur and W. Paulson. Ann Arbor: University of Michigan Press.

—(2006), 'Revisiting The Natural Contract'. http://www.ctheory.net/articles. aspx?id = 515

—(2007), *The Parasite*. Translated by L. R. Schehr. Minneapolis: University of Minnesota Press.

—(2008), *Le Mal Propre: Polluer Pour S'Approprier*. Paris: Le Pommier.

Thompson, E. (2007), *Mind in Life: Biology, Phenomenology, and the Sciences of Mind*. Cambridge: Harvard University Press.

Ziarek, E. (2010), 'Feminine 'I Can': On Possibility and Praxis in Agamben's Work.' *Theory and Event*, 13:1.

Zizek, S. (1998), 'A Leftist Plea for "Eurocentrism"', *Critical Inquiry*, 24:4 (Summer 1998), pp. 998–1009.

Chapter 7

Deleuze on Bergsonian Duration and Nietzsche's Eternal Return

Nathan Widder

The thing is, I became more and more aware of the possibility of distinguishing between becoming and history. It was Nietzsche who said that nothing important is ever free from a 'nonhistorical cloud'. This isn't to oppose eternal and historical, or contemplation and action: Nietzsche is talking about the way things happen, about events themselves or becoming. What history grasps in an event is the way it's actualized in particular circumstances; the event's becoming is beyond the scope of history (Deleuze, 1995, p. 170).

One of the remarkable aspects of Deleuze's *Bergsonism* (1991) is its positive portrayal of two of Bergson's most controversial and, for many, weakest works, *Duration and Simultaneity* (1999) and *The Two Sources of Morality and Religion* (1956). The first seems not only patently to misunderstand the implications of Einstein's special theory of relativity, but also to be a regression of Bergson's thought back to his early work, *Time and Free Will* (1910). The second seems to represent an aging Bergson's turn to mysticism and transcendence – although these already appear in Bergson's 1911 Huxley Lecture, which opens *Mind-Energy* (1920, pp. 1–28). Against such views, Deleuze contends that *Duration and Simultaneity* does not invoke a new psychologism but challenges the physicist for confusing different types of multiplicity and continuing to treat time as a counting of instants, with Bergson offering an alternative metaphysics needed by modern physics; and he argues that the significance of Bergson's later work is that it demonstrates the process by which duration, as difference actualizing itself, underpins social and moral history. Both defences accord with Deleuze's larger thesis that duration's structure of a virtual pure past contracted into an actual present and propelling time itself into an open future expresses a conception of internal difference, which Deleuze deploys explicitly against a

Hegelian conception of internal difference as contradiction. Duration, of course, is at the centre of all of Bergson's philosophical endeavours, and in the development of his thought it comes to define both the separation and the connection of space and time, matter and memory, body and mind, the closed systems of scientific enquiry and the unpredictable open systems of life and evolution, which surpass all scientific analysis. Deleuze's reconstruction of Bergson's thought makes clear that time, as a differentiation of difference that is more than a chronological passage of instants, is the foundation of all fields of becoming. Bergson and Deleuze, in this respect, clearly occupy the same terrain.

Nevertheless, despite Bergson's presence throughout Deleuze's work, and against the many scholars who see Bergson as Deleuze's principal inspiration, the multiplicity and differentiation that characterize duration play only a limited role in Deleuze's philosophy of time. This is clear in *Difference and Repetition* (1994), where duration is linked only to the second of three syntheses of time, and in *Cinema II* (1989), where Bergson all but vanishes once the chapter on 'The Powers of the False' is reached. In both cases, Nietzsche is the figure who replaces Bergson, and the eternal return replaces duration, with Deleuze holding that the latter concept of time only grounds time's chronological passage, whereas the former effects time's ungrounding. This turn to Nietzsche is not a radicalization of Bergson's thought or a "Bergsonization" of Nietzsche, as has been claimed by some.[1] Rather, Deleuze's early reading of Bergson, as will be seen, is more an attempt to introduce into Bergson's thought themes that only find a proper home in Nietzsche. In this way, Deleuze's turn to Nietzsche, I will argue, represents a fundamental break with key features of Bergson's thought: the priority given to the pure past, which, Deleuze argues, implies a continuing form of transcendence; the thesis of continuity, which in Bergson sustains a revised concept of the ego; and the way in which the new emerges in time. Deleuze opposes Bergson on all these points through the introduction of an intensive discontinuity that is absent in Bergson's duration. The early Deleuze does seek to ascribe this discontinuity to Bergson's thought, but Deleuze eventually gives up on the attempt: thus, the claims made in both *Bergsonism* and 'Bergson's Conception of Difference' (1999) that there are in fact quantitative intensities to be found in Bergsonian duration are replaced in *Difference and Repetition* with the view that Bergson's critique of intensity "seems unconvincing".[2] After these early works, Bergson assumes no more than a middle position in the unfolding of Deleuze's ontology of time, and Deleuze never returns in a serious way to either *Duration and Simultaneity* or *The Two Sources*.[3]

Bergson's early formulation of duration in *Time and Free Will* asserts an absolute separation between space, associated with quantity, and time, associated with quality. Later he attempts various rapprochements between them, but these reconciliations, as will be seen, all maintain the priority of quality over quantity, which serves to sustain Bergson's assertions of duration's continuity and ego's purdurance. Deleuze initially tries to attribute to Bergson a position that overturns this priority, before turning to Nietzsche and finding the resources he needs in Nietzsche's conception of "difference in quantity". And thus it is to Nietzsche and the eternal return that Deleuze finds his final formulation of the structure of time. In the eternal return, the continuity characteristic of duration persists, but as a surface effect of a more profound discontinuity and ungrounding. This move to Nietzsche, as will be seen, has profound consequences for the relationship between the event and history, as the event can no longer be assigned to a pure past that delineates some sense of historical truth. Indeed, Deleuze will maintain that those conceptions that tie the event to reminiscence – even where the event does not occur in historical time – reinvoke a Platonist notion of the ground. By contrast, the eternal return's concern solely with the future reveals the eventness of the event, the becoming by which it escapes and ungrounds history, thereby inaugurating the new.

Bergson on Quantity and Quality

Time and Free Will opens with a critique of the concept of intensive quantity, defined as quantity that while 'not admitting of measure … can nevertheless be said that it is greater or less than another intensity' (1910:3). Bergson holds the idea to be self-contradictory, since 'as soon as a thing is acknowledged to be capable of increase and decrease, it seems natural to ask by how much it decreases or by how much it increases' (p. 72). He therefore maintains that all conscious states that may appear to relate to one another in terms of more and less are in fact qualitatively different in kind. This forms the prelude to Bergson's presentation of duration as a continuous succession of distinct but interpenetrating qualitative states, one that appears discontinuous and quantitative only when time is abstractly and symbolically represented in space, thereby becoming extended, divisible and numerable. The illusion of quantity arises easily enough from the way the self relates to the extended, external world, which allows quantitative changes associated with bodily experiences to be linked to inner states, ultimately to the point where these become confused (pp. 163–64). The error is consolidated by language and the way extensity is introduced into inner life in order to designate inner states.

> [W]hen we turn to our conscious states, we have everything to gain by keeping up the illusion through which we make them share in the reciprocal externality of outer things, because this distinctness, and at the same time this solidification, enables us to give them fixed names in spite of their instability, and distinct ones in spite of their interpenetration. It enables us to objectify them, to throw them out into the current of social life. (p. 231)

The ego is the linchpin connecting these two orders. Its substantiality, for Bergson, is never in doubt, but he believes its form is frequently misunderstood. Contacting the extended world at its surface (p. 125), its true nature is found not in space but in time: 'Pure duration is the form which the succession of our conscious states assumes when our ego lets itself *live*, when it refrains from separating its present state from its former states' (p. 100). Associationism's error is to separate the ego from its states, conceiving the former as an indifferent thread holding together a discrete multiplicity of the latter, and 'thus substituting the symbol of the ego for the ego itself' (p. 226). By contrast, the concrete ego is not something static; rather, it changes without passing away and thus is something that *endures*.

Bergson insists on the absolute divide between these two worlds: 'The fact is that there is no point of contact between the unextended and the extended, between quality and quantity' (1910, p. 70); also, 'If magnitude, outside you, is never intensive, intensity, within you, is never magnitude' (p. 225). Inner life can be ascertained only by purifying it of erroneous forms, so that 'in order to view the self in its original purity, psychology ought to eliminate or correct certain forms which bear the obvious mark of the external world.... Intensity, duration, voluntary determination, these are the three ideas which had to be clarified by ridding them of all that they owe to the intrusion of the sensible world and, in a word, to the obsession of the idea of space' (p. 224). But this insistence takes Bergson into a series of quandaries. He maintains that only the ego endures, that the only duration existing outside us is the present moment, but he must then treat the undeniable perception of external change as something mysterious: 'we must not say that external things *endure*, but rather that there is in them some inexpressible reason in virtue of which we cannot examine them at successive moments of our own duration without observing that they have changed' (p. 227). And he can only gesture towards the deep psychic life that his absolute division requires: 'certain states of the soul seem to us, rightly or wrongly, to be self-sufficient, such as deep joy or sorrow, a reflective passion or an aesthetic emotion. Pure intensity ought to be more easily definable in these simple cases, where no extensive element seems to be involved' (pp. 7–8). Unsurprisingly, the articulations Bergson attempts to give of these self-sufficient states carry seemingly ineliminable traces of extensity and magnitude. He asserts that aesthetic feelings of beauty and moral feelings of pain go through a series of purely qualitative changes (pp. 14–19) – as though their progress did not involve and perhaps depend upon, say, physical sensations such as an empty feeling in the pit of the stomach from the start – but admits by the conclusion of his discussion that, 'there is hardly any passion or desire, any joy or sorrow, which is not accompanied by physical symptoms; and, where these symptoms occur, they probably count for something in the estimate of intensities' (p. 20). When addressing the affective sensations of pleasure and pain, he simply asserts, without any justification or argument, that while the succession seems to become greater as more parts of the body are involved and in sympathy with the affected part – 'we estimate the intensity of a pain by the larger or smaller part of the organism which takes interest in it' (p. 35) – this is preceded by a purely qualitative series of changes (pp. 47–48). Perhaps nowhere is the mixture of quantity and quality more obvious than in Bergson's frequent use of simple motion to illustrate duration and its continuity, since despite Bergson's insistence that such movement, being successive, is durational (p. 114), it is nevertheless visual and thus extended.[4] Ultimately, Bergson can sustain the separation of quality and quantity only by invoking a crude idealism. He states, for example, that 'there will always be an irreducible psychic element in anger, if this be only the idea of striking or fighting … which gives a common direction to so many diverse movements' (p. 29). And he holds that 'sound would remain a pure quality if we did not bring in the muscular effort which produces it or the vibrations which explain it' (p. 46), as though sound was anything other than vibration – a confusion reminiscent of the error Nietzsche (1967, 1.13) identifies of thinking that lightning is something distinct from its flash and the associationist error Bergson himself criticizes of dividing the ego from its states.

In later works, Bergson retreats from this absolute separation in favour of a reconciliation between quality and quantity. An obvious route is available: a synthesis à la Hegel's (1975, §§ 89–111) that, based on how sufficient changes in quantity yield changes in quality, unifies quantity and quality in the concept of measure. Such a resolution, however, would quite clearly be anathema to Bergson – and would significantly lessen his value to Deleuze.

So Bergson pursues two other interrelated paths. With the first, which appears initially in *Matter and Memory*, Bergson holds that science can move closer to consciousness and life by going beyond an abstract mechanics that denies movement its unity, indivisibility and qualitative heterogeneity (Bergson, 1991, p. 41), and he praises modern physics for treating the universe in terms of forces rather than atoms, thereby rediscovering the essential continuity of space (pp. 196–201). The worlds of internal duration and external space and movement are still irreducible, and the translation of the latter into the former remains an enigma, but this is only the case 'between quality on the one hand and pure quantity on the other' (p. 202). This opens the way for Bergson to ask whether 'real movements present merely differences of quantity, or are they not quality itself, vibrating, so to speak, internally, and beating time for its own existence through an often incalculable number of moments?' (ibid.). He answers by holding that the continuous flow of qualitative sensations in consciousness and the extended movements that occur in space both can be seen to involve the contraction of innumerable vibrations (pp. 202–208). The way modern physics and energetics dissolve the atom into wavelengths and frequencies of force thus provides a common foundation for the distinct worlds of consciousness and matter, ensuring that 'we grasp, in perception, at one and the same time, a *state* of our consciousness and a *reality* independent of ourselves' (pp. 203–204).

But Bergson is quite aware that the modern physicist does not abandon quantity. Indeed, these vibrations, which he holds to be innumerable, continuous and qualitative, are characterized by alternation – hence discontinuity – and are constantly being quantified. In principle, they must be numerable, since they demonstrate that there are, 'beneath the apparent heterogeneity of sensible qualities, homogenous elements which lend themselves to calculation' (Bergson, 1991, pp. 204–205). But Bergson maintains – carrying forward an argument from *Time and Free Will* (1910, pp. 122–23; p. 226) – that the actual calculation of these elements presupposes a consciousness with a quality of duration adequate to the task of tallying them.[5] Having suggested that duration itself might be vibration ('real movements … vibrating, so to speak, internally, and beating time for its own existence'), it is now separated from vibration and becomes its ground. To say that light waves vibrate 400 billion times a second, an alternation that cannot be grasped by our own lived duration, means that either there must be a real consciousness able to grasp this in a single intuition with the same ease with which we count the ringing of clock bells, or we must dismiss the number as a fiction given to us by a still too quantitative science. *Matter and Memory* affirms the first possibility with the idea of multiple rhythms of duration (Bergson, 1991, pp. 206–208), whereas *Duration and Simultaneity* dismisses it. Both views are based on the same principle: that quality and consciousness have primacy over quantity and measurement. Thus, in the later work, the physicist's vibrations and reciprocal forces are held illicitly to introduce discontinuity into the universe and amount to 'interposed human convention' (Bergson, 1999, p. 25). And a universal, single pace of duration is asserted, at least for all human consciousness (p. 32), allowing Bergson to dismiss the different rates of aging posited by the special theory of relativity for Peter on earth and Paul in his spaceship as nothing more than "mathematical fictions" (p. 20). The affirmation or rejection of constitutive vibrations and of the existence of different paces of duration all rest on the claims that reality is fundamentally qualitative and that quantity is necessarily an abstract and external view of quality.

This same principle also governs Bergson's other proposed reconciliation of quantity and quality. It is prefigured in *Matter and Memory*, where Bergson suggests that 'the interval between quantity and quality [might] be lessened by considerations of *tension*' (1991, p. 183); continues in the 1903 essay 'Introduction to Metaphysics', which appears in *The Creative Mind*, where the diversity of durations is considered in terms of compression and dilation (Bergson, 1983, pp. 187–88); and reaches full articulation in *Creative Evolution*, where Bergson distinguishes consciousness and matter by how tightly they compact durational succession. Duration is now never fully absent from matter (Bergson, 1998, p. 201), but matter and spirit are defined as two opposing tendencies, the latter compressing the past into the present in order to explode forward in creative evolution, the former relaxing this compression and coagulating into relatively inert substance. Thus, 'we pass from [spirituality] to [materiality] by way of inversion, or perhaps even by simple interruption' (ibid.), and 'physics is simply psychics inverted' (p. 202). But the primary tendency is spiritual and hence qualitative, with Bergson portraying the relationship of spirit with matter in terms of a jet of steam thrown into the air, with droplets forming through condensation and falling back to earth, though they are still pressed upwards by the continuous force of the uncondensed part of the steam jet. 'The evolution of living species within this world', he declares, 'represents what subsists of the primitive direction of the original jet, and of an impulsion which continues itself in a direction the inverse of materiality' (p. 247). Thus, even though the genesis of intelligence and of matter are inseparable (p. 199), the former retains priority over the latter. Ironically, then, while physics seems to have moved closer to life in *Matter and Memory*, in *Creative Evolution* Bergson holds that positive science in principle bears on reality only 'provided it does not overstep the limits of its own domain, which is inert matter' (p. 207).

All this undercuts the early Deleuze's claims that Bergson's critique of intensity in *Time and Free Will* is ambiguous and not necessarily even directed at intensive quantity as such but only the intensities normally associated with psychic states (Deleuze, 1991, pp. 91–2); that for the Bergson of *Matter and Memory*, 'there are numbers enclosed in qualities, intensities included in duration' (p. 92); and that 'one of Bergson's most curious ideas is that difference itself has a number, a virtual number, a sort of numbering number' (Deleuze, 1999, pp. 44). Deleuze's early readings of Bergson's philosophy seek to save it from self-contradiction by distinguishing its methodological and ontological aspects. Bergson's method, he argues, isolates space and time by insisting on their difference in kind, denying quantitative differences of degree between conscious states and establishing a strict dualism between inner and outer worlds. Bergson's ontology relates time and space in terms of different tendencies to contract or relax, duration contracting into itself all levels and thus accounting for the genesis of both time and space, but this unity remaining virtual and thus only potentially numerical. Invoking the virtual in this way, Deleuze contends that quantity is indeed reintroduced into quality, not as the numerically distinct differences of degree Bergson criticizes from his earliest work, but as "degrees of difference" – degrees of more and less, where the number is not discrete but virtual. These degrees of difference differentiate levels of duration and distinguish duration and space, all within an ontological monism.

This division of Bergson's philosophy into methodological and ontological may indeed answer some of its apparent contradictions. But whether intensive quantity really re-emerges in Bergson's thought is another matter. That Bergson himself does not recognize this is evidenced by the paucity of textual support Deleuze can muster to demonstrate it. None is cited in the key pages where the position is advanced *Bergsonism* (1991, pp. 91–4). In 'Bergson's Conception of Difference', Deleuze partially quotes a passage in *The Creative Mind* where Bergson states that physics is 'more and more clearly revealing to us differences in number behind our distinctions of quality' (Bergson, 1983, pp. 58–9, partially quoted in Deleuze, 1999, p. 44). However, examination of Bergson's text shows that this point applies only to 'the world of inert matter' (1983, p. 59) and that it remains dependent on 'the choice of a certain *order of greatness* for condensation' (ibid.) that consciousness realizes when it contracts material vibrations into a perception in order to grasp these qualities. Moreover, Bergson's peculiar stance on modern science, as already discussed, surely indicates that if, as Deleuze says, his philosophy 'triumphs in a cosmology where everything is a change in tension and nothing else' (Deleuze, 1999, p. 59), it remains very different from the measurable change in tension of modern physics. Having suggested in the early pages of his essay that Bergson introduces virtual number into quality, Deleuze fails to carry this theme into his discussion of degrees of difference. Indeed, by linking vibration strictly to relaxation, Deleuze seems to reinforce the opposite idea – that quantitative difference appears only when the qualitative internal difference of a fully contracted, simple duration is externalized, engendering a repetition that pertains only to external, actualized differences, never to internal difference.

> To say that the past is conserved in itself and that it is prolonged into the present is to say that the next moment appears without the previous one having disappeared. This supposes a *contraction*, and it is contraction that defines duration. Opposed to contraction is pure repetition or matter: repetition is the mode of a present which only appears when the other has disappeared, the instant itself or exteriority, vibration, relaxation. Contraction, by contrast, designates difference, because in its essence it makes repetition impossible, because it has destroyed the very condition of any possible repetition (Deleuze, 1999, pp. 56–7).

Certainly the passage refers only to material or bare repetition that is rightly external to duration, and Deleuze goes on to say that duration, as difference, both differs from material repetition and is the infinite repetition of the past and memory,[6] one that contracts its layers in such a way that novelty necessarily arises (p. 60). But again, the link between these virtual repetitions of the past and quantity, as well as between different levels of duration and quantity, is never demonstrated, and Bergson's own words indicate that despite the terminology of contraction and relaxation, of more and less, he really considers these differences to be qualitative. Thus, the passages Deleuze (1999, p. 59) quotes from 'Introduction to Metaphysics', where Bergson speaks of a continuous multiplicity of durations above and below human duration, are followed a few pages later in Bergson's text by a dismissal of infinitesimal calculus as a science of symbols and magnitudes and a call for metaphysics *'to operate differentiations and qualitative integrations'* (Bergson, 1983, p. 191).

Bergson would not have been incorrect to worry that a reintroduction of quantity, even as a virtual quantity, would undermine key aspects of his philosophy. It implies a fundamentally different relationship not only between metaphysics or ontology and science, but also between time and the self. In

Deleuze's turn from Bergson, time becomes a fractured and discontinuous structure for an "aborted cogito" (Deleuze, 1994, p. 110). It does this through the introduction of intensive quantity taking the form not of an extensive and discrete break but an immanent "irrational cut" (Deleuze, 1989, p. 277). Deleuze is certainly able to identify in Bergson's thought forms of all the major ideas in his own philosophy of time, including a structure of internal difference and a repetition immanent to time that engenders the new. But through his engagements with Nietzsche, each of these elements is transformed.

Difference in Quantity and Will to Power

Nietzsche shares Bergson's view that the mechanistic conception of the world is deeply flawed. Seeking purely quantitative analyses of all phenomena, it can only describe the world, not know it,[7] and even this depends on fanciful and essentialist hypotheses that posit the atom as a seat of motion, accept the "sense prejudice" (Nietzsche, 1968, § 635) of motion in empty space, and ascribe, without demonstration or justification, mysterious powers of attraction and repulsion to independently existing material entities (pp. 620–21). On the one hand, as Deleuze points out, Nietzsche's critique of atomism 'consists in showing that atomism attempts to impart to matter an essential plurality and distance which in fact belong only to force' (Deleuze, 1983, p. 6). The concept of force is thus one that is inherently relational: 'the essence of force' is 'the relation of force with force' (p. 40). On the other hand, removing the fiction of the atom is insufficient, because mechanism's 'purely quantitative determination of forces' still remains 'abstract, incomplete and ambiguous' (p. 43). The physicist's 'victorious concept "force," … still needs to be completed: an inner will must be ascribed to it, which I designate as "will to power," i.e., as an insatiable desire to manifest power; or as the employment and exercise of power, as a creative drive, etc.' (Nietzsche, 1968, § 619). But despite general similarities, Nietzsche's will to power differs in fundamental respects from Bergson's supplemental driving forces of duration and *élan vital*.

Nietzsche parallels Bergson in holding that 'in a purely quantitative world everything would be dead, stiff, motionless' (Nietzsche, 1968, § 564). Nevertheless, this is only the beginning of an extensive rethinking of quantity and quality. Mechanistic theory holds all qualities perceived by the senses to be reducible to quantitative formulae. Yet on the one hand, 'everything for which the word "knowledge" makes any sense refers to the domain of reckoning, weighing, measuring, to the domain of quantity; while ... all our sensations of value (i.e., simply our sensations) adhere precisely to qualities' (§ 565); and on the other hand 'we need "unities" in order to be able to reckon: that does not mean we must suppose that such unities exist' (§ 635). While mechanism correctly locates knowledge in quantity, through its uncritical assumption of unity (the atom), it reduces quality directly to quantity and establishes an absolute division between knowledge (what can be "objectively" quantified) and value (the "subjective" interpretation or assessment of this "objective" reality). Units enable counting and calculation, but also abstract away constitutive relations. Thus, on a concrete level where no unities or things pre-exist their relations, quantity cannot be a number but only a relation. As Deleuze declares: *'Quantity itself is therefore inseparable from difference in quantity'* (1983, p. 43). This difference in quantity is intensive, an ordinal relation of more and less. Nietzsche calls it 'order of rank', which is also an order of power, of strength and weakness, 'but it should be kept in mind that "strong" and "weak" are relative concepts' (Nietzsche, 1974, § 118). As an intensive difference, it cannot be measured along a fixed numerical scale that could reduce the differences between forces to equality: as Deleuze maintains, 'To dream of two equal forces ... is a coarse and approximate dream, a statistical dream in which the living is submerged but which chemistry dispels' (1983, p. 43). Difference in quantity thereby designates a fundamental heterogeneity within force relations.

However, although a world of forces is one of differences in quantity that are only later organized into unities, Nietzsche maintains that quantitative difference is never experienced as such, but instead is felt in terms of quality: 'Our "knowing" limits itself to establishing quantities; but we cannot help feeling these differences in quantity as qualities ... we sense bigness and smallness in relation to the conditions of our existence ... with regard to making possible our existence we sense even relations between magnitudes as qualities' (Nietzsche, 1968, § 563). Deleuze thus holds quality to be 'distinct from quantity ... because it is the aspect of quantity that cannot be equalized, that cannot be equalized out in the difference between quantities' (1983, pp. 43–4). Qualities are therefore heterogeneous, just like forceful differences in quantity, but while qualities are entirely a matter of perspective – 'It is obvious that every creature different from us senses different qualities and consequently lives in a different world from that in which we live' (Nietzsche, 1968, § 565) – they are not merely subjective interpretations of an independent quantitative world. The link between quality and concrete difference in quantity thereby subverts mechanism's partitioning of knowledge and value: values may not be reducible to fixed quantities, but they remain immanent to the domain of quantity, since values refer to power relations and are constituted so as to be 'our perspective "truths" which belong to us alone and can by no means be "known"' (ibid.). Consequently, 'the reduction of all qualities to quantities is nonsense: what appears is that the one accompanies the other, an analogy' (§ 564).

Once mechanism's abstractions of unity and numerical quantity are eliminated, Nietzsche holds, 'no things remain but only dynamic quanta, in a relation of tension to all other dynamic quanta: their essence lies in their relation to all other quanta, in their "effect" upon the same' (Nietzsche, 1968, § 635). But if the connection between difference in quantity and the feeling of quality is accepted, then the will to power must be acknowledged, simply because 'mere variations of power could not feel themselves to be such: there must be present something that wants to grow and interprets the value of whatever else wants to grow' (§ 643). This makes the will to power 'not a being, not a becoming, but a *pathos* – the most elemental fact from which a becoming and effecting first emerge' (§ 635). The various meanings of the Greek *pathos* – 'occasion, event, passion, suffering, destiny' (§ 635, translator's note) – are all significant. The will to power arises with the event of clashing forces, and, indeed, an event is nothing other than the clash: 'The degree of resistance and the degree of superior power – this is the question in every event' (§ 634). It is an affect or feeling of power that is inseparable from the clash, and it defines a perspective that carries it forward. No force could be or become without this feeling of power and the non-subjective compulsion to discharge itself, and this discharge is governed by the principle that each force, which is what it is by virtue of its relations to other forces, expresses itself so that its feeling of power can be satisfied and augmented. For Deleuze, although the will to power emerges from clashing forces, it is also their genetic and creative element, both determining the difference in power between related forces and the corresponding qualities (active and reactive) of each force in the relationship: 'The will to power here reveals its nature as the principle of the synthesis of forces. In this synthesis – which relates to time – forces pass through the same differences again or diversity is reproduced' (Deleuze, 1983, p. 50). In the terminology of *Difference and Repetition*, the will to power is a 'differenciator' that 'relate[s] different to different without any mediation whatsoever by the identical, the similar, the analogous or the opposed' (Deleuze, 1994, p. 117), or a 'dark precursor ... [a] difference in itself or difference in the second degree which relates heterogeneous systems and even completely disparate things' (p. 120). The will to power creates a discontinuity that cannot be found in Bergson, nor in Deleuze's reading of Bergson.

The language of synthesis appears in Bergson and in Deleuze's early reading of Bergson only negatively: duration is not a synthesis of unity and multiplicity (Bergson, 1983, p. 175; pp. 184–85; Deleuze, 1991, pp. 42–6; 1999, p. 53); such a synthesis, which constitutes number and motion, instead depends on duration, but it is also through it that duration assumes the form of an homogenous medium and is confused with space (Bergson, 1910, p. 75; p. 93; pp. 124–25); synthesis, being a unity of separate elements, is incompatible with duration's unity and indivisibility (Bergson, 1998, p. 29n), though duration remains nonetheless both a unity and a multiplicity (1983, pp. 168–69). Deleuze, however, does eventually adopt the terminology, holding duration to be the second of the two "passive" syntheses of time. It is passive because in it, 'time is subjective, but in relation to the subjectivity of a passive subject' (Deleuze, 1994, p. 71). But this also marks its inadequacy. Deleuze holds that concrete synthesis must be conceived in terms of disjunction. 'The whole question' he states, 'is to know under what conditions the disjunction is a veritable synthesis' (1990, p. 174). But it must therefore be a synthesis that is neither active nor passive, as it dissolves the subject.[8] The significance of the will to power in this respect is that its drive is one of overcoming, such that even its negative form ultimately surpasses itself (Deleuze, 1983, p. 70), and even if only the negative will to power is knowable, its essence is found in the affirmative will to power that exceeds it (pp. 172–73). In this way, the will to power's disjunctive synthesis breaks with Bergson's commitment to the ego's endurance and continuity. If endurance continues to appear, it is only as a surface effect of a foundational disjunction. But as a consequence of this, the emergence of the new goes hand-in-hand with the appearance of continuity.

From Duration to Eternal Return

Deleuze's first break with Bergson is therefore to treat duration as a synthesis. He first identifies a passive synthesis, associated with Hume, which connects successive independent instants into a line of time, without which the active powers of memory recall and intellect would be impossible. The first synthesis of time is analogous, Deleuze notes, to the synthesis Bergson recognizes as constituting motion and number and leading to the erroneous spatialization of time (Deleuze, 1994, pp. 71–2). And like Bergson, Deleuze holds it to depend on duration, arguing that the first synthesis cannot account for the passage of the present and the flow of time. The present's passage, Deleuze maintains, can only occur by virtue of the continuation and inherence of the past within it, such that each moment is both present and past at once: 'No present would ever pass were it not past "at the same time" as it is present; no past would ever be constituted unless it were first constituted "at the same time" as it was present' (p. 81). Duration, as a synthesis of multiple layers of memory compressed into the present, thereby serves as the transcendental ground of time and its passage: 'The claim of the present is precisely that it passes. However, it is what causes the present to pass, that to which the present and habit belong, which must be considered the ground of time. It is memory that grounds time' (p. 79). However, beyond the virtual inherence of the past in the present, duration introduces a dimension of 'pure past' in which both present and past moments are 'two asymmetrical elements of this past as such' (p. 81). The pure or *a priori* past, which never passes, remaining ever present but unrepresentable (p. 82), constitutes the milieu within which past presents are felt and recalled, and is the mechanism in which 'the entire past is conserved in itself' (p. 84). The form in which the pure past makes itself felt in the present, the form in which it is lived, is reminiscence, 'an involuntary memory which differs in kind from any active synthesis associated with voluntary memory' (p. 85). Although it is here, Deleuze says, 'that Proust intervenes, taking up that baton from Bergson' (p. 84), comparable ideas are certainly to be found in the pure memory in *Matter and Memory* and the creative emotion of dynamic religion in *The Two Sources*.

The present is the most contracted form of this pure past, but between successive presents, each of which compresses and so repeats the entirety of its respective past, there are 'non-localisable connections, actions at a distance, systems of replay, resonance and echoes, objective chances, signs, signals and roles' (Deleuze, 1994, p. 83), so that 'however strong the incoherence or possible opposition between successive presents, we have the impression that each of them plays out "the same life" at different levels' (ibid.). Duration thereby assures a repetition 'in which difference is included' (p. 84). But for Deleuze, this repetition does not yet engender the new. It retains the coherence and continuity of the ego, as Bergson explicitly intends, and the pure past functioning as time's transcendental ground retains a trace of transcendence. Having linked duration to Platonic reminiscence in *Bergsonism* (Deleuze, 1991, p. 59), in *Difference and Repetition* Deleuze identifies a pure past in Plato that is 'necessarily expressed in terms of a present, as an ancient *mythical* present' (Deleuze, 1994, p. 88). This implies an equivocation already implicit in the second synthesis of time. For the latter, from the height of its pure past, surpassed and dominated the world of representation: it is the ground, the in-itself, noumenon and Form. However, it still remains relative to the representation that it grounds.... It is irreducible to the present and superior to representation, yet it serves only to render the representation of presents circular or infinite (ibid.).

This transcendence of the past suggests that Bergson does not so much overturn a linear, chronological order of time as simply complicate it, introducing an unrepresentable dimension into is structure, but also circumscribing the discontinuity of this pure past for the sake of knowledge. On the one hand, 'the shortcoming of the ground is to remain relative to what it grounds, to borrow the characteristics of what it grounds, and to be proved by these', so that it remains 'a correlate of representation' (ibid.). On the other hand, to the degree that the pure past remains related to actual past and present moments, it lacks a synthetic connection to them, which allows it to assume a transcendent status. Despite his rejection of a static being beyond the physical world, Bergson nevertheless duplicates a Platonic gesture when he holds intuition of a past that was never present to provide a mechanism to grasp the absolute.

By contrast, the third synthesis, understood as eternal return, fractures both time and the self that exists within it. Deleuze introduces it through Kant's insistence against Descartes that the cogito's self-determination as a "thinking thing" must take place within time. As a result, its spontaneity of thought can be understood 'only as the affection of a passive self which experiences its own thought – its own intelligence, that by virtue of which it can say *I* – being exercised in it and upon it but not by it' (Deleuze, 1994, p. 86), and the ego is thereby fractured by its own temporality. Instead of a self that is unified by the continuous succession and retention of its past, the eternal return posits the self as a disjunctive synthesis, a relation of disparate differences brought together through a differenciator that sustains their heterogeneity. For this reason, eternal return is not simply the repetition/return of difference within time, a version Deleuze sometimes offers when opposing the standard reading of Nietzsche's doctrine as the endless recurrence of identical events. The eternal return cannot refer to a dissymmetry recurring in time, but instead must designate the dissymmetrical structure of time itself. This structure, Deleuze contends, involves at least two temporal series, which are not successive but coexistent and which come together through a caesura, differenciator or dark precursor that circulates through them.

No series serves as a foundation for the others, and the various series do not refer to the same subject, so that together they express a 'power of the false' absent in Bergsonian duration, a power that 'poses the simultaneity of incompossible presents, or the coexistence of not-necessarily true pasts' (Deleuze, 1989, p. 131).

Deleuze offers as illustration a revised version of Freud's Oedipal story, in which the Oedipal trauma, which need not refer to a real childhood event, both separates and joins together two sexual orders, one infantile and pregenital, the other adult and genital, within the unconscious. The orders have divergent body images and both real and imaginary objects of desire, memories of the past and expectations of the future, and they are linked through an event that can only be expressed by the phallus, the signifier of the mysterious paternal Law, which is never fully comprehensible. Constituting the separate series through a radical break, it cannot be localized within either series but instead resides in the margins of each. But the phallus also does not establish an identity between the series, as it has no identity itself, and so it is univocal across the series, but its univocity is that of an enigma. The phallus therefore functions as a differenciator, connecting temporal series that 'are not distributed within the same subject' (Deleuze, 1994, p. 124). In place of a subject, then, is a self that is out of sync with itself, caught up in diverse lines of time referring to different subjectivities within the same, not so unified being. These disparate subjectivities come together by way of their repetition and resonance with one another – the adults one knew or expected to be as child subjects, Deleuze says, resonate in the unconscious with the adult subjects one is among other adults and children (ibid.) – and they communicate through a traumatic event that is never fully defined and located for any of them. But this multiplicity can easily be effaced – and indeed, it regularly is – leaving an apparently singular subject living a single line of successive events. The enigma of the traumatic event may then appear as an original or early childhood event that later events repeat well or badly, rather than an untimely element that sustains the heterogeneity of the different temporal series. Deleuze maintains that this reduction of multiplicity is due to the way the differenciator of difference necessarily projects an original term in the process of differing from and hiding itself as it circulates through the series it brings together (pp. 105–106). The result is the appearance of the continuities that characterize the first and second syntheses of time. In this way, the eternal return engenders a structure in which identity and continuity always float on the surface of disparate disjunctions of difference.

The Event and History

When realized in action, Deleuze holds, the third synthesis presents a temporal order in which 'the present is no more than an actor, an author, an agent destined to be effaced; while the past is no more than a condition operating by default' (Deleuze, 1994, p. 94). The past provides the default conditions for the act of overcoming – the willing of eternal return – but the performance of so great an act in the present requires a consolidation and unification of the ego that makes it equal to the task. Yet, while overcoming finds its origin in this unified ego, 'the event and the act possess a secret coherence which excludes that of the self; ... they turn back against the self which has become their equal and smash it to pieces, as though the bearer of the new world were carried away and dispersed by the shock of the multiplicity to which it gives birth: what the self has become equal to is the unequal in itself' (pp. 89–90). The overt form of willing the eternal return involves transforming every 'it was' into 'thus I willed it' and, ultimately, into 'thus I will its eternal return'. It thereby retains the appearance of circularity and continuity, but beneath this it carries out a profound transmutation, which dissolves the ego and opens the self to multiplicity. In this way, the eternal return institutes a creativity, realized in thinking and the thought of eternal return, that makes possible a break with the past. In the end, therefore, the eternal return concerns only the future, by virtue of its 'expelling the agent and the condition in the name of the work or product; making repetition, not that from which one "draws off" a difference, nor that which includes difference as a variant, but making it the thought and the production of the "absolutely different"; making it so that repetition is, for itself, difference in itself' (p. 94).

Diverse theories of the event converge in linking the event to the past, even if this is a past that was never present, and determining it as the ground of historical "truth". This is the case with Bergson, as evidenced by his accounts of creative evolution and moral and religious development; and with Lacan, who, while criticizing Bergson's 'naturalistic inadequacy' (Lacan, 1977, p. 28) and 'intuitionist mystification' (p. 48), posits the traumatic encounter with the Real as an event whose conditions of emergence dictate that it must appear to come from the past, in such a way that it reveals how 'it is the truth of what this desire has been in his history that the patient cries out through his symptom' (p. 167). Unsurprisingly, one can find in Bergsonian memory and Lacanian recollection whiffs of Platonic transcendence.[9] But for Deleuze, the event's eventness necessarily locates it in the future; the event enters history from the future, and even where history seems to be a mundane continuity, the new is engendered. The structure of time, as eternal return, guarantees this novelty.

Notes

[1] See, for example, Ansell-Pearson (2002, ch. 7), Borradori (2001), Boundas (1996), and Moulard (2002).

[2] 'This is why the Bergsonian critique of intensity seems unconvincing. It assumes qualities ready-made and extensities already constituted. It distributes difference into differences in kind in the case of qualities and differences in degree in the case of extensity. From this point of view, intensity necessarily appears as no more than an impure mixture, no longer sensible or perceptible. However, Bergson has thereby already attributed to quality everything that belongs to intensive quantities. He wanted to free quality from the superficial movement which ties it to contrariety or contradiction (that is why he opposed duration to becoming); but he could do so only by attributing to quality a depth which is precisely that of intensive quantity' (Deleuze, 1994, p. 239). Deleuze's critique of and break with Bergson has parallels with Bachelard's call in *The Dialectic of Duration* for the development of a 'discontinuous Bergsonism' that would 'arithmetize Bergsonian duration' (2000, pp. 28–29). On these parallels, see Widder (2008, pp. 40–49).

[3] Both texts occasionally reappear in passing, mostly in footnotes. But the positive portrayals the early Deleuze articulates are absent, with the partial exception of a footnote in *Cinema I* (1986, pp. 226n:15) where Deleuze repeats that *Duration and Simultaneity* does not challenge Einstein's theories themselves but only questions their ability to construct a theory of real time.

[4] Simple motion, particularly the lifting of one's hand, remains Bergson's favourite example throughout his work, even though he occasionally admits that the movement is in fact not simple at all (see Bergson, 1998, p. 299). Despite some claims that he privileges the auditory (see, for example, Ansell-Pearson, 2002, p. 12), Bergson states explicitly that sight and touch are superior to sound in demonstrating the fullness and continuity of experience (1991, pp. 196–197). Russell is thus quite correct in stating that 'Bergson is a strong visualizer, whose thought is always conducted by means of visual images' (1946, p. 826).

[5] 'The duration lived by our consciousness is a duration with its own determined rhythm, a duration very different from the time of the physicist, which can store up, in a given interval, as great a number of phenomena as we please. In the space of a second, red light ... accomplishes 400 billion successive vibrations. If we would form some idea of this number, we should have to separate the vibrations sufficiently to allow our consciousness to count them or at least to record explicitly their succession.... A very simple calculation shows that more than 25,000 years would elapse before the conclusion of the operation. Thus the sensation of red light, experienced by us in the course of a second, corresponds in itself to a succession of phenomena which, separately distinguished in our duration with the greatest possible economy of time, would occupy more than 250 centuries of

our history. Is this conceivable? We must distinguish here between our own duration and time in general' (Bergson, 1991, pp. 205–206).

[6] 'Repetition is thus a sort of difference; only it is a difference that is always exterior
to itself, a difference that is indifferent to itself. Inversely, difference is in turn a
repetition' (Deleuze, 1998, p. 58).

[7] 'It is an illusion that something is known when we possess a mathematical formula
for an event: it is only designated, described; nothing more!' (Nietzsche, 1968,
§ 628). Also: '"Mechanistic interpretation": desires nothing but quantities; but
force is to be found in quality. Mechanistic theory can therefore only describe
processes, not explain them' (§ 660).

[8] Notably, Deleuze never refers to the third synthesis, linked to eternal return, as
passive.

[9] On this point, see Widder (2008, pp. 50–62).

Bibliography

Ansell-Pearson, K. (2002), *Philosophy and the Adventure of the Virtual: Bergson and the Time of Life.* London: Routledge.

Bachelard, G. (2000), *The Dialectic of Duration.* Translated by M. McAllester Jones. Introduction by C. Chimisso. Manchester, UK: Clinamen Press.

Bergson, H. (1910), *Time and Free Will: An Essay on the Immediate Data of Consciousness.* Translated by F. L. Pogson. London: George Allen and Unwin.

—(1920), *Mind-Energy: Lectures & Essays.* Translated by H. Wildon Carr. London: MacMillan and Co., Ltd.

—(1956), *The Two Sources of Morality and Religion.* Translated by R. Ashley Audra and C. Brereton, with W. Horsfall Carter. Garden City, New Jersey: Doubleday.

—(1983), *An Introduction to Metaphysics: The Creative Mind.* Translated by M. L. Andison. Totowa, New Jersey: Rowman & Allanheld.

—(1991), *Matter and Memory.* Translated by N. M. Paul and W. S. Palmer. New York: Zone Books.

—(1998), *Creative Evolution.* Translated by A. Mitchell. Mineola, New York: Dover Publications.

—(1999), *Duration and Simultaneity: Bergson and the Einsteinian Universe.* Translated by L. Jacobson, with M. Lewis and R. Durie. Edited by R. Durie. Manchester, UK: Clinamen Press.

Borradori, G. (2001), 'The temporalization of difference: reflections on Deleuze's interpretation of Bergson'. *Continental Philosophy Review*, 34:1, pp. 1–20.

Boundas, C. V. (1996), 'Deleuze-Bergson: an ontology of the virtual', in P. Patton, (ed.), *Deleuze: A Critical Reader.* Oxford: Blackwell, pp. 81–106.

Deleuze, G. (1983), *Nietzsche and Philosophy.* Translated by H. Tomlinson. London: Athlone Press.

—(1986), *Cinema I: The Movement-Image.* Translated by H. Tomlinson and B. Habberjam. London: Athlone Press.

—(1989), *Cinema II: The Time-Image.* Translated by H. Tomlinson and R. Galeta. London: Athlone Press.

—(1990), *The Logic of Sense*. Translated by M. Lester, with C. Stivale. New York: Columbia University Press.

—(1991), *Bergsonism*. Translated by H. Tomlinson and B. Habberjam. New York: Zone Books.

—(1994), *Difference and Repetition*. Translated by P. Patton. London: Athlone Press.

—(1995), *Negotiations*. Translated by M. Joughin. New York: Columbia University Press.

—(1999), 'Bergson's Conception of Difference'. Translated by M. McMahon, in J. Mullarkey, (ed.), *The New Bergson*. Manchester: Manchester University Press, pp. 42–65.

Hegel, G. W. F. (1975), *Hegel's Logic: Being Part One of the Encyclopaedia of the Philosophical Sciences*. Translated by A. V. Miller. Forword by J. N. Findlay. Oxford: Oxford University Press.

Lacan, J. (1977), *Écrits: A Selection*. Translated by A. Sheridan. New York: W. W. Norton.

Moulard, V. (2002), 'The time-image and Deleuze's transcendental empiricism', in *Continental Philosophy Review*, 35:3, pp. 325–45.

Nietzsche, F. (1967), *On the Genealogy of Morals*. Translated by W. Kaufmann and R. J. Hollingdale. New York: Vintage Books.

—(1968), *The Will to Power*. Translated by W. Kaufmann and R. J. Hollingdale. New York: Vintage Books.

—(1974), *The Gay Science, with a Prelude in Rhymes and an Appendix of Songs*. Translated by W. Kaufmann. New York: Vintage Books.

Russell, B. (1946), *History of Western Philosophy and Its Connection with Political and Social Circumstances from the Earliest Times to the Present Day*. London: George Allen and Unwin.

Widder, N. (2008), *Reflections on Time and Politics*. University Park, Pennsylvania: Penn State University Press.

Chapter 8

Time Out of Joint

Elizabeth Grosz

Time is perhaps the most enigmatic, the most paradoxical, elusive and "unreal" of any form of material existence. This may be why physicists, whose goal it is to explain material existence, have often relegated the perception of passing and change, time, as subjective illusion, mere appearance or matter encoded by the attributes of human perception. Yet, as Kant demonstrated in *The Critique of Pure Reason*, time is neither given to inner apprehension, nor to external sense: it is neither subjective nor objective but the a priori condition of the presentation of objects and subjects, the precedence or precession of pure temporality.

What Kant demonstrated was that time cannot be subordinated to movement – whether the movement of objects or the movement of ideas – without changing its nature, without converting its intensive features into an extensive form. Movement does not inscribe time; rather time inheres or subsists in movement; movement presupposes time and comes to be understood, not as a determination of an object, but as the outline of space itself. The tangibility, reality and materiality of movement only make sense, can only be regarded as spatial and/or temporal, insofar as time and space inhere in, and are presupposed by movement. In this sense, the world of matter, of bodies, is itself the materialization or actualization of incorporeals, virtuals, forces which precede and surpass them: matter itself can be construed as the uncanny double, the phantasm or simulcra of these intangibles.

Rather than marking out, dividing, regulating and ordering movement, which occurs when time becomes the translation, the representation, the measure of things, Kant comes to think time in its ordinal rather than its cardinal outline, as not simply the ordinal passage from one moment to the next, from one to two to three, but the accumulation of all past moments, the movement from the first to the second which incorporates it and to a third which includes them both. Time is no longer equivalent to the succession of moments, which mark the object's transition from one position in space to another, the movements by which cosmological bodies travel in circular motion for the Greeks, or the movements by which atomic particles oscillate for the Pre-Socratics. Rather, in Kant's formulation, it becomes the empty form, the retroactive imposition of the succession of determination on every possible movement; in other words, the synthesis by which movement is understood as unified, singular, movements "of" or attributable to a thing or object, the success by which a thing gains its identity (for identity itself can only be conceived, even in its most minimal sense, as a relative cohesion over time and over space). Time is no longer defined by the relations of the movements it measures; rather movement must be defined in relation to time, which conditions it. Succession is now construed as an effect rather than the essential characteristic of time.

Everything moves or changes, moves or changes in time, but time itself does not move or change, nor does it measure or accompany movement and change. It must be understood to inhere in movement, underlie and explain its possibility, without being identified with it. We systematically misconstrue the force of time, which is the force of dispersion, when we see ourselves as the repositories of time, when we reduce time to the psychological or the subjective. As Bergson makes clear in his conversions of Kantianism into an ontology of becoming, time is not in us, for we are in time, it is our limit and our condition for action. The time we live is impersonal, inhuman, pre-subjective, even if we must construe it as presence, transparency and directed through will.

Gilles Deleuze has argued that there is a strange affinity between Kant's positioning of time (and space) as a priori intuitions and Shakespeare's Hamlet: '*The Critique of Pure Reason* is the book of Hamlet, the prince of the north' (*Essays Critical and Clinical*, p. 28; see also Deleuze's preface to the English translation of *Kant's Critical Philosophy*). Hamlet is the first hero, not of doubt, of scepticism or inaction; he is the hero of a new kind of time, a time that is still with us. Deleuze describes this time as 'the time of the city and nothing other, the pure order of time' (p. 28). Time is freed from cause, from law, from nature; it comes to have its own positivity, its own force and impact. Hamlet needs time to act, whereas for Oedipus or Antigone, for Greek tragedy, time is subordinated to movement, functioning as inevitable consequence, the passive implication, of a chain of events set off in advance. Acts produce time: but for Hamlet, time enables acts. For the Greeks, time is relentless inevitability, modelled on the certainty and perfection of the movements of the heavenly bodies themselves. For Hamlet, however, time is delay, interruption, interval or pause.

For Shakespeare, it is time itself which acts, when Hamlet cannot: 'The time is out of joint,' (Hamlet, Act 1, Scene 5). A new kind of time, the time of the city, comes into existence, yet this time is somehow unhinged from the circle, the movements of celestial repetition, from the line that is historical progress or development, from law that announces itself and from nature that gives itself. It is an unnatural time, a deviation of and within time, that Shakespeare invokes and Kant theorizes: a possessed time. Time acts, it has its own forces, which cannot be described as either worldly or subjective, for it is the condition of their very opposition. This new or other time, the unhinging or derangement of time, time as active positivity, as impersonal force, is the displacement of the subject, of God, of the order of the Cosmos, of all agency, of causality.

To have a life of its own, time deviates, splits, divides itself, into a present whose limit is never given in advance, and the perpetual fissuring of the present that its placement on the threshold of past and future entails, its division into Chronos and Aion, in the language of the Stoics. As Bergson recognized in *Matter and Memory*, to retain and protract itself, to stretch itself so that it can be conceived in terms of a past, present and future, time is not divisible into three orders, but only into two. Time splits into two trajectories: one virtual, the other actual; one that makes the present pass, and the other that preserves itself as past while still part of the present. One forms memory, the other perception; one is oriented towards reminiscence and the past, the other opens out to anticipation and the unknowable future. What needs to be explained in this time of the city is not the pre-eminence of the future, which is the unargued-for starting point, but the capacity of duration to function "simultaneously" as present and as the past of that present. Time is this very split, 'the powerful, non-organic Life which grips the world.' (Deleuze, 1989, p. 81). In short, to reformulate the Bergson of *Creative Evolution*, the Bergson whose aim was the inversion of Kant's understanding: it is we who are in time, rather than time that is in us. Time is not an effect of the subject's imposition onto the world. Quite the contrary: time is the resistance of the world to the subject. Time is the form of interiority without itself being interior, the form of objects without being objective, the form of subjects without being subjective, the form of matter without being material. It is a strange "substance" without substance, a force without measurable energy, a form without outlines. It is the paradoxical itself.

If time, historical time, the time that has marked our time and its rise as relentless inevitability, is perhaps best represented as being perpetually out of joint, then this may explain Deleuze's fascination with cinema and his reconceptualization of the movement-image in terms of the time-image in his two volumes dealing with cinema. Cinema is that strangely paradoxical form which both functions as a perpetual present, the present being equated with the projection of light through celluloid onto the screen, and an ever-moving but also pre-scripted past that this luminous present always carries with it. Deleuze calls this divided structure 'the crystals of time'. Located between two times – the time of production and the time of screening – each with their own virtualities, each with their own separate past and future, each with their own crystal circuits between virtual and actual, cinema for us, as much as Hamlet was for the advent of the modern city, expresses, time's dynamism, time's life, time's own internal crystalline structure. Like Hamlet, cinema functions only in-between two times, as time divided, 'a bit of time in the pure state, the very distinction between two images which keeps on reconstituting itself' (Deleuze, 1989, p. 82). The history of cinema is the history of this moving dynamic of pasts and presents; and each cinematic production is the framed, viewable fission of time, time fractured and restored, only to be fractured again. Film itself crystallizes time; time's dynamism is that which film most ably expresses.

Can we live in a time out of joint? This is perhaps the burning social question of the present: Can we live at the speed we are required to, with the forms of slowness that we also require? Is the technology, which is supposed to enhance and make our lives easier, simply providing another task to undertake, another labour to perform, another benchmark for speeding up? Is cinema, as far as the exploration of time can go, the pure art of temporality? Can there be a new kind of cinema, a new kind of performance, a new kind of art that elaborates and complicates perception by forcing it to encounter time's moving force?

Clearly, the exploration of time and the development of models more subtle and complex to understand its effects and operations is an ongoing process, one which only the future itself can address. Science, in its ever more minute explorations of material forces, is almost daily discovering or producing strange experiments whose implications for an ontology of time await development (for example, scientists announced that they had "frozen" light, that is, stopped its movement and then restarted it. Yet the inalterable character of light has provided the terms by which time itself has been scientifically measured in the post-Einsteinian universe. How can light be frozen if it is the measure of time? What does "frozen" or "stopped" even mean without a concept of time?) These are profoundly open questions, questions for which science requires philosophical and artistic elaboration. Although scientific investigations of matter will no doubt modulate and transform conceptions of time, cinema nevertheless, in spite of its own complications – those of finance, distribution, reception, narrative structure, cinematic genres – remains thus far the very assemblage for the expression of time, the machinery by which time manifests itself and is perceptible most visibly. It may be that Bergson was right all along in understanding science as the elaboration of slices of time; and the art as a potential immersion in and celebration of its always forward-oriented continuity. It may be that new modes of apprehension of time await a new kind of history, a new kind of knowledge, new forms of art and perhaps even more artful forms of science.

Bibliography

Bergson, H. (1944), *Creative Evolution*. Translated by A. Mitchell. New York: Random House.

—(1988), *Matter and Memory*. Translated by N. M. Paul and W. S. Palmer. New York: Zone Books.

Deleuze, G. (1984), *Kant's Critical Philosophy. The Doctrine of the Faculties*. Translated by H. Tomlinson and B. Habberjam. London: The Athlone Press.

—(1989), *Cinema 2. The Time-Image*. Translated by H. Tomlinson and R. Galeta. Minneapolis: University of Minnesota Press.

—(1997), *Essays Critical and Clinical*. Translated by D. W. Smith and M. A. Greco. Minneapolis: University of Minnesota Press.

Kant, I. (1970), *The Critique of Pure Reason*. Translated by N. K. Smith. London: Macmillan.

Chapter 9

The Crumpled Handkerchief

Jane Bennett and William Connolly

In a recent book, the philosopher Graham Harman extracts a metaphysics from Bruno Latour's body of work: not metaphysics 'in the bad, old-fashioned sense' of 'taking one layer of reality to be the genuine article' and reducing all others to 'flickering shadows' in the cave, but metaphysics as a contestable image of how the cosmos works, of what kind of order it tends towards and what propensities and potentia are contained within it (Harman, 2010b, p. 5). Metaphysics matters: a sense of how the universe arranges itself and its affairs, how it 'does its thing', colours the way we humans negotiate our various microcosmic worlds.[1] Harman places Latour alongside Whitehead, Bergson, William James, Deleuze, Serres, Simondon and Tarde, all of whom emphasize the capacity to become-otherwise of things; each endorses a metaphysics of Becoming more than Being, of flow, generative process, creative evolution, ruckus.

Harman goes on to identify two camps within this group, depending upon whether the putative focus is on the generative process or its actualized entities. In the first camp are Bergson and Deleuze who are concerned, he says, with 'a generalized becoming' that 'precedes any crystallization into specific entities'. In the second camp are Whitehead and Latour, whose objects of analysis include 'actual freight trains and apricots' (Harman, 2009, p. 101). Harman prefers the second camp, but to him neither gives objects their full ontological due. Deleuze and Bergson tend to present objects as mere epiphenomena of the Virtual or Duration, and Deleuze especially veers too close to 'the pure monism of a single lump universe' (Harman, 2009, p. 160).[2] The camp gathered around Latour better attends to discrete entities, but here the culprit is "relationism" or the view that an object is 'no more than what it modifies, transforms, perturbs, or creates', is 'completely actualized in any moment, inscribed without reserve in its current scheme of alliances' (Smith, ND).[3] To really give objects their due, says Harman, would be to highlight their ability to perdure, a resilience tied to the fact that they harbour a differential between their inside and outside, or in other words, retain an irreducible moment of (withdrawn-from-view) interiority. Harman, drawing upon Heidegger, asserts that it is in 'the nature of objects to withhold their full secrets from each other' (Harman, 2010a, p. 169).[4] Harman thus offers an 'object-oriented ontology' as a better way to acknowledge the strange force of objects and to counteract human hubris at both an epistemological and a practical level.[5]

Why do we rehearse Harman's critique of "lump ontology" and "relationism"? We think that Harman is off base in his reading of Deleuze and Guattari, ignoring, for example, the concepts of haecceity and the Refrain and the many specific things (horses, shoes, orchids, packs, wasps, priests, metals, capitalist orders, etc.) that have starring roles in *A Thousand Plateaus*; and we think his critique of relationism or process goes too far (Harman, 2009, p. 159).[6] But Harman's dogged focus on things-themselves – his object-orientedness – does push us to reflect critically upon the tendency to privilege process over product within ontologies of Becoming and to continue to refine our theorizations of the periodic and differentiated quality of Becoming.[7]

Those tasks provide a focus on our essay. But let us preface them with an explicit acknowledgement of the (aesthetic, affective, ethical) appeal that an ontology of Becoming holds for us: we confess an attraction to the idea that freedom, movement, creativity are installed at the very heart of things, we are drawn to the call to try to ride the waves of *natura naturans* and diffuse the urge to master a sea of Life that was not designed for us, and we find an ontology of Becoming to confirm our everyday experience of change as quite fundamental to life and of time as proceeding 'more like the flight of [a]... wasp than along a line' (Serres et al., 1995, p. 65). We also acknowledge that such allure may sometimes distract attention from the persistence and resilience of form, or, better, of what Walt Whitman calls "shapes": 'The shapes arise! Shapes of doors giving many exists and entrances' (Whitman, 2002). If references to an ever-free Becoming, or a Nietzschean world of energetic flows, or a Deleuzean vibratory cosmos or a Bergsonian world of creative evolution have tended politically to focus on exposing the possibility of things becoming otherwise, we will attempt to focus also on the uncanny fact that individuated entities emerge, collaborate and manage to withstand the hustle and flow for a while. How do shapes manage to distinguish themselves from the onto-field – how, in Serres' words, 'is Venus born from the sea, how is time born from the noisy heavens' (Serres, 1995, p. 26)? What initiates the congealing that makes objects? Is it possible to identify phases within formativity, plateaus of differentiation? If so, do the phases/plateaus follow a temporal sequence? Or, does the process of formation inside Becoming take the shape of a non-chronological kind of time? And, in addition to thinking about the impetus to or process of emergence, how do things manage to persist? What Harman does for us, then, is to call us to think more actively about things hanging together in a world of Becoming.

Manuel De Landa and others have pursued this question via Deleuze and Guattari, whose notion of the machinic was one attempt to name the 'processes that act on an initial set of merely coexisting, heterogeneous elements, and cause them to come together and consolidate' (De Landa, 1997).[8] We too find the Deleuzean frame illuminating, but will combine it with the work of Michel Serres, which offers a rich conceptual-metaphorical repertoire for thinking the shapes and systemic dimensions of Becoming. We begin with Serres' notion of *noise*, the name he gives to that onto-field of generativity and its impersonal force of operation. We then turn to his account of how the process parses itself into phases and ultimately into discrete and persistent phenomena. Finally, we address his notion of (non-linear) time as a "crumpled handkerchief" and place it alongside Deleuze's (Nietzschean) concept of 'the powers of the false'. At the end of the essay, we draw out some implications of these notions for the practice of historical analysis.

Noise

Noise is an archaic French word that does not quite coincide with noise in the auditory sense. The term would be known to modern French speakers through the expression 'cherchez le noise', which means: to look for the murmuring messiness or inconsistency in the texture of a person, action or event, and then to do something (obliquely, indirectly) that exposes that static – perhaps just to chide someone, perhaps out of a vague sense of loyalty to the element of indeterminacy in life. Cherchez le noise is to stir up a settled form, to foreground for a moment the sand in its gears.

Noise, in the sense that Serres wants to evoke, is the fluctuating ado that is the strange substance of any discrete, differentiated shape; it is 'the matter and flesh of manifestations' (Serres, 1995, p. 14). Instead of a single "big bang" (Serres, 1995, p. 61) marking the transition from formless potentiality to actual individualities, Serres posits a continuous noise in and between phenomena. *Noise* is not the primordial precondition of things, but is coterminous with them; it is the quivering flock of "dovetails", 'the multiplicity of the possible [that] ... rustles in the midst of the forms that emerge from it'. (Serres, 1995, pp. 23–4). Serres offers an assortment of other naturalistic

images of noise: it is a 'sheeting cascade' out of which phenomena sometimes fall (Serres, 1995, p. 18). It is restless matter, but because it lacks the
sharpness or clarity of "motion", its fuzzy activity is better described as "percolation". *Noise* is also named as 'the court of the undifferentiated'[9] – but
here Serres seems to misspeak, and he immediately takes back the suggestion of a smooth ontological field lacking in difference. While noise is 'the
multiple as such ... undefined by elements or boundaries', it is not a flat
plain, uniform soup or lump ontology. Here, where Deleuze might have
inserted a reference to 'pre-individual singularities' in order to denote an
intrinsic heterogeneity, Serres invokes variable degrees of "viscosity" (Serres,
1995, pp. 4–5).[10]

Noise is a syrupy material, snotty fluid. Is it, then, an emptiness or a fullness, a black absence or a superabundance of presence? (Serres, 1995,
p. 30) Serres says it is both, and exhibits no interest in debates between
'ontologies of lack' and 'ontologies of abundance'.[11] *Noise* also includes lots
of auditory sounds, which together form the hum, buzz, or 'background
noise' of life. These murmurs include the 'intropathetic noise' made by our
bodies as they run their engines of metabolism, digestion, thinking, breath-
ing, circulation. It is interesting to compare Serres' claim that 'no one can
live without noise' (Serres, 1995, p. 61) to an anecdote told by John Cage:
'For certain engineering purposes it is desirable to have as silent a situation
as possible. Such a room is called an anechoic chamber, its six walls made of
special material, a room without echoes. I entered one at Harvard several
years ago and heard two sounds, one high and one low... [The engineer]
informed me that the high one was my nervous system in operation, the low
one my blood in circulation. Until I die there will be sounds. And they will
continue following my death. One need not fear about the future of music'
(Perloff, 2005, p. 104).

We turn now to Serres' delineation of the various phases of formativity, a
kind of structural skeleton of Becoming.

Phases

In his 1977 *The Birth of Physics*, Serres used a Lucretian or ancient atomist
account to describe the cosmological process through which shapes arise:
in the beginning there was a sheeting rain of primordia; this is followed by
a series of random swerves as primordia deviate ever-so-slightly from their
linear trajectory; these eccentric deviations create crash encounters between
primordia, some of which result in conjoinings; conjoinings can pile up,

and a confused milieu of turbulence arises; then there can follow a stage where the matter-bits congeal into bodies; these bodies sooner or later decay, decline and disseminate. This process describes how all individual things come into being, things natural as well as political.[12]

Five years after the publication of that book, however, Serres re-visits in *Genesis* the question of how shapes arise within an undesigned, vibratory cosmos. This time his poetic expression of the turbulent structuration of Becoming relies little on an atomistic imaginary. Swerving atoms are replaced by noise. Serres does, however, retain his (Lucretian) vow to remember the aleatory – to not forget its role in history and life.[13] Thus, Serres' tale of formativity follows the logic of 'could happen': at each phase of noise, shapes could be arising or maybe not. This logic of 'it depends' (Serres, 1995, p. 60) is uncannily familiar, for physical nature abounds with examples of it. Take a field of seed-corn: 'The seed-corn dies, and it dies. The seed-corn dies, and it sprouts. It sprouts and it is meager.... It sprouts and it multiplies, exponentially, it overruns the place'. In other words, sometimes noise expresses 'a welter of aborted beginnings' (Serres, 1995, p. 69), but sometimes noise burps out 'a tiny little cause, which, making its way through the intersections, tries its luck at living, heads to the left, tails to right ...'(Serres, 1995, pp. 58–59).

Just what is that 'tiny little cause', that initiating ancestor of a shape? In *Genesis*, Serres calls this most immature phase of differentiation a "surge". A surge is a minimal intensification within the "pell-mell" of noise (Boisvert, 1998, p. 482). As an example of this tiny act of self-distinguishment, Serres cites that ever-so-slightly-higher pitch of sound we sometimes hear above the background noise of the wind, or that barely perceptible little dance of water that turns out to be a premonition of a swell. What can happen once a surge exists? Sometimes a surge will repeat itself. And if it does so enough times, it can become a "fluctuation". Like the surge, the phase called fluctuation is unstable, although it has managed to maintain a stronger pulse of repetition.[14] A fluctuation can then, or maybe not, become a "bifurcation", or series of branching-outs with a generic kind of directionality, as in the successive forking of trees or the spilling out of an epidemiological contagion.[15]

What could happen (but maybe not) next? We already have said that *noise*, as a ruckus, has a natural tendency to double back on itself in repetitions or "redundancies", and that an initial redundancy or pulse can become a fluctuation and then a bifurcation. Or that each repetition can fizzle out. If the repetition of a branching-series does intensify, then it can become a "rhythm or cadence". Some times this beat will persist to form a "vortex" or whirlpool that carves out a region amid the pandemonious noise. Serres calls this persistent swirl of activity "turbulence", which names that 'irregular bombardment of circumstances' wherein the force of repetition, the force of formed forms and the force of decay have achieved a certain "synchrony" (Serres, 1995, p. 109). It is through this cauldron of turbulence that noise thickens into lumps of "phenomena", and the bubbling swirl keeps those shapes upright while they, like a child's spinning top, remain in motion. Serres uses the figure of "turbulence" to displace descriptions of noise as profound disorder: noise is 'perhaps ... a more exquisite order still, one our banal stupidity cannot manage, stiff as a board as it is, to conceive, since it is still given over to concepts ...' (Serres, 1995, p. 109).

Turbulence can spin out "phenomena" or what Serres prefers to call the "invariances" in/of noise. Serres distinguishes three types of invariances: there is the 'stupid, heavy, even, odd, standing there' kind of invariance, such as a statue or a sandbag; there is the invariance that is the effect of a more or less steady rate of motion, such as the spinning top or the revolving Earth; and there is the 'more intelligent invariant' that persists as movement itself, such as the river that 'remains in equilibrium all along its bed' or the I that grows old but still continues to 'resemble myself' (Serres, 1995, p. 120). Note that in Serres' typology of things the human–non-human divide is very smudged: a self can sometimes act with a sandbag invariance and a river can sometime be the 'more intelligent' kind of variance.

The Handkerchief and the Powers of the False

Noise, surge, fluctuation, bifurcation, cadence, vortex, turbulence, invariances: these are the modes of consistency produced by the repetition-redundancies of noise. Though we can distinguish between the modes, we cannot do so clearly or definitely, for each is less a segment of a smooth totality than a phase of an open whole. A phase is a style that persists beyond its heyday and bleeds over into its before and after; the demise of a phase is not a definitive death but a fading that overlaps with what emerges out of it.[16] As phase-states, then, surge, fluctuation, bifurcation, echo, cadence, vortex and invariances are always to some degree contemporaries of each other. And because the structure of Becoming is phasal, even relatively strong "invariances" – even phenomena or objects – remain multi-temporal in the sense of carrying other modes of consistency along with them. Serres illustrates this point by speaking of time as a crumpled handkerchief:

If you take a handkerchief and spread it out in order to iron it, you can see in it certain fixed distances and proximities ... Then take the same handkerchief and crumple it, by putting it in your pocket. Two distant points are suddenly close, even superimposed. If, further, you tear it in certain places, two points that were close can become very distant (Serres et al., 1995, p. 60).[17]

The crumpled handkerchief shows how time readily accommodates heterogeneous objects as well as how each object can enclose within itself opposite or opposing modes. His example here is his self: 'I am young and old' (Serres, 1995, p. 60).[18] The crumpled handkerchief also displays how events very far from each other in chronology sometimes act as contemporaneous intimates, as, for example, when 'the Nazis, in the most scientifically and culturally advanced country, adopted the most archaic behavior', or when Lucretius's ancient poem about primordia co-operated with a modern theory of fluids. Serres goes so far as to say that we are always 'simultaneously making gestures that are archaic, modern, and futuristic' and that every 'historical era is likewise multitemporal, simultaneously drawing from the obsolete, the contemporary, and the futuristic. An object, a circumstance, is thus polychronic, multitemporal, and reveals a time that is gathered together, with multiple pleats' (Serres et al., 1995, pp. 57–60).[19]

Can we say more about this aspect of time, whereby elements from the past, slumbering for months, years, centuries or millennia, quicken again to life? Perhaps the idea of the cinematic flashback can help. Take, for instance, the flashback at work in *Citizen Kane*.[20] After the death of the flamboyant, populist newspaperman, we flash back to a scene from Kane's childhood in which his parents, at the front of the visual field, discuss their son's future with a wealthy banker. Through a small, bright window in the back of the room, we see little Kane playing outside in the snow with his sled. The viewer takes in the scene and uses it to try to make sense of Kane's life. Later in the film, that flashback recurs, but this time on the screen of our imagination rather than the theatre: it is repeated with a variation, as we visualize the first flashback while we are shown in the movie a scene in which that sled burns in a fire at Kane's cluttered estate, this time with the trade name "Rosebud" clearly visible. "Rosebud" was the cipher that the reporter reviewing the life of Kane had been assigned to decipher, because that word had been uttered by Kane just before he died. This second flashback, a visualization without film image, enters into the protraction of the present as we ponder how moments and levels of the past help shape the future without themselves always assuming the shape of a representation. This cipher from the past leaped into Kane's memory as he sensed how it had helped to form his character, how life with the sled had helped him to become what he was after it. The initial flashback to his childhood is now called forward again by us at the end of the film (in the form of a visualization), to help us feel how layers of the past can be at work despite being too protean to be represented. Rosebud is real without being fully decipherable by Kane or us. It is an instance of what Gilles Deleuze, working with themes in Nietzsche, calls 'the powers of the false'. It worked upon the life of Kane (and us) without either of us being able to represent its full range of meanings and affects. These powers are not that far away from what Freud calls 'memory traces' or what Serres invokes when he speaks of the 'welter of aborted beginnings' intrinsic to the life of noise.

Before we explore further the powers of the false in the realm of human history, we note that they also operate in non-humans, in for example, magma. Surges of magma on the ocean floor can impel two tectonic plates to rub up against each other more actively. One such plate, say that of the pacific rim, can then push up against the west coast of North America, producing stresses here and there, stresses real enough to be activated later but too vague now to be what later becomes the San Andreas fault. Only if the general pressures amass in specific combinations will some stresses become a fault line, and that fault can become the site of earthquakes. The stress point, however, was not an earthquake waiting to happen, for if other events still in the future did not appear, it would just simmer with its indefinite potentia. We are again in the realm of what Serres called the logic of 'it depends' or 'could happen, maybe not': the stress point could become an earthquake or it could become the birthplace of a new kind to rock at its vague site of receptivity. It takes tectonic pressures and the stress point together to generate a fault, and those two in conjunction with new pressures yet to generate an earthquake at a particular place and time. These events can be separated by thousands of years in the folds of a "handkerchief" of time. That zone of indiscernibility between a fault line and a rock formation of uniform strength is one of the sites of what Nietzsche and Deleuze call the powers of the false. Again, these powers are real enough to exert multiple effects under variable conditions (many of which may never occur), but they are often too vague to qualify as a definite actuality, or even a preformed possibility.

The powers of the false can also be seen to reside in carbon. Carbon atoms have a natural propensity to bond easily, with hydrogen, oxygen and nitrogen, and to form molecules that are both stable and flexible. There was no inevitability that carbon-based molecules would evolve into life: numerous contingent combinations were needed even for what we (only retrospectively) call "pre-life" forms. Just the right mix of other elements had to emerge alongside carbon if the incipient capacity festering in a complex formation as "pre-life" was to vibrate in a new way. The "power" of the false is the potentia of that which is merely simmering in a formation; it is not implicit in the sense of tending on its own to become only one thing. The powers of the false refers to that which quivers with a potential that can be defined authoritatively only after the fact of its emergence and evolution. It becomes what it will have been, and it might have become otherwise had it been nudged in different directions.

Such fecund powers are critical to the ontologies of Nietzsche, Deleuze and Serres, and they operate in both nature and culture. As Deleuze makes clear in Chapter 6 of *Cinema II: The Time Image*, the idea of the false need not be set only on an epistemic register, the register through which we separate what is true in a schema of knowledge from what falls outside it. That is one sense of the word, but the false now acquires another meaning too: one where the false does not take the form of an entity stable enough to qualify as existing "outside" or beyond a frame of knowledge. This false has the capacity to make a difference in the world without having had to pass through to the phase of phenomenon. On this ontological register, the powers of the false consist of energetic remainders (noise) that do not fit a particular regime of cultural equalization but nonetheless enter into novel vibrations at key moments in nature-culture.

Now let us return to the powers of the false within the layering of human memory and the practice of history. Our example now is the conduct of what Stuart Kauffman calls the 'quantum brain' (Kauffman, 2008). The human brain rotates back and forth between two types of activities: one a restless searching for points of stabilization and the other a stabilization of perceptions, trains of thought or coherent conversations. Consider, within this image of the quantum brain, what happens in Proust's *Time Regained* when the protagonist slips on a couple of uneven stones as he is about to join a party of aristocrats he has not seen for years. Marcel is hurled back to a moment long ago when something had been sensed without being perceived, partly because of the diverting pressure of action-oriented perception at the time. This incipience festered for years as a non-event, as perhaps what Serres would call a fluctuation. But it now enters into a pattern of resonance with a new slipping event, and thus into a phase of bifurcation or even rhythm. The vibratory pressure of the incipient past unfolding in the protraction of this moment opens up the possibility of a feeling, thought or action that was neither available for the first time nor could exist now without the first time. In the protraction of the present, the two sensed times, separated by years, reverberate together in a new way, opening Marcel to a rich experience of duration that had heretofore escaped him.

The "false" in human memory, like the pluripotentiality residing in the "memory" of magma or carbon, is that which is not consolidated enough at inception to assume the shape of a phenomenon. It exerts its strongest power when, many years later as if out of nowhere, it becomes a trigger on the edge of sensory awareness that makes a difference to thought, feeling, judgement and action. The false sows a seed from which new ideas, strategies or tempers can be ushered into the world in a new setting. It is thus not merely that which exceeds us or is the negative: the lack, the other or the insoluble gap between concept and thing. The false encompasses and exceeds those themes because even as it escapes our powers of perception, it also helps propel new turns of becoming at strategic moments: the productive powers of the false.

But the previous example does not sufficiently reveal the strange efficacy of these vague, intense triggers, nor does it show just how precarious the quantum brain is in its delicate oscillation between culturally organized trains of activity and breaks in the train through which layers of the past surge into the present to stimulate new thought or generate an impasse. Consider, then, another scene from *Time Regained*, when we meet a person who has lost that fragile balance between following a train of thought and responding to subliminal triggers that nudge the train in a new direction. This example illuminates the delicate poise required for thinking between coherence and innovation, between composing a narrative and allowing it to be reset, between insisting upon the integrity of a theory and responding to strange markers that carry it along a new trajectory. The powers of the false enable this creativity, even as they can also disable thought.

At that same party, Marcel encounters Charlus after a hiatus of many years. The arrogant intellectual he had known as a young man has now dissolved into a new being carrying traces of its former self. Charlus has aphasia. When he and Marcel enter into conversation this time, something strange happens. The earlier Charlus and the current Charlus now contend desperately against each other in a way that Marcel can only experience in terms of the disconcerting breaks and stutters that emerge from Charlus. The triggers for these stutters are too buried to be detected even vaguely. Neither the early Charlus nor the new Charlus can now be without the presence of the other, but neither can prevail because of the other. The two Charluses now contend radically with and against each other:

Of the two, one, the intellectual one, passed his time in complaining that he suffered from progressive aphasia, that he constantly pronounced one word or letter by mistake for another. But as soon as he actually made such a mistake, the other M. de Charlus, the subconscious one, who was as desirous of admiration as the first was of pity and out of vanity did things that the first would have despised, immediately, like a conductor whose orchestra had blundered, checked the phrase which he had started and with infinite ingenuity made the end of his sentence follow coherently from the word which had in fact uttered by mistake ...; his vanity impelled him, not without the fatigue of the most laborious concentration, to drag forth this or that ancient recollection ... which would demonstrate to me that he had preserved or recovered all his lucidity of mind (Proust, 1993, pp. 247–48).

The sentences of the novel increasingly take on the character of the contest Marcel describes. They increasingly incorporate elements, which strain against each other as they maintain a precarious balance, for our benefit. The poise that Charlus has lost, due to the interaction of forces pulling in different directions, also discloses the kind of torsion that must be in play to some degree when we are thinking and conversing at our best. Here the false consists of odd triggers too buried to be discernible and too insistent to be latent or ineffective.[21] Charlus cannot describe or characterize these perverse powers below awareness that keep disrupting his monologue; he can merely display their effects in one persona as he complains about them in another.

Proust understood through close attention to experience, even before Deleuze or Stuart Kauffman theorized it, that the human brain functions best when it maintains a delicate equipoise between its quantum state (where layered, ideational energies disturb and penetrate one another) and its collecting of itself into a mode of coherence. The first moment lasts only a half-second most of the time, though it may be extended a bit with practice. The second, equally important, may last longer; but it runs the risk of being stuck in a rut that cannot be reset. Stutter and stammer, as you allow a strange word or phrase to emerge from a trigger too deep and vague to be captured, but not too much or too often. An excess of either stifles the element of creativity in thought; the lack of either does the same. Both Charlus, the aphasiac and the loquacious ideologue, have lost the delicate balance required, though in different ways.

Because we periodically participate in quantum moments of creation that make a difference to life and world, we are junior partners in a world of becoming composed of numerous force-fields that exceed us, that act upon us in multiple ways and that we intervene into at multiple levels (See Connolly, 2011). We cannot control or master a world that includes the powers of the false. But because our own thought also includes them, we can learn how to inflect them and perhaps even put them to use. We can experiment with ways to enhance our sensitivity to that which hovers in the zone of indiscernibility between the actual and the real-but-not-actual. Sometimes that sensitivity will take the form of being responsive to sensory experience below the threshold of capture; sometimes it will take the form of responding to effects that express triggers below sensory attention; sometimes it will take the form of exploring a new train of thought that has almost miraculously opened up before us. In each case, the powers of the false are at work. To cite Deleuze and Guattari here, experiment with a degree of caution.[22] When Nietzsche and Deleuze speak of the "innocence" of becoming, they include the powers of false in that portrayal. The world is not marked, in the first instance, by original sin, primordial guilt or divine judgement. Neither is it one in which we are entirely responsible for what we think or do. It is, instead, a world in which, periodically and at our best, we move back and forth between experiments in thought and action as new circumstances arise and recoil back upon those activities to reflect upon their effects. It is thus a risky world, one in which the powers of the false make it impossible to drain out all the risk: the powers of the false prowl in cultural equalizations that have been forged through us and in non-human force fields that impinge upon us as well as each other. These also set some of the reasons that thinkers who emphasize the (ontological) powers of the false resist folding too much systematicity into ethics or an ethos of politics. Systematic morality weighs too heavily upon time.

The Practice of History

Let us turn now to which figures of human action and interaction would be appropriate to a world in which time periodically becomes crumpled and the powers of the false come into play. We are speaking now of the self as a durable object, a self in the phase of the 'more intelligent invariant' that persists as movement itself (*Genesis*, p. 120). We will try, pace a strong tendency in Harman, to remain faithful to this human thing as we consider in particular the role it can play in inflecting the noise by listening, narrating, interpreting and inflecting the course of history. Latour might speak here of the participation of "actants" which are neither pure objects nor full subjects but "interveners" (Latour, 2004, p. 75); Deleuze refers to 'quasi-causal operators' that, by virtue of their specific location in an assemblage, can make the difference or become a decisive force catalyzing a new event (De Landa, 2005, p. 123). Serres describes this stance as one of an "aperture" or "listening post": while noise is a self-generating power and is 'not dependent on me, not dependent on anyone', its phases are 'contingent on an observer, they hinge on a listening post, on a channel, on an aperture'. (Serres, 1995, pp. 62–3) Within the noise, a small differentiation happens, the cascade thickens in spots and knots, and the flow suddenly takes on a "direction": but 'what the flux is hurrying toward is the receiver, which is not yet certain to let it pass through', The human observer can 'attract the directional flux', as my ears can be drawn to refrains amidst a generalized din (Serres, 1995, p. 64).[23]

One example of this human activity, which Serres himself pursues, is the historian's attempt to discern which operators, born years or centuries apart, have now become adjacencies in folded time. Latour, in a conversation with Serres, asks him to elaborate on this practice: How can one know when a cross-period adjacency is at work? 'What allows you to establish the rapprochement? This is the great difficulty for your readers, who may have an impression of free association, of arbitrary rapprochements. The problem is understanding the operator you extract.... [What is] the key [for example] that allow you to link together a piece of Lucretius and a piece of physics' (Serres et al., 1995, 63)? Serres responds by invoking the need for analogy based on the intuition of a certain structural "correspondence" between events or entities otherwise assigned to different categories, such as physics and poetry, or ancient and modern.[24] Serres was suddenly struck, he says, by an uncanny resemblance between what Archimedes was saying about fluids and what Lucretius was saying about Athens: both writers told of a "vortical" structure of generativity at work. Serres noted this resemblance and took it as a call to place these two thinkers into dissonant conjunction, 'to explicate, that is, "to unpleat"' the fold that they seem to be sharing. Serres thus seems to add a new wrinkle to his ontology of noise: a world of noise, with its inherent tendency towards repetition and redundancy, is a world of fractal similitudes,[25] a kind of de-theologized version of what Foucault described in *The Order of Things* as the 'prose of the world'.

In what, then, might historical practice alert to crumpled time look like? Perhaps in attempts to make experimental, analogical connections between events or bodies separated by time and place that suddenly appear to resemble one another. That, says Serres, is 'Hermes's very method: he exports and imports; thus, he traverses. He invents and can be mistaken – because of analogies, which are dangerous ... – but we know no other route to invention' (Serres et al., 1995, p. 66).[26]

The medievalist Eileen Joy defends a model of historiography close to the one Serres recommends. Objecting to scholarship that 'labors to inscribe a definitive "break" between "now" and "then"', Joy calls for a practice of history alert to the way 'every present moment is inhabited by and also inhabits (consciously and unconsciously) multiple, heterogeneous temporalities – some at a distant remove and other more contiguous'. The task of the historian, says Joy, 'might be to make those heterogeneous temporalities more visible and more traceable, in order to aid us in cultivating a deeper attention to, not the genealogies of history, but its entanglements. For time is all knotted up, and we, we are knotted up with time.... [A]ll scholarly studies are really excavations, in one form or another, of the site of the Now, which has folded within it, all of time'.[27]

Joy shares our view of time as crumpled and periodically driven with powers of the false that jump across temporal zones. While she and other historians are better equipped to explore the implications of this image of time for historiography, we will conclude by enacting our role as listening posts/operators by narrating what we think may be an emerging bifurcation of noise. In the summer of 2010, we saw a London production of the musical Hair, which had first opened on Broadway in 1968 and ran for 1750 performances: a span of 32 years. One of us has seen the play both times. The audience in London, made up of all ages, was strongly affected by the performance of this story, by the sexual and political energies of young people facing an unpopular war and the tension between a longing to belong (to nation, to city, to family, to Earth) and the fact that none of these collectives seemed to fit or satisfy the longing. Why was the 2010 audience so moved by the story of the Vietnam War and the summer of 1968?

Two dimensions, we think, jump across chrono-times to become proximities in the folds of time. The first is the sickening waste of life and imposition of suffering caused by wars, wars deemed necessary by those who stand above them and act not as listening posts or apertures but as putative masters of the universe. The second adjacency, perhaps, is of two rhythms of energetic sound, one produced by the score in 1968 and another produced by the "same" score in 2010. Doubtless, some of the vibrations that jump across the two contexts operate below human audibility but not below our capacity to resonate with them, as when inaudible vibrations in organ music still affect the mood of those in the room. The music, in its layered expressions, induces one set of images and aspirations in 1968 – towards participatory democracy within the container-space of a nation – and another in 2010. Because the latter seems not yet to have fully entered the phase of "phenomena", we are uncertain about what it is. But our intuition in the theatre that evening was that something is afoot. A something that is not reducible to nostalgia. So, in a creative act of analogy, we surmise that a non-nation-based locus of belonging is emerging today, perhaps a belonging to time as becoming that can augment and extend those other more familiar modes of belonging (Wong, 2010).

We like the ordinariness of the image of a crumpled handkerchief with viscous clots, and we appreciate the boldness of the idea that falseness has power: together these images speak to both the persistence of shapes and to flows of communication and miscommunication within and between phases of invariance. We prefer to keep this dual focus alive, rather than pursue alone Harman's focus on the "object". Harman's object-oriented-ness seems designed in part for an ethical task: to provide a philosophical bulwark against the ever-present tendency of epistemological and practical hubris on the part of humans. We share his concern. But we find that Serres and Deleuze enable us to foreground the incalculability and element of opacity in things while also acknowledging the operation of (what Serres calls) the 'multiple as such' or that protean flow of Becoming, the ado rattling around in and around us and other things. Attending to this double process – a field of generativity and stabilizations (as in the oscillating, quantum brain) – is essential to a sensitive grasp of history and to a thoughtful politics.

Notes

[1] We tend to agree with Michel Serres who, as Steven Connor notes, 'assumes that every metaphysics is founded upon a physics, a particular theory of the operation of forces and materials' (Connor, 2004, pp. 105–17.).

[2] Purer cases of this monism include, says Harman, Pythagoras, Parmenides, Anaximander. Although Deleuze tries, says Harman, to define a 'realm beneath experience' – the virtual – that is not a flat blob but a heterogeneity 'animated in advance by different 'pre-individual' zones', this attempt only ends up dooming 'specific realities' to 'a sort of halfhearted existence somewhere between one and many' (Harman, 2009, p. 160).

[3] See Brian Smith's review of Graham Harman's *Prince of Networks*. In Harman's words, Latour treats objects as so singular that they 'vanish instantly with the

slightest change' in their relations within a network (Harman, 2009, p. 6). Harman seeks an even more 'more radical democracy in which the comet itself, a deep reality currently unexpressed in all of the comet's relations, and equally inexpressible in all possible relations that it might enter in the future, also has its foot jammed in the door of the world.... For this reason, we must end the popular denunciations of substance, the ... attempts to reduce the reality of things to their effects on other things ... [There exists]... not just some dark and shapeless matter that rationality can never reach, but a menagerie of inscrutable objects hidden from birds and sand-grains just as much as from us' (Harman, 2010b).

4   Because Latour treats objects as purely operational entities, he fails to think their withdrawing depth. By Harman's analysis, so too does Deleuze fail, for his highly motile, self-transforming virtual realm renders any actuality that emerges a surface formation on the ever-changing sea of the Virtual. Thanks to J. D. Dewsbury for this point.

5   Jane Bennett pursued a parallel project (independent of speculative realism and object-oriented ontology) in *Vibrant Matter: A Political Ecology of Things* (2010). Bennett and Harman are both interested in theorizing a material agency irreducible to the role things play in a symbolic order and both are willing to experiment with thinking thingness even in the wake of critiques of unmediated access made in the names of Kant, Heidegger, Adorno, and social constructivists.

6   In an April 22, 2010 blog posting, Harman says that he doesn't not think that Deleuze's ontology is 'a lump, I just don't think his ontology fully recognizes the need for fully-formed individuals. I realize that they are unfashionable, but I think people will start realizing that they are necessary; too many problems result if you don't have them. Deleuze is a lot of fun, but is not quite one of my heroes (What I like best, I think, is his tone.)'. [http://doctorzamalek2.wordpress.com/page/7/]

7   *A Thousand Plateaus*, for example, often directs the reader's attention away from res extensa towards intensities (becomings-animal, becomings-woman, Bodies without Organs). These are not functional, bounded entities but sets of 'speeds and slownesses between unformed particles [having only] ... the individuality of a day, a season, a year, a life.' (Deleuze and Guattari, 1993, p. 262). For Harman's object-oriented ontology, a stronger theory of individuation is needed: after all, concrete objects regularly do withstand the ontological flow or flux: 'Unless a philosophy can account adequately for the fact that not all changes make a difference, then its sense of individuals is too weak...' Graham Harman, April 29, 2010. [http://doctorzamalek2.wordpress.com/page/7/]

8   Deleuze himself invokes Nietzsche as his inspiration here: Nietzsche explored 'a world of impersonal and pre-individual singularities, a world he then called Dionysian or of the will to power.... Being is not an undifferentiated abyss [for Nietzsche], it leaps from one singularity to another, casting always the dice...' (Deleuze, 1990, pp. 106–107).

9   'I call forth the absences, the nudities, the blank pages, the matrices. I summon the phantoms which fade away the further they come forward. I call forth the court of the undifferentiated' (Serres, 1995, p. 42).

10   As Raymond Boisvert notes, Serres's' term noise lacks the 'privative prefixes' that philosophy has traditionally used to name the multiple: for example, as 'the indeterminate, the unformed, disorder, the indefinite, and the apeiron' (Boisvert,

1998). Serres rejects the word 'disorder' altogether and prefers to speak of states of relative 'distribution' and states of relative 'gathering' in noise (Serres, 1995, p. 109).

[11] 'The dance is born out of blankness, bareness, or on the contrary, out of clamors' (Serres, 1995, p. 36). We can never know which it is: 'When there is an infinity of dispersed information in the well, it is really the same well as if it were devoid of information' (Serres, 1995, p. 18).

[12] Innumerable versions of the process proceed simultaneously: different rainfalls, different vectors of swerve, different configurations of turbulent forces, different sets of shapes, different rates and sequences of decay and decline. But the same strange 'logic' holds each time: the sequence of stages repeats in a spiral repetition: the 'stroke of genius' in Lucretian political theory/physics, says Serres, is that 'there is no circle, there are only vortices ..., spirals that shift, that erode' (Serres, 2000, p. 58.).

[13] For example, *Genesis* repeatedly tells of shapes that emerge by virtue of 'an insufficient reason,' a 'quasi-nonexistent cause' (Serres, 1995, p. 60) whose quite real efficacy remains somewhat inexplicable (Serres, 1995, p. 57).

[14] It has become 'frequentative' (Serres, 1995, p. 68).

[15] 'The expansive fizzle of sea noise is broken up into fluctuations. A given one of them, dwarfish, singular begins gathering followers.' And the direction-less fluctuation becomes vectoral. We cannot know why or when a vector will form but we should be on the lookout for them because there is a natural tendency towards 'redundancy, echo, imitation' (Serres, 1995, p. 69) intrinsic to noise, a 'fractal breeze' within. (Serres, 1995, p. 63).

[16] In popular parlance, a phase names a style of comportment (say that of a teen-aged girl) marked by distinctive, identifiable repetitions or tendencies (towards introspection, attraction to horses, hair, scents): 'What's the matter with her, for pity's sake?' asked Herold ... 'Perhaps it's a phase. Young girls often pass through it' W. J. Locke, Stella Maris (1913), cited in the definition of 'phase' in the Oxford English Dictionary. Serres himself does not speak of phases, invoking instead the links of a 'chain' of formativity. Each linkage forms by the 'insufficient reason' of an 'interference' or instability whose existence we are led to posit by the evidence of its effects. Each link is itself a brittle formation, as fragile as its connection to the others; the chain is a sticky stream of flotsam that 'slide over one another, as though viscous ... This is not a solid chain, it is simply a liquid movement, a viscosity, a propagation that wagers its age in each locality. Here we are in liquid history and the ages of waters' (Serres, 1995, p. 71).

[17] Steven Connor notes that Serres apprehends time as 'an 'implicate order', as a complex volume that folds over on itself, and in the process does not merely transform in time, but itself gathers up and releases time, as though time were like the intricately folded structure of a protein' (Connor, 2004, pp. 105–17).

[18] 'Only my life, its time or its duration, can make these two propositions coherent between themselves.' 'Any object in the world,' says Serres, 'insofar as it resists the tendency to entropy, is a complex clock associating several times' (Serres, 2000, p. 163).

[19] Serres uses the crumpled handkerchief to illustrate the non-linearity of time, the strange contemporaneity of past and present, the way time proceeds in 'folds

or twists'. But in order to emphasize the peculiar motility or movement-style of time, Serres moves from the hankie-object to a series of homely processes, such as coffee-brewing ('Time doesn't flow; it percolates'), bread-making (time moves through a series of folding, stretching, and doubling-back repetitions), and insect flight ('Follow the flight pattern of a fly. Doesn't time sometimes flow according to the breaks and bends that this flight seems to follow or invent?').

20 The film *Citizen Kane* was directed by Orson Wells, produced in 1941.

21 Some triggers subsist on the edge of sensory awareness, and others exert effects below that threshold, as chemical-electrical pressures that make a difference without being felt. The latter are like those vibrations in organ music that make a measurable effect on our moods but are inaudible. Subtract those vibrations and the mood changes, though the kind of difference they make also varies with the settings in which they occur.

22 'But once again, so much caution is needed to prevent the plane of consistency from becoming a pure plane of abolition or death, to prevent the involution from turning into a regression to the undifferentiated' (Deleuze and Guattari, 1993, p. 298).

23 The obvious referent here is the human observer, though there is nothing in Serres to exclude non-human observers, such as the oyster's lure for the one grain of sand from the vast plain of the ocean floor.

24 For Serres, the logic of turbulent generativity – the becomings of noise – applies to all scales of order: to organisms, societies, ecosystems; to the meteorological, the biological, the psychological, the political, the historical. He writes in a way that does not so much reject as simply doesn't feel the force of the distinction between a moral and a geological discourses, between a poem and a treatise, between the ancient and the modern. He mingles and confounds, sometimes in the same sentence, terms and claims from different archives and centuries.

25 A world of noise calls for a practice of writing that is a 'fractal meander'(Serres, 1995, p. 114).

26 Jonathan Gil Harris argues that the crumpled handkerchief is in part the product of 'an act of strategic proximation – it requires the artful labor of the critic, a labor that goes beyond mere empirical description of things as they really are or were. Serres thus allows us to recognize how our untimely mediations create the past and the present, less in the sense of making them up, than of persistently transforming the web of relations that tether the past to us – and us to it' (Harris, ND).

27 See posts by Eileen Joy and the reply by Jeffrey J. Cohen (ND). Michael Shortland argues that Serres figures history as 'a series of convergences in different frames of reference; there is no universal time: 'each thing has its own time. ... a temporal polymorphism.' Consequently, Serres's historiography is contemporaneist: his past is not consigned to history but is still active and relevant. Not, then, so much the 'history of the present' ... but rather the 'presence of the past'.... Serres's histoires travel here and there across time, always on the move, exchanging registers, exploring experiences, and analysing styles of life. This is hugely disorientating, like time travel without a map or compass, and a far cry from the neatly categorized and lucid 'ratified' and 'lapsed' history ... one associates with Bachelard and Canguilhem' (Shortland, 1998, pp. 335–53).

Bibliography

Bennett, J. (2010), *Vibrant Matter: A Political Ecology of Things*. Durham: Duke.

Boisvert, R. (1998), 'Review of Michel Serres' Genesis', in *Zygon*, *Vol. 33*, no. 3 (September), pp. 481–83.

Connolly, W. (2011), *A World of Becoming*. Durham, NC: Duke University Press.

Connor, S. (2004), 'Topologies: Michel Serres and the Shapes of Thought', in *Anglistik, Vol. 15*, pp. 105–17.

De Landa, M. (1997), 'The Machinic Phylum', in *TechnoMorphica*. Accessed May 10, 2010 at http://www.v2.nl/archive/articles/the-machinic-phylum.

—(2005), *Intensive Science and Virtual Philosophy*. New York: Continuum.

Deleuze, G. (1989), *Cinema II: The Time Image*. Translated by H. Tomlinson and R. Galeta. Minneapolis: University of Minnesota Press.

—(1990), *The Logic of Sense*. New York: Columbia University Press.

Deleuze, G. and Guattari, F. (1993), *A Thousand Plateaus: Capitalism and Schizophrenia*. Minneapolis: University of Minnesota Press.

Foucault, M. (1970), *The Order of Things*. Pantheon Press.

Harman, G. (2009), *Prince of Networks: Bruno Latour and Metaphysics*. Melbourne, re.press.

—(2010a), *Guerrilla Metaphysics*. Peru: Open Court.

—(2010b), *The Metaphysics of Objects: Latour and his Aftermath*, p. 5, [draft]. Accessed May 8, 2010 at http://www.pucp.edu.pe/eventos/congresos/filosofia/programa_general/viernes/sesion15-16.30/HarmanGraham.pdf.

Harris, J. G. (ND), 'Untimely Mediations', in *Early Modern Culture*, no. 6. Accessed at http://emc.eserver.org/1-6/issue6.html.

Joy, E. and Cohen, J. J. (ND), http://www.inthemedievalmiddle.com/2009/03/signaling-to-each-other-from.html.

Kauffman, S. (2008), *Reinventing the Sacred*. New York: Basic Books.

Latour, B. (2004), *The Politics of Nature*. Cambridge: Harvard University Press.

Perloff, M. (2005), '"Multiple Pleats": Some Applications of Michel Serres's Poetics', in N. Abbas (ed.), *Mapping Michel Serres*. Ann Arbor: University of Michigan Press, pp. 99–112.

Proust, M. (1993), 'Time Regained', in *In Search of Lost Time*. Translated by A. Mayor and T. Kilmartin. New York: The Modern Library, *Vol. VI*.

Serres, M. (1995), *Genesis*. Ann Arbor: Michigan University Press.

—(2000), *The Birth of Physics*. Manchester: Clinamen Press.

Serres, M. and Latour, B. (1995), *Conversations: on Science, Culture, and Time*. Ann Arbor: University of Michigan Press. Shortland M. (1998), 'Review of Conversations on Science, Culture, and Time by Michel Serres and Bruno Latour and of A History of Scientific Thought by Michel Serres', in *British Journal for the History of Science, Vol. 31*, no. 3 (Sep., 1998), pp. 335–53. Accessed Feb 17, 2010 at http://www.jstor.org/stable/4027816.

Smith, B. (ND), 'Review of Graham Harman's Prince of Networks', in *The Philosopher's Magazine*, http://www.philosophypress.co.uk/?p = 611.

Whitman, W. (2002), 'Song of the Broad-Axe', in M. Moon (ed.), *Leaves of Grass*. Oxford: Norton.

Wong, M. (2010), *Belonging to Time*. Johns Hopkins University [doctoral dissertation].

Chapter 10

A Physical Theory of Heredity|Heresy:
The Education of Henry Adams

Bernd Herzogenrath[*]

Both a grandson and a great-grandson of American presidents, Henry
Brooks Adams was a fourth-generation member of what was by far the most
important and influential political dynasty in American history. He received
the finest formal education available in his time, graduating from Harvard,
where he was later appointed a professor of medieval history. During the
Civil War, he served as a secretary to his father Charles Francis Adams Sr.,
who was appointed as the ambassador of United States to England, and he
was later the editor of the North American Review. Nonetheless, his autobiography *The Education of Henry Adams* shows a deep sense of failure and
raises the question of how to cope with the erosion of all certainties and the
collapse of the idea of teleological progress. During Adams's lifetime, the
virtues of the American republic, its moral and spiritual basis, were being
submerged under the rising tide of capitalism. Industrialization exploded
after the Civil War and with the growth of industry and business came
urbanization, and the cities were flooded with young farmers and
European immigrants. Such developments also led to a new American
upper class, consisting of entrepreneurs such as the Carnegies and the
Rockefellers who built enormous fortunes by exploiting natural resources
and cheap labor. Here Charles Darwin's [or Herbert Spencer's] survival
of the fittest meant a ruthless selfishness and the striving for profit by any
means. A new generation of Americans had to deal with the problems
born of capitalism, industrialization, and social and economic change.
The old republic, with its party system of Republicans and Federalists, was
transformed into a new 'mass democracy', with Democrats and Whigs.

* The original version of this essay was published as 'The Education of 'Henry Adams:
A Physical Theory of Heredity|Heresy', in *Organs, Organisms, Organisations: Organic Form
in 19th Century Discourse*, edited by T. Rachwal and T. Slawek, Frankfurt: Peter Lang, 2000:
159–68. This recent version is reprinted from my book *An American Body|Politic. A Deleuzian
Approach*, Hanover: Dartmouth College Press, 2010: 208–33, with kind permission.

The old republic had restricted popular participation in politics by permitting only property owners to vote and through the hierarchical structure of parties, including the provision that only the members of the party elites could nominate candidates. In contrast, the new democratic system relied more on grass-root support and shaped politics according to the people's will. However, selfish economic individualism also entered democratic politics. Corruption was so much the order of the day that Whitman, in 'Democratic Vistas', complained that 'never was there, perhaps, more hollowness at heart than at present, and here in the United States ... The official services of America, national, state, and municipal, in all their branches and departments, ... are saturated in corruption, bribery, falsehood, mal-administration ... The great cities reek with respectable as much as non-respectable robbery and scoundrelism' (Whitman, 1996, p. 961). In short, even in the new mass democracy—with its promise of a government of the people and by the people, where the representers were thought not to be aloof from the represented—the gulf widened continually: 'I say that our New World democracy, however great a success in uplifting the masses out of their sloughs, in materialistic development, products, and in a certain highly-deceptive superficial popular intellectuality, is, so far, an almost complete failure' (p. 962).

Adams's writings, I argue, are important for a discussion of the Body|Politic because he can be regarded as the last republican, situated at a historical point where, after the Civil War, the republic of the founding fathers [in which his ancestors played a fundamental role] was about to be replaced with modern democracy. The republican tradition had embodied the ethos of a Body|Politic rooted in 'civic virtue', the absence of corruption and overly commercial interests, ensured by a system of checks and balances and able leaders. The shift from a politics of virtue to a politics of [self-] interest necessitated a new structure for the Body|Politic in the new era of modernity, in which the world became faster and smaller, and people's experiences became increasingly fragmented and alienated. It called for a new science as well: sociology. The work of 'socio-evolutionists' such as Auguste Comte [who actually coined the word sociology] and Spencer developed simultaneously with Darwin's theory of evolution, and took nineteenth-century biology and physics as its scientific models—exactly the sciences that Adams also turned to in order to make sense of the seismic shift to modernity, a transition he also equates with the trajectory from unity to multiplicity, and from order to chaos [it must be noted, however, that he is ambivalent about at least the concepts of multiplicity and chaos]. In his *Education*, Adams repeatedly focuses on the energy that multiplicity and chaos provide, and the staleness and inertia of order, and connects these musings with political observations. The residual Puritan in him not only claimed that 'anarchy, by definition, must be chaos' (Adams, 1995, p. 385), but also conceded that 'chaos often breeds life, when order breeds habit' (p. 239). To counter stifling habit, Adams saw the need for reforms, since 'the whole government, from top to bottom, was rotten with the senility of what was antiquated and the instability of what was improvised ... the whole fabric required reconstruction as much as in 1789, for the Constitution had become as antiquated as the Confedera-tion. Sooner or later a shock must come, the more dangerous the longer postponed. The Civil War had made a new system in fact; the country would have to reorganize the machinery in practice and theory' (ibid.). For Adams, the American nation is deeply indebted to the 'power of the people.' His histories of the United States during the administrations of Jefferson and Madison, which cover one of the most important periods in the founding of the American nation, are a hymn to the power of 'the people of the United States, ... [who] were trying an experiment which could succeed only in a world of their own' (Adams, 1986b, p. 1020). Thus, if Adams seems at times to be deeply pessimistic about the development of American democracy, he always saw that its problems were the fault of the corruption of political rep-resentatives, and not of the people: 'The better test of American character was not political but social, and was to be found not in the government, but in the people' (Adams, 1986a, p. 1336). Ultimately, for Adams, 'after all sys-tems of Government are secondary matter, if you've only got your people behind them. I never have as yet felt as proud as now of the great qualities of our race, or so confident of the capacities of men to develop their capacities in the mass' (Adams, 1982–1988, 1, p. 458).

Though Adams is not a political theorist in the narrow sense of the word, and though he does not present a unified and coherent theory of the Body|Politic, his writings contain much of use and value for an assessment of the trajectory of the Body|Politic from the republic of the founding fathers to the modern democracy of the twentieth century.[1] For Adams, a historian, 'democracy is the only subject for history. I am satisfied that the purely mechanical development of the human mind in society must appear in a great democracy so clearly, for want of disturbing elements, that in another generation psychology, physiology, and history will join in proving man to have as fixed and necessary development as that of a tree; and almost as unconscious' (Adams, 1947, pp. 80–1). As Richard Hofstadter has put it, 'while it is no doubt true to some degree everywhere that history doubles for political theory ... it is perhaps more keenly true in the United States' (Hofstadter, 1968, p. 4). Adams was a not only a historian but also a man of letters, novelist, and political journalist, and his *Education,* though partly indebted to the discursive strategies of the autobiographical form, is actually an extended meditation on the social, technological, political and intellectual changes that marked the transition from the nineteenth century to the twentieth. For Adams, the story of the individual provides the story of the nation—the 'biological evolution' of the individual body has to be read in conjunction with the 'democratic evolution' of the Body|Politic: 'American types were especially worth study if they were to represent the greatest democratic evolution the world could know. Readers might judge for themselves what share the individual possessed in creating or shaping the nation, but whether it was small or great, the nation could be understood only by studying the individual' (Adams, 1986a, 1335). As both novelist and historian, Adams made use of the scientific concepts of his times. He did not adhere so much to their quality as rigorous scientific and [quasi-]objective theories as to their usefulness as heuristic and conceptual models. His use of such concepts 'reveal[s] a desperate search for new terms and appropriate metaphors for describing twentieth-century forces' (Rowe, p. 50). Attacks on the inaccuracy of Adams's application of scientific concepts miss the point. As Melvin Lyon has suggested, their use should be read as the attempt to create convenient fictions exemplifying Adams's quest for powerful metaphors.[2] In this chapter, I want to show how some later developments in the human and natural sciences would have provided a fruitful subtext for Adams's doubts and ramifications, developments he sensed but could not conceive of within the scientific framework of his own time. Adams himself sees the close connection between science and politics in their attempts to come to terms with the 'evidence of growing complexity, and multiplicity, and even contradiction, in life. He could not escape it; politics or science, the lesson was the same, and at every step it blocked his path whichever way he turned. He found it in politics; he ran against it in science; he struck it in everyday life, as though he were still Adam in the Garden of Eden between God who was unity, and Satan who was complexity, with no means of deciding which was truth' (Adams, 1995, 377). This seemingly simple distinction between the discrete entities of 'unity' and 'multiplicity' is complicated throughout the whole text by chiastic claims such as 'the greater the unity and the momentum, the worse became the complexity and the friction ... the multiplicity of unity had steadily increased, was increasing' (ibid.). Ultimately, 'order and anarchy were one, but ... the unity was chaos' (p. 385). I am not insinuating that Adams was a complexity theorist *avant la lettre*. However, while contemporary [human and natural] scientists have generally regarded Adams as a brilliant but weirdly erratic figure in American thought, these quotations show that his interest in the interrelations of chaos and order, multiplicity and complexity, at least points in the direction of this new discipline. In 'A Letter to American Teachers of History,'[3] Adams claimed that the 'department of history needs to concert with the departments of biology, sociology, and psychology some common formula or figure to serve their students as models for the working of physico-chemical and mechanical energies' (Adams, 1920, pp. 261–62).

To read the 'physicist-historian' (p. 310) Adams in the light of current scientific findings repeats his gesture to 'make sense' of the past by the present, a gesture that, according to Roland Barthes, is the ultimate gesture of criticism: 'One can say that the critical task ... is purely formal: not to 'discover' in the work or the author something 'hidden,' 'profound,' 'secret' which hitherto passed unnoticed (by what miracle? Are we more perspicacious than our predecessors?), but only to adjust the language his period affords him ... to the language, i.e., the formal system of logical constraints elaborated by the author according to his own period' (Barthes, 1972, pp. 258–59). Since Adams himself struggled with Darwinism and the theory of evolution, with genealogy and its vicissitudes, I want to situate his rhetoric of education and its failure, unity and multiplicity, within the contexts of complexity theory[4] and molecular biology—as a neo-Darwinian approach to the question of evolution. Here, I will draw in particular on the texts and theories of Deleuze, Serres and Stuart Kauffman.

The discourse of genealogy, or the question of heredity and family lines, provides an important structural paradigm for Adams's text, and it is this discourse that this chapter will mainly focus on. It might even be apt to say that *The Education of Henry Adams* tells a story of heredity as much as it tells a story of education. Even before the beginning, so to speak, the text of *The Education* focuses on the question of 'the self'—both on the relation of the self to history, society, and knowledge, and on the relation of the self to itself. *The Education*, curiously enough, begins with two prefaces. While the first is composed by a 'fake editor' [Adams himself wrote it] and provides a short introduction to the overall topic of the book and the history of its author, the second, 'real' preface revolves around the problematics of the ego. Referring to Rousseau's *Confessions*, Adams calls this book 'a monument of warning against the Ego' (Adams, 1995, p. 8). Here, the ego is seen as a 'manikin on which the toilet of education is draped in order to show the fit or misfit of the clothes'. Adams does not believe in the individual ego as a center for knowledge and language; for him, 'the object of study is the garment, not the figure. The tailor adapts the manikin as well as the clothes to his patron's wants. The subject of education, however–the 'real body' for which the ego-manikin serves as a 'model,' the 'young man himself,' or Henry Adams–is 'a certain form of energy; the object to be gained is economy of his force' (ibid.). In this oscillation between center and energy|economy, Adams's second preface structurally repeats the tension he refers to in his 'Editor's Preface', the tension between his study *Mont Saint Michel and Chartres* [1904] and the *Education* as a whole. While Adams refers to the first book as 'a Study of Thirteenth-century Unity', he labels *The Education* 'a Study of Twentieth-century Multiplicity' (p. 5).[5]

Educated in a long tradition of conservative Bostonians to which he felt he belonged— 'his education was warped beyond recovery in the direction of puritan politics ... the old Puritan nature rebelled against change' (p. 29)—Adams felt quite lost when faced with the 'paradigm shift' of modernity brought about after the Civil War and the assassination of Lincoln, seeing 'before him a world so changed as to be beyond connection with the past' (p. 202). 'Unity' had been the main attractor of Adams's education, in his interest in medieval theology and also in the fact that members of the Adams family had been devout fighters for the cause of unity in the political sense: Adams's great-grandfather was John Adams, the second president of the United States, the 'colossus of independence', as Thomas Jefferson called him, and a believer in a centralized government with strong checks and balances of popular power. Adams's education along the paths of 'unity' had not prepared him for the 'multiplicity' he encountered. Whereas former generations could rely on 'old forms of education, that [generation] which had its work to do between 1870 and 1900 needed something quite new' (p. 30), simply because the world as Adams knew it had completely changed: 'In 1900 he entered a far vaster universe, where all the old roads ran about in every direction, overrunning, dividing, subdividing, stopping abruptly, vanishing slowly, with side-paths that led nowhere, and sequences that could not be proved' (p. 379). Adams sensed that he had lost what he thought had been a past of fixed and orderly certainties. He stood on the brink of 'a new multiverse' (p. 433) of uncertainties, a radically polycentric world of intersecting forces, a new version of the world that once and for all replaced medieval monotheism—'a new world which would not be a unity but a multiple' (ibid.). This multiverse was discontinuous with Adams's personal past and amounted to a sudden historical break. He was faced with absolute newness; for him, 'this new exploration along the shores of Multiplicity and Complexity promised to be the longest' (p. 425). A historian born to a family of politicians, describing himself as a 'student of multiplicity' (p. 424), Adams was highly concerned with multiplicities and complexity and their relation to the Body|Politic [and the domain of complexity theory, closely related to the similar interests of Deleuze and Serres] as early as 1907, when these 'new sciences' did not yet exist per se. This chapter is not so much concerned with the accuracy of Adams's explorations as it is with his attempt to conceive of a 'dynamic theory' by adapting and mutating the physical sciences of his time.

The first chapter of *The Education*, following the two prefaces, begins with an impressive and extensive litany of names and places that unmistakably establish the main coordinates of the tradition and cultural background in which Henry Brooks Adams was situated at birth: 'Under the shadow of Boston State House, turning its back on the house of John Hancock, the little passage called Hancock Avenue runs, or ran, from Beacon Street, skirting the State House grounds, to Mount Vernon Street, on the summit of Beacon Hill; and there, in the third house below Mount Vernon Place, February 16, 1838, a child was born, and christened later by his uncle, the minister of the First Church after the tenets of Boston Unitarianism, as Henry Brooks Adams' (p. 9). This safe insertion into a privileged cultural background is immediately paralleled by Adams's recourse to a bodily, organic metaphor. Commenting on his birth and the ritual of christening, Adams connects this act to an apparently more brutal Jewish ceremony of circumcision: 'Had he been born in Jerusalem under the shadow of the temple and circumcised in the Synagogue by his uncle the high priest, under the name of Israel Cohen, he would scarcely have been more distincly [sic] branded, and not much more heavily handicapped in the races of the coming century' (ibid.). Two chapters later, Adams explicitly draws the connection to the idea of 'education' when he states that 'the surface was ready to take any form that education should cut into it' (p. 43, my emphasis), and in his reference to education as being 'stamped' (ibid.) onto the body. Education, the law of the symbolic register, qua representation cuts into the continuum of the body. From such a perspective, the body is seen as inert, passive matter awaiting conceptual differentiation from the outside, and not as an informed body that differentiates itself— the body is regarded as something that is [man-]made, not something that is alive, that grows. As John Carlos Rowe has observed, in *The Education*, 'education becomes the successive activities of draping, cutting, and fitting the garments and studying their "fit or misfit"' (Rowe, 30) on the manikin, which also is the result of a primal cut [analogous to circumcision], a cut that introduces the subject to the realm of representation, culture and tradition. It is indeed this cut that makes the subject come into existence as subject in the first place. The question is, however, to use Adams's metaphor of the second preface, how closely the Body|Politic's desire for unity and representation can be linked to the 'certain form of energy' that the subject is, without 'cutting off' the connection.

Throughout the text, Adams repeatedly builds up an opposition between country and town, summer and winter, closely connected to the respective family lines of the Adams family and the Brooks family. While summer, country, and the Brooks family are associated with freedom and play, winter, town, the Adams family represent rules and regulations, the law. As Lyon has observed, 'by associating Boston and school with winter, [Adams] also creates the first link between his unity-multiplicity dichotomy and the book's pervasive water symbolism. For winter is rigid unity, a frozen time of ice and snow. This symbolic use leads directly into the snow, ice, and glacier imagery which appears later in the book' (Lyon, p. 134). However, within this 'rule of phase,' so to speak, Adams [as the subject 'Henry Adams' within the text of *The Education*] opts for yet another phase state, an alternative between frozen rigidity and fluid turbulence. In a self-reflective passage in which he comments on the process of writing, Adams states: 'The pen works for itself, and acts like a hand, modeling the plastic material over and over again to the form that suits it best. The form is never arbitrary, but is a sort of growth like crystallization, as any artist knows too well; for often the pencil or pen runs into side-paths and shapelessness, loses its relations, stops or is bogged. Then it has to return on its trail, and recover, if it can, its line of force' (Adams, 1995, pp. 369–70). Still, it is exactly the variety, the deviance of the rigid main lines that Adams repeatedly highlights both in the text of *The Education* and in his account of his own genealogy. The discourse of teleological heredity is repeatedly infected by the discourse of heresy. In the first chapter, Adams states that 'the atmosphere of education in which he lived was colonial, revolutionary ... , as though he were steeped ... in the odor of political crime. Resistance to something was the law of New England nature' (p. 12). Here, Adams foreshadows that strange chiastic formulation he later uses to express what he sees as a universal formula: 'Chaos was the law of nature; Order was the dream of man' (p. 427). In these phrases, lawlessness itself turns into a kind of law. And it comes as no surprise, bearing in mind the opposition of rigidity and fluidity that Adams sets up throughout the first chapters, that later accounts of outlawry should sometimes overlap with Adams's recourse to water imagery.

In Rome, where he receives 'accidental education' (p. 84) on his European tour, Adams discusses the example of the Italian patriot Garibaldi. He retrospectively describes himself as a 'young American who had no experience in double natures' (p. 95), in those ambiguities that a character such as Garibaldi presented to him, which 'seemed to teach the extreme complexity of extreme simplicity.' Adams's observations of Garibaldi's 'compound nature of patriot and pirate' (p. 95), are later taken up in his repeated self-characterization as 'conservative Christian anarchist' (p. 384; p. 446). In this earlier chapter, he comments on the fact that his family heritage had once provided two quite similar examples of patriot and adventurer, so that even in his 'unitary' tradition, multiplicity|complexity inheres: 'Minister Adams remembered how his grandfather had sailed from Mount Wollaston in midwinter, 1778, on the little frigate 'Boston', taking his eleven-year-old son John Quincy with him, for secretary, on a diplomacy of adventure that had hardly a parallel for success. He remembered how John Quincy, in 1809, had sailed for Russia, with himself, a baby of two years old, to cope with Napoleon and the Czar Alexander single-handed, almost as much of an adventurer as John Adams before him' (p. 111). No wonder, then, that Adams's 'highest ambition was to be pirated and advertised free of charge, since, in any case, his pay was nothing. Under the excitement of the chase, he was becoming a pirate himself, and liked it' (p. 271).

However, the most striking example of 'outlawry' is provided by Adams's grandmother Louisa, wife of 'The President,' John Quincy Adams. Born in London to an Englishwoman and an American merchant from Maryland, she is the personification of an alien element that somehow had 'intruded' into the New England line of descent of the Adams genealogy— 'the old Puritan nature rebelled against change', whereas to 'outsiders, immigrants, adventurers, it was easy' (p. 29) to rebel against 'old forms of education' (p. 30). Louisa was such an 'outsider, immigrant, adventurer'—not born a New England woman, which 'defect was serious' (p. 22). For Adams, this turbulent disturbance of an otherwise seemingly straight line of descent makes him a 'half exotic' (p. 24) in a double sense: 'As a child of Quincy he was not a true Bostonian, but even as a child of Quincy he inherited a quarter taint of Maryland blood' (p. 24), and it is safe to assume that this constituted the charm of Adams's beloved 'Quincy education'. Louisa's impact on his education is described by Adams as immense. As a child, he 'never dreamed that from her might come some of those self-doubts and self-questionings, those hesitations, those rebellions against law and discipline, which marked more than one of her descendants; but he might even then have felt some vague instinctive suspicion that he was to inherit from her the seeds of the primal sin, the fall from grace, the curse of Abel' (p. 23). However ambiguous this inheritance might have seemed to the child Henry Adams, in the adult's rhetoric of heredity, as he sets it up from the very first pages of his *The Education*, this inheritance is almost explicitly connected to his version of the Virgin Mary—it might in fact be read as a clue that his outsider position is effected by that 'quarter taint of Maryland blood'.

It becomes clear that the Virgin, Adams's prime example of 'unity', is not 'orderly' at all: the Virgin is not a symbol of perfection [indeed, she is anything but], though she has been repeatedly read as such. Unity and multiplicity, order and chaos, are not clearly separated entities. In fact, Adams sees Louisa as clearly connected to those same 'lawless impulses' that he had somehow inherited from her, 'The Madam' (p. 21). The heretical impact of the Virgin can be found in Adams's *Mont Saint Michel and Chartres*—here Adams reveals that 'the Virgin embarrassed the Trinity ... Mary concentrated in herself the whole rebellion of man against fate; the whole protest against divine law; the whole contempt for human law as its outcome; the whole unutterable fury of human nature beating itself against the walls of its prison house, and suddenly seized by a hope that in the Virgin man had found a door of escape. She was above law' (Adams, 1983, p. 596). In contrast to the cruel regiment of the law, Mary dwelled in grace and 'sympathy with people who suffered under law' (p. 597). As a result, 'Mary filled heaven with a sort of persons little to the taste of any respectable middle-class society' (ibid.), those immigrants, outsiders, and adventurers who were little to the taste of twentieth-century Boston bourgeois society either, but who had nevertheless somehow infected the Adams lineage—an infection that Adams himself considered quite benevolent: the 'fluid order' (J. 81) of the Virgin resolved the rigidity of the father's law and represented, in R. P. Blackmur's words, a 'flexibility various enough to receive and react to new impressions' (Blackmur, p. 17).

Adams's conception of the Virgin has an unmistakably Lucretian ring to it. In his famous chapter on 'The Virgin and the Dynamo', Adams quotes Lucretius's invocation of Venus— 'not one of Adams's many schools of education had ever drawn his attention to the opening lines of Lucretius, though they were perhaps the finest in all Latin literature, where the poet invoked Venus exactly as Dante invoked the Virgin: "Quae quoniam rerum naturam sola gubernas" (Adams, 1995, p. 365; 'Since you alone govern the nature of things'). Venus was not only, as Adams suggests, a model for Dante's invocation of the Virgin, but also Adams's own infatuation—in fact, just as he 'translat[ed] rays into faith' (p. 364) by drawing the analogy between the dynamo and the Virgin, Adams—and indeed the whole Christian tradition—translated the heathen goddess of love, Venus|Aphrodite, into the Christian virgin mother of Christ. For Adams, the Virgin [like Lucretius's Venus] is the very force that creates nature and human culture out of chaos with 'her creative touch' (Hamill, p. 11): 'She was Goddess because of her force; she was the animated dynamo; she was reproduction—the greatest and most mysterious of all energies' (Adams, 1995, p. 365). However, as Adams laments, 'in America neither Venus nor Virgin ever had value as force' (p. 364); in fact 'this energy was unknown to the American mind' (p. 365). In connection with Adams's discussion of unity and multiplicity, order and chaos [and their interrelation], the reference to Venus|the Virgin engenders chaos and multiplicity: forceful disorder is female and is related to sexuality as a scandal, an 'unmoral force' (p. 366). Ultimately, sexuality, reproduction, growth, the Many—in short: life—are posed against the logic of the One. No wonder, then, that Adams can spot only some vestiges of that intense force in art: 'He could think only of Walt Whitman; Bret Harte, as far as the magazines would let him venture; and one or two painters, for the flesh-tones. All the rest had used sex for sentiment, never for force' (p. 366).

Serres's reading of Lucretius provides an obvious reference for Adams's invocation of Venus. Serres has argued that Lucretius's poem 'De Rerum Natura' did indeed anticipate modern science, in particular modern physics and chaos theory. According to Serres, Lucretius's idea of the clinamen can be read as an infinitesimally small deviation that induces a slight turbulence in the eternal fall of the atoms. The impact of the clinamen anticipates the sensitive dependence on initial conditions that plays such an important role in chaos theory and complexity theory. As such, this turbulence 'interrupts the reign of the same, invents the new reason and the new law ... gives birth to nature as it really is' (Serres, 1982, p. 100). What this 'new law' of multiplicity replaces is the logic of unity, which is 'repetitive, and the train of thought that comes from it infinitely iterative, is but a science of death' (ibid.). It was such a 'science of death' that Adams saw in Darwin's theory of evolution, a theory that should have made sense of family trees, heredity, and genealogy and its vicissitudes, as Adams experienced them, on a macroscopic and universal level—but which, in Adams's view, ultimately failed.

When Darwin published his seminal study *On the Origin of Species* in 1859, it had a wide impact not only on the natural sciences, but on society as a whole. The church in particular was offended by a theory that attempted to explain creation by tracing man back not to God, but to a monkey. Above all, Darwin himself was a theologian turned scientist, a fact that made things worse since it branded Darwin as a heretic. However, even if the theory of evolution found wide acceptance, the rigid causal mechanics of his theory were too neat for Adams: 'Unbroken Evolution under uniform conditions pleased everyone—except curates and bishops—and it was the very best substitute for religion; a safe, conservative, practical, thoroughly Common-Law deity' (Adams, 1995, p. 217). The emphasis here is on the word uniform—for Adams, the very concept of something rigidly linear had something oppressive to it, and resulted in a 'science of death' that deserved such a label not just on a metaphorical level. He cynically adds: 'Such a working system for the universe suited a young man who had just helped to waste five or ten thousand million dollars and a million of lives, more or less, to enforce unity and uniformity on people who objected to it; the idea was only too seductive in its perfection' (ibid.). Although 'steady, uniform, unbroken evolution from lower to higher seemed easy' (p. 218), Adams was deeply dissatisfied with the idea of gradual evolution in Darwin's theory. Against this all-too-smooth theory of heredity, 'Adams hinted his heresies in vain' (p. 219), heresies that were in part influenced by the counter theories of the 'catastrophists' and by Louis Agassiz, a key influence on Adams's attitude towards Darwinism, who is reported to have stated that 'the possibilities of existence run so deeply into the extravagant that there is scarcely any conception too extraordinary for Nature to realize' (quoted in Heinrich, p. 42). Unable to detect evolution 'in life', 'all [Adams] could prove was change' (Adams, 1995, p. 222), and it was indeed the idea of 'change' that 'attracted his mind' (p. 223). He 'wished to be shown that changes in form caused evolutions in force' (p. 379), something that Darwinism had failed to prove to him. A quite similar 'science of death', what Serres calls the 'stable, unchanging, redundant ... recop [ying of] the same writing in the same atoms-letters' (Serres 1982, p. 100), Adams saw revealed in the principles of [Bostonian] bourgeois education. In line with his metaphor for education [the cut, or stamp, which implies an almost mechanical, assembly-line form of education], Adams repeatedly comments on what he calls 'education, but in the type' (Adams 1995, p. 39). In his chapter 'Harvard College', Adams observes that 'the school created a type, not a will', and as a result, 'its graduates could commonly be recognized by the stamp' (p. 57). Even in his childhood, his brothers and sisters were becoming 'modes or replicas of the same type, getting the same education' (p. 39). Against this background, Adams preferred to see|construct himself as different: whereas 'his brothers were the type; he was the variation' (p. 12).[6]

In his rhetoric of 'type' and 'variation', the discourses of heredity and education get intertwined in Adams's text again and again: as Adams himself states, 'his education was chiefly inheritance' (p. 30). The story of education gets mixed up with the story of evolution and longs for a story of mutation. And it is here, I argue, that later developments in Darwinism and genetics might have provided Adams with the powerful metaphor of mutation that is always lurking in the back of his text, but that never is clearly expressed. Later in his book, Adams acknowledges that 'any doctrine seemed orthodox ... A little more, and he would be driven back on the old independence of species' (p. 379) which at least accounted for 'variety'. In line with his recurrent emphasis on lawlessness and play, Adams presumably would have embraced the Mutations theory proposed by the Dutch biologist Hugo de Vries in the early twentieth century. De Vries, rediscovering the Mendelian laws of heredity, had pointed out 'the role of "sports" or mutations, sudden and drastic variants in individual organisms, in the process of adaptation' (Hofstadter 1944, p. 97). In pointing out the abrupt and often catastrophic character of evolution, de Vries introduced a 'strong contrast to the slow, legato, and minuscule variations of Darwin's evolution' (ibid.). It was up to still later developments in biology and genetics to show that such a mutation is in fact not the accidental exception to the rule, but a coextensive part of it. The reason both de Vries and Adams have a problem with accepting natural selection is that they regard it as ultimately conservative, eliminating only negative mutations and lacking the productive force needed to create entirely new organisms. De Vries came up with a concept that integrated the occurrence of sudden changes—leaps—in the traits of a cell that were not caused by common genetic recombination of traits and that led to new species, to aberrant varieties that he called 'mutations'. This observation changed the understanding of the workings of evolution by emphasizing spontaneous mutation as a creative principle and a source of discontinuity in evolutionary change. In opposition to the prevailing Darwinian idea that species slowly and gradually evolve into new ones, with natural selection steering evolution in the favorable direction of the survival of the fittest, evolution came to be seen as a two-step process of the chance occurrence of a mutation, followed by its persistence or elimination (selection). Even in its variant form, natural selection is still seen as the sole force and agent in evolution—everything in the natural world can ultimately be explained by mutations within the genome and the subsequent selection of the fittest adaptation by the environment, a gradual process that is completely reliant on external conditions.

Yet de Vries's findings, alongside with his rediscovery of Mendel's laws, prepared the ground for the development of genetics and molecular biology. In his account of the discoveries of molecular biology, *Chance and Necessity*, Jacques Monod emphasizes the role of chance in evolution. In his study, Monod comments on the fact that Darwinism has been awaiting a 'physical theory of heredity' (Monod, p. xi) to counter metaphysical explanations, in order to clarify man's position in and relationship with the universe [the title of this chapter is a mutation of Monod's phrase]. The theory of the genetic code provided exactly this: heredity depends on 'long messages written with a four-letter alphabet' (Ruelle, p. 6). In this, it does not differ much from the 'science of death' that Serres commented on, the endless reproduction of the same 'atoms-letters'. However, there is one important twist: 'When cells divide, these messages are copied, with a few errors made at random; these errors are called mutations' (ibid.).

According to Monod, the 'physical theory of heredity' is marked by a kind of heretical aberration from the law, by a few errors made at random. It is exactly the intrusion of chance into necessity [that is, the intrusion of a 'reading mistake' of the information that normally ensures the exact reduplication of the genetic material] that causes the diversity of the species: 'We call these events accidental; we say that they are random occurrences. And since they constitute the only possible source of modifications in the genetic text, itself the sole repository of the organism's hereditary structures, it necessarily follows that chance alone is at the source of innovation, of all creation in the biosphere. Pure chance, absolutely free but blind, at the very root of the stupendous edifice of evolution: this central concept of modern biology is no longer one among other possible or even conceivable hypotheses. It is today the sole conceivable hypothesis' (Monod, pp. 112–13). *Chance and Necessity* shares with Adams's *Education* not only an emphasis on the importance of chance and 'play' with regard to the concept of laws and rules, but also some key metaphors. Like Adams's outlaw and pirate, Monod's subject is 'a gypsy, [who] lives on the boundary of an alien world' (pp. 172–73), a world marked by the 'definitive abandonment of the 'old covenant'' (p. 171), facing the 'necessity of forging a new one' (ibid.). Thus, for Monod, it is absolute randomness, the 'side-paths' that introduce a degree of freedom from the rigid deterministic order of natural selection: 'The ancient covenant is in pieces; man knows at last that he is alone in the universe's unfeeling immensity, out of which he emerged only by chance. His destiny is nowhere spelled out, nor is his duty' (p. 180). Such a foregrounding of randomness only, against natural selection only, misses the complex interplay of chaos and order, multiplicity and unity. It still assumes a binary opposition between two extremes and does not focus on the in between, where chaos and order meet. It is here that I suggest a return to Venus.

For Serres, Venus is an important conceptual persona, figuring prominently in both *The Birth of Physics* and *Genesis*. She becomes the icon for a new kind of science—the 'physics of Venus' [Serres's name for complexity theory] (Serres, 2000, p. 110), the antidote to what he sees as the physics of

Mars, a science for a world without clinamen [and without newness], where 'the new is born of the old, the new is just the repetition of the old' (p. 109).[7] The science of Mars sees matter as passive and sees the connection between man and matter—between Adams's clothed manikin and the 'certain form of energy'—as irretrievably broken. In what almost sounds like a direct reply to Monod's 'ancient covenant ... in pieces', Serres states that 'many ... sciences are founded ... on the violation of the contract. Man is a stranger to the world, to the dawn, to the sky, to things ... His environment is a dangerous enemy to be fought and kept in servitude. Martial neuroses' (p. 131). However, Lucretius, following Epicurus, sees the world as an ever-changing, open system, in which order arises out of chaos, in which matter is self-organizing because of its complexity. Here 'man is in the world, in matter and of matter. He is not a stranger, but a friend, a familiar, a companion and an equal. He maintains an Aphroditean contract with things' (p. ibid.).

The ultimate reason why for Adams an 'American Virgin would never dare command; an American Venus would never dare exist' (Adams 1995, p. 365) lies in Serres's observation that 'groupings ... seem to enjoy a bit of the status of Being only when they are subsumed beneath a unity ... We want a principle, a system, an integration' (Serres 1995, p. 2)—exactly what Adams feels has been lost in America after the Civil War. Ultimately, 'the laws of Venus-nature are indecipherable to the children of Mars' (Serres 2000, p. 108). However, in order to accept multiplicity, and the intricate interplay of chaos and order, 'the physics of Venus [have to be] chosen over that of Mars,' a physics in which 'turbulence ... troubles the flow of the identical, just as Venus disturbs Mars' (p. 110). Simply because we want a unity, 'we always see Venus without the sea; or the sea without Venus' (Serres 1995, p. 18), whereas in fact Venus and the sea [unity and multiplicity] are intimately linked: 'Venus ... is not transcendent, like the other gods, she is immanent to this world, she is the being of relation' (Serres 2000, p. 123) —order is not transcendent to multiplicity, but coextensive with it. Thus, 'we turn away from the waves to admire the wave-born' (Genesis p. 2), when instead we should ask the important question 'how is Venus born from the sea ...? How are forms born from the formless' (p. 26)?

For Deleuze, Lucretius's 'hymn to Venus-nature' is a hymn to multiplicity, to 'Nature as the production of the diverse ... [to a] sum which does not totalize its own elements' (Deleuze 1990, p. 267). Nature—life —according to Venus 'is not attributive, but rather conjunctive ... Harlequin's cloak, made entirely of solid patches and empty spaces; she is made of plenitude and void, beings and nonbeings,' and not a totalizing 'Being, the One and the Whole' (p. 267). For Adams, to believe in a totalizing whole and to dismiss multiplicity were exactly the 'faults of the patchwork fitted on [the generation of the] fathers' (Adams 1995, p. 8)—the new garment of multiplicity should rather look like Harlequin's coat [a patchwork of ands] of which even the manikin itself [the former unified and transcendent ego] is a part. As Serres puts it, 'le moi est un corps mêlé ... Voilà que revient le manteau d'Arlequin, cousu d'adjectives, je veux dire de termes placés côte à côte.'[8] Order and chaos, side by side—and, not either|or: nature is 'a chaotic multiplicity of orderly or unitary multiplicities and chaotic multiplicities' (Serres 1995, p. 110). And the individual is part of that turbulence; it is an open, dynamic system as well. For Deleuze, the individual is not a fixed form but 'collections of sensations, each is such a collection, a packet, a bloc of variable sensations' (Deleuze and Parnet, pp. 39–40), or in Adams's words, 'a bundle of disconnected memories' (Adams 1995, p. 202). The ego is not so much a transcendent unity as it is 'a bicycle-rider, mechanically balancing himself by inhibiting all his inferior personalities'—the individual is regarded as 'complex groups, like telephonic centres and systems' (p. 411). The focus on the interplay of order and chaos [ultimately, of order born from chaos] has far-ranging consequences for the theory of evolution as well. If Adams dismisses doctrines of 'sudden conversions, due to mere vital force acting on its own lines quite beyond mechanical explanation' (p. 379), it is because he cannot accept suddenness—mere randomness and chance—as a satisfying explanation for evolution. Such a doctrine, as Deleuze points out in a discussion of evolutionism and biology, would 'conceive of existence as a brute eruption, a pure act or leap which always occurs behind our backs and is subject to a law of all or nothing' (Deleuze 1994, p. 211). The creativity and productivity of evolution cannot be reduced to the production of identical members of the species, with the occasional random mutation to account for variety—evolution as production cannot be reduced to a negativity, to a simple response to external selection, but must follow a different dynamics. As Deleuze says, it cannot 'proceed by elimination or limitation, but must create its own lines of actualization in positive acts' (Deleuze 1991, p. 97). Darwin, Deleuze acknowledges, inaugurated 'the thought of individual difference. The leitmotiv of *The Origin of Species* is: we do not know what individual difference is capable of!' (Deleuze 1994, p. 248). But natural selection puts a halt to this experimentation and 'fixes' certain differences. In contrast to the Darwinist doctrine of differences that are ultimately created externally only, by the pressure of natural selection, Deleuze posits virtualities, 'internal differences'—that is, he argues that function is the 'driving force' of evolution, so that mutations are not accidents that befall evolution but are the result of a multiplicity in matter itself from which order is created by self-differentiation. Every species, even every individual, is a fixation and arresting of that movement of multiplicity, but regarded as an a priori unity—just like the figure|body of Venus-without-sea. The question 'What is the formula for this 'evolution'?' (p. 255) becomes important. Deleuze's answer is that, for a complex system, 'the more the difference on which the system depends is interiorized in the phenomenon ... the less it depends on external conditions which are supposed to ensure the reproduction of the 'same' differences' (p. 256).

Here Deleuze comes close to a conception that complexity theory has brought to modern biology. As the biologist Brian Goodwin has stated, 'we could, if we wished, simply replace the term natural selection by dynamic stabilization, the emergence of the stable states in a dynamic system' (Goodwin, p. 51). The theoretical biologist Stuart Kauffman goes even further in claiming that order in evolution is not the result of natural selection, as orthodox Darwinism would have it, nor is evolution due to mere accident—order is achieved by the self-organizing dynamics of matter's internal multiplicity of differences. The emergent properties of self-organization are 'so profoundly immanent in complex regulatory networks that selection cannot avoid that order' (Kauffman 1993, p. xvii)—the molecular variants produced by evolution provide 'order for free' (Kauffman 1995a, p. 71), order emerges immanently. Kauffman aims at a theory of evolution that 'incorporates self-organization into the weave of evolutionary theory' (Kauffman 1993, p. vii). For him, natural selection cannot be the only source of order in organisms, but order is also too prevalent to be a result of chance only, as Monod would have it. Thus, Kauffman examined Monod's 'chance' for underlying, 'orderly' behavior—and found it. For an organism to work, Kauffman claims, 'there'd have to be an extraordinary amount of selection to get things to behave with reliability and stability. It's not clear that natural selection could ever have gotten started without some preexisting order. You have to have a certain amount of order to select for improved variants' (Kauffman 1995b, 336). Selection builds on the emergent properties generated by self-organization and stabilizes them. For Kauffman, 'selection achieves and maintains complex systems poised on the boundary, or edge, between order and chaos. These systems are best able to coordinate complex tasks and evolve in a complex environment' (Kauffman 1993, p. xv). The self-organizing dynamics intrinsic to evolution follow a different logic than that of natural selection, but not completely unrelated to it. As a consequence, for Serres, the individual who emerges out of this Venusian physics arises, wave-born, out of a turbulent nature that 'is a multiplicity of local unities and of pure multiplicities', a Harlequin's coat that is coextensive with the Harlequin-manikin of the individual body—'my body, my corporeal-order, my corporeal-disorder, life and death, perhaps it is after all, too, only a temporary turbulence, linking up smaller turbulences, in a unitary, though ramshackle, fashion' (Serres 1995, p. 110). Ultimately, then, compared to Monod's notion of man as a 'gypsy … on the boundary of an alien world', because of the fact that evolution is as dependent on chance as on an underlying order, a turbulent order that in fact is born from chaos, Kauffman can see man 'at home in the universe' (Kauffman 1995a, p. 189). Adams himself seems to anticipate [or wish for] such an 'Aphroditean contract' based on the turbulence in both nature and man. In the final paragraph of *The Education of Henry Adams*—a paragraph that has puzzled critics because it comes unexpectedly and because its conciliatory character stands in marked contrast to the rest of the text [and to the times that followed], a paragraph that almost is an emergence of newness from within the text—Adams hopes that 'perhaps some day—say 1938, their centenary—they [Adams, John Hay, and Clarence King] might be allowed to return together for a holiday, to see the mistakes of their own lives made clear in the light of the mistakes of their successors; and perhaps then, for the first time since man began his education among the carnivores, they would find a world that sensitive and timid natures could regard without a shudder' (Adams 1995, pp. 476–77). As already noted, Adams's rhetoric of 'type' and 'variation' also has to be read with regard to the Body|Politic. In the type's proliferation of 'the same', such a Body|Politic resembles what Deleuze|Guattari call the 'cancerous BwO' (Deleuze|Guattari 1993, p. 163) with its 'totalitarian and fascist' (p. 165) nature. According to John Protevi, the cancerous BwO is a 'runaway self-duplication of stratification. [It] breaks down the stratum on which it lodges by endlessly repeating the selection of homogenized individuals in a runaway process of 'conformity.' Social cloning. Assembly-line personalities' (Protevi, pp. 171–72). Adams voices a similar concern when he envisions a pessimistic future of a society 'reserved for machine-made, collectivist' (Adams 1995, p. 423) individuals—a cancerous B[ody|Politic]wO. Just like Deleuze|Guattari's Kafka, Adams sensed the 'diabolical powers that are knocking at the door' (Deleuze|Guattari 1986, p. 41), be it the 'American technocratic apparatus or the Russian bureaucracy or the machinery of fascism' (p. 12). With regard to the theory of evolution, in which the outcome is never predictable, these 'diabolical powers' are not a chance mutation, an accident that befalls an otherwise smooth evolution process, but virtual vectors already at work in the Body|Politic that are actualized only later. The result of such a development, for Adams, is ultimately entropic,[9] since 'machine-like types' 'brought up together under like conditions have nothing to give each other' (Adams 1995, p. 58).[10] The maximum state of entropy in a closed system results in a complete lack of exchange energy, and as a consequence in a lack of care, sympathy, and grace—exactly those virtues the Virgin|Venus [and thus complexity and multiplicity] stand for, and what Adams connects with an 'ideal democracy' as a tendency to counter this process of degradation, a strategy that ultimately points to a 'becoming-democratic that is not the same as what States of law are' (Deleuze|Guattari 1994, p. 113).

Kauffman has pointed at the possibilities of complexity theory for 'a deep new understanding of the logic of democracy' (Kauffman 1995a, p. 28), a democracy as a politics of self-organization, evolving as a response to problems and conflict. Democracy is regarded as an inherently 'experimental' politics, played out in the space in between conflicting orientations and opinions of individuals and|or groups—a rhizomatic multiplicity rather than a controlling unity. For Adams, 'there are moments in politics when great results can be reached only by small men,—a maxim which, however paradoxical, may easily be verified. Especially in a democracy, the people are apt to become impatient of rule, and will at times obstinately refuse to move at the call of a leader, when, if left to themselves, they will blunder through all obstacles, blindly enough, it is true, but effectually' (Adams 1879, p. 432). Thus, ultimately, only the force of a becoming-minor can effectuate changes in the Body|Politic. Although Adams simultaneously expresses the convictions of a believer in American democracy and points towards its limitations, for him, the democratic Body|Politic ultimately moves in the direction not of entropic degradation, but towards complexity—the rising action of Adams's *History* had focused on the emergence of American democracy in a highly affirmative tone. Adams here is in accord with Spencer, who claims that a Body|Politic changes from a simple structure to a 'continually-increasing complexity of structure' (Spencer, p. 201). And although Spencer's social Darwinism [his philosophy of social evolution in fact predated Darwin's biological evolution] is ultimately responsible for the laissez-faire capitalism that so troubled Adams's faith in real, existing American democracy, the question of authority and control in the Body|Politic is also at the heart of Adams's musings. Spencer's use of the Body|Politic concept differs markedly from its employment by Plato and Hobbes, for example, in that it focuses on coordination versus control; diffused sources of order versus one source of order; and a bottom–up versus a top–down organization. The fundamental problem with the traditional metaphor of the Body|Politic, for Spencer, was that Plato and Hobbes not only likened the Body|Politic 'simply to the organization of a living body in general, but to the organization of the human body in particular' (p. 200),[11] and that it was 'explained on the hypothesis of manufacture, rather than that of growth' (p. 195).[12] Spencer's critics were quick to point out an apparent contradiction in the analogy of the freely growing social organism: the analogy itself implied a central control. The political scientist Ernest Barker sums up the dilemma: 'An organism is a unity with a nerve-centre; that nerve centre regulates the whole body; and of a sudden the "growing" organism which should not be regulated becomes a bureaucratic or socialistic state under control of the central brain. Starting with a conception of organic growth intended to justify individualism, Spencer ends with a conception of organic unity which tends to justify socialism' (Barker 96). Yet Spencer, with the help of modern science, deals with the problem of order and authority as related not to 'manufactured' political individualism, but to biological individuality. Ultimately, he asks if an individual's 'order' [or 'unity'] results from the subordination of its constitutive 'elements' [cells, or individuals respectively] to a controlling agency, or rather from the interaction of those very elements. Critics who claim there is a contradiction in Spencer's work argue from the perspective of an organism regulated by a nervous center that controls the rest of the body. But Spencer sees the sources of 'nervous authority' as diffused as he believed the sources of political authority ought to be: 'In some of the lowest animals, characterized by the absence of a nervous system, such sensitiveness as exists is possessed by all parts' (p. 205).[13] Thus, for Spencer, the Body|Politic has not evolved by divine providence or by the control of 'central' lawmakers, and its organizations are 'neither supernatural, nor are they determined by the wills of individual men' (p. 196). On the contrary, they are the result of growth, of 'general natural causes'. The Body|Politic, a 'complex body of mutually dependent' 'elements', has 'spontaneously evolved' (ibid.) because of the increasing complexity of its structure.[14]

The increase of complexity, the tendency of a democratic evolution —of democracy as evolution—is also the topic of Adams's anonymously published novel *Democracy*.[15] In this novel, Nathan Gore, a Massachusetts historian, is asked if he thinks 'democracy the best government' (Adams 2006, p. 37), and he replies: 'I believe in democracy. I accept it. I will faithfully serve and defend it. I believe in it because it appears to me the inevitable consequence of what has gone before it. Democracy asserts the fact that the masses are now raised to a higher intelligence than formerly. All our civilisation aims at this mark. We want to do what we can to help it. I myself want to see the result. I grant it is an experiment, but it is the only direction society can take that is worth its taking; the only conception of its duty large enough to satisfy its instincts; the only result that is worth an effort or a risk. Every other possible step is backward, and I do not care to repeat the past. I am glad to see society grapple with issues in which no one can afford to be neutral' (p. 36). Kauffman voices a similar hope when he says that 'democracy may be far and away the best process to solve the complex problems of a complex evolving society' (Kauffman 1995a, p. 28).[16] If democracy is understood as a complex interplay of chaos and order, as a Body|Politic emerging from self-organizing properties, it makes sense that Adams, in his novel, refers to the 'slowly eddying dance of democracy' (Adams 2006, p. 43)—in his histories, he sees democracy as a dance of eddies in a 'democratic ocean' (Adams, 1986a, p. 1334), as small islands of stability emerging out of turbulence.

The rise of modern mass democracy went hand in hand with the fall of politics as statecraft in the old sense. Whereas the politics of republican statecraft had been related to virtuous leaders, the new American political character was one of a virtual democracy in the Deleuzian sense of the word, its potentiality related to its underlying multiplicity of forces [individual, economical, institutional, etc.]: 'Modern politics is, at bottom, a struggle not of men but of forces. The men become every year more and more creatures of force, massed about central power-houses. The conflict is no longer between the men, but between the motors that drive the men, and the men tend to succumb to their own motive forces' (Adams 2006, 400).[17] However, for Adams, the question arises if there is an alternative to either the 'Old Unity' [the republic of the founding fathers, irreversibly lost] or the 'New Multiplicity' [modern democracy as ultimately disorganized and corrupt]. Kauffman comments on a similar problem in scientific terms when he claims that 'eighteenth-century science, following the Newtonian revolution, has been characterized as developing the sciences of organized simplicity, nineteenth-century science, via statistical mechanics, as focusing on disorganized complexity, and twentieth- and twenty-first-century science as confronting organized complexity. Nowhere is this confrontation so stark as in biology' (Kauffman 1993, p. 173). This describes Adams's dilemma perfectly and Adams was looking for solutions in evolution theory, solutions that Darwinism could not offer because it was still embedded in that dichotomy between 'organized simplicity' and 'disorganized complexity', which Adams could make sense of only as a movement that was blind, but effective.

Adams was hoping for an alternative to the strategy of 'running order through chaos, direction through space, discipline through freedom, unity through multiplicity' (Adams 1995, p. 17); to external control, 'the despotism of artificial order which nature abhorred' (p. 433); and to the fear of multiplicity as mere disorder. Adams senses that the 'conservative Christian anarchist [Adams himself] could have no associate, no object, no faith except the nature of nature itself' (p. 386)—and this "larger synthesis" (ibid.) was validated not by Hegel, but by the findings of an emerging new science. It can be argued that Adams's work at times comes close to accepting a downward determinism: he is concerned with entropy to almost hysterical dimensions, as the chapter from *The Education*, 'A Dynamic Theory of History', and essays such as 'The Tendency of History' [1894], 'The Rule of Phase Applied to History' [1909] and 'A Letter to American Teachers of History' [1910] reveal. These essays are Adams's attempt to come up with a theory of history in congruence with the science of his times. If unity is lost in the new 'multiverse,' the only option for Adams seems to have been the acceptance of 'disorganized complexity'.[18] However, he also senses that taming the multiplicity, which has been the 'task of education, as it is the moral of religion, philosophy, science, art, politics, and economy' (Adams 1995, p. 17), cuts off the connection to life and production, to that 'certain form of energy'. Thus, against the 'despotism of artificial order' and the 'science of death', of entropy's repetition of sameness and identity, Adams posits both a 'prudent hopefulness' (Levenson p. 93) for democracy, as voiced in the comments of Mrs. Madeleine Lee and Nathan Gore in *Democracy*, and his hope for 'another Newton' (Adams 1920, p. 263) to find a way out of entropic determinism, to open the way for 'organized complexity'.

According to Deleuze, the concept of entropy, in its tendency to reduce differences and to unitize differences, expresses 'a strange alliance at the end of the nineteenth century between science, good sense and philosophy. Thermodynamics was the powerful furnace of that alloy' (Deleuze 1994, p. 223). The concept of entropy was based on a set of commonsensical definitions, such as 'the given as diverse; reason as a process of identification and equalisation tending towards identity; the absurd or irrational as resistance of the diverse to that identificatory reason' (pp. 223–24). Against this repetition of sameness, Deleuze posits a repetition of difference, which amounts to exactly the notion of 'organized multiplicity' that Adams was too early in history to be able to appeal to:

> When we seek to define energy in general, either we take account of the extensive and qualified factors of extensity—in which case we are reduced to saying 'there is something which remains constant,' thereby formulating the great but flat tautology of the Identical—or, on the contrary, we consider pure intensity insofar as it is implicated in that deep region where no quality is developed, or any extensity deployed. In this case, we define energy in terms of the difference buried in this pure intensity and it is the formula of 'difference of intensity' which bears the tautology, but this time the beautiful and profound tautology of the Different. Energy in general will not then be confused with a uniform energy at rest, which would render any transformation impossible. Only a particular form of empirical energy, qualified in extensity, can be at rest; one in which the difference in intensity is already cancelled because it is drawn outside itself and distributed among the elements of the system (p. 240–41).

Like orthodox Darwinism, the concept of thermodynamic entropy allowed nature to become an object of prediction—the second law of thermodynamics 'provides a rule according to which ... different objects tend to equalise themselves and the different Selves tend to become uniform' (p. 226). However, it is inadequate as a concept both because it deals only with closed systems in equilibrium and because it [mis]takes the conditions of such a system for the intensity itself. Thus, the 'organized multiplicity' that counters thermodynamics is in fact a 'self-organized multiplicity', the production of intensity being a result of|immanent to [extensive] entropic processes, including the generation of 'structural stability and morphogenesis' [René Thom's phrase] that governs the creation of organisms. Deleuze envisions a physics based on becoming and heterogeneity rather than being [stable identity] and homogeneity. Adams, in his parallelization of biology and politics, biological and democratic evolution, sensed that the 'movement from unity into multiplicity ... would require a new social mind' (Adams 1995, p. 470) as well. He sensed the politics needed for a 'democratic ocean' (Adams 1986a, p. 1334), but in his account of things, 'man could go no further. The atom might move, but the general equilibrium could not change' (pp. 1334–335). He could not believe that states far from equilibrium, on the edge of chaos, could not make what Serres calls the shift from turba to turbo, from turbulence to the vortex— 'the first is simply disorder and the second is a particular form of movement' (Serres 2000, p. 28), but, since order may emerge out of chaos, the two are one.[19] For Serres, the cone, or the top, a children's toy, is a perfect illustration for this vertical movement that is both stable and unstable, order and disorder— 'the simplicity of complexity, first and foremost, an additive machine; a synthesis of contradictions' (p. 29). Maybe Adams envisioned something similar when he further described the 'new social mind' by claiming that 'evidently the new American would need to think in contradictions' (Adams 1995, p. 470), in terms of difference and heterogeneity rather than unity and homogeneity.

If 'the Different' was more active than 'the Identical', if multiplicity was 'more fundamental' than unity, then the represented multitude was more important than the representers, the social more important than the 'political proper'.[20] At the beginning of *Democracy*, the central character with political aspirations, Mrs. Madeleine Lee, a wealthy young widow, wants 'to see with her own eyes the action of primary force ... She was bent upon getting to the heart of the great American mystery of democracy and government' (Adams 2006, pp. 4–5). This 'primary force', this 'motive power' (p. 5), is seen as the consequence of a 'clash of interests, the interests of forty millions of people and a whole continent, centering at Washington; guided, restrained, controlled, or unrestrained and uncontrollable, by men of ordinary mould; the tremendous forces of government, and the machinery of society, at work' (ibid.). However, Adams was not so sure that this 'machinery' was still working. In *The Education*, he states that 'the political dilemma was as clear in 1870 as it was likely to be in 1970. The system of 1789 had broken down, and with it the eighteenth-century fabric of a priori, or moral, principles ... Nine-tenths of men's political energies must ... be wasted on expedients to piece out,—to patch,—or, in vulgar language, to tinker,—the political machine as often as it broke down. Such a system, or want of system, might last centuries, if tempered by an occasional revolution or civil war; but as a machine, it was, or soon would be, the poorest in the world,—the clumsiest,—the most inefficient' (Adams 1995, pp. 268–69). According to Adams, 'the sum of political life was, or should have been, the attainment of a working political system. Society needed to reach it. If moral standards broke down, and machinery stopped working, new morals and machinery of some sort had to be invented' (ibid.). However, to accept corruption—the very absence of morals—as the 'new morals' that made the 'new machinery' work, was out of the question. In an article written on the occasion of the 1869 gold scandal and Black Friday, Adams pointed out the dangers of emerging capitalism for a democratic system:

For the first time since the creation of these enormous corporate bodies, one of them has shown its power for mischief, and has proved itself able to override and trample on law, custom, decency, and every restraint known to society, without scruple, and as yet without check. The belief is common in America that the day is at hand when corporations far greater than the Erie—swaying power such as has never in the world's history been trusted in the hands of private citizens, controlled by single men like Vanderbilt, or by combinations of men like Fisk, Gould, and Lane, after having created a system of quiet but irresistible corruption—will ultimately succeed in directing government itself. Under the American form of society no authority exists capable of effective resistance. The national government, in order to deal with the corporations, must assume powers refused to it by its fundamental law,—and even then is exposed to the chance of forming an absolute central government which sooner or later is likely to fall into the hands it is struggling to escape, and destroy the limits of its power only in order to make corruption omnipotent. Nor is this danger confined to America alone. The corporation is in its nature a threat against the popular institutions spreading so rapidly over the whole world. Wherever a popular and limited government exists this difficulty will be found in its path; and unless some satisfactory solution of the problem can be reached, popular institutions may yet find their existence endangered (Adams, 1891, pp. 365–66).[21]

Maybe, ultimately, the 'new morals' that had to be invented were not to be found in the government, but rather in 'the governed'. In a move similar to Spinoza's distinction between potentia [force, strength and creative activity] and potestas [command and authority], Adams's narratorial voice slightly criticizes Mrs. Lee precisely for confusing 'the force of the engine ... with that of the engineer, the power of the men who wielded it' (Adams 2006, p. 5)—a criticism that might also be a self-criticism. By concentrating on the ruling elite, the 'representers' [e.g., Jefferson and Madison in Adams's histories], Adams had concentrated on the fittest, the 'great men' that were most able to represent 'the people'. However, when the representers cut their connection with the multitude on which their 'survival' depends, the multitude that already provides autopoietic 'order for free', and when they themselves mistake the potentia of the engine for the potestas of the engineer, this leads to self-interest and corruption, exactly those traits in modern democracy that Adams so vehemently despises. As he puts it quite cynically in his novel, 'democracy, rightly understood, is the government of the people, by the people, for the benefit of Senators' (p. 14)—in particular for the benefit of Senator Ratcliffe, the corrupt politician in the novel. Mrs. Lee sees that a return to that potentia is necessary, that her desire for power [potestas] and control is ultimately at war with democracy itself. Like Adams, she has hopes that the potentia of the multiplicity|multitude provides 'order for free' from which a more stable order might arise: 'Underneath the scum floating on the surface of politics, Madeleine felt that there was a sort of healthy ocean current of honest purpose, which swept the scum before it, and kept the mass pure' (p. 96). At the end of *Democracy*, she turns her back to Washington: 'She had got to the bottom of this business of democratic government, and found out that it was nothing more than government of any other kind. She might have known it by her own common sense, but now that experience had proved it, she was glad to quit the masquerade' (p. 166). Instead she turns 'to the true democracy of life, her paupers and her prisons, her schools and her hospitals' (ibid.), to the self-organizing turbulence out of which order—albeit a different order than that of representation, control, and unity, an order 'far from equilibrium'—arises.

Writing from the other end of the twentieth century, Gregoire Nicolis and Ilya Prigogine state in *Exploring Complexity* that 'today, wherever we look, we find evolution, diversification, and instabilities. We have long known that we live in a pluralistic world in which we find deterministic as well as stochastic phenomena, reversible as well as irreversible ... the complex processes we discover in the evolution of life or in the history of human societies' (Nicolis and Prigogine, pp. 2–3)—these observations almost sound like a direct reply to Adams's quest. Ultimately, for Adams, the movement from unity to multiplicity would not only require a 'new social mind' but a new Body|Politic as well: a transition from the founders' republic, with a central authority and checks and balances that held 'mob rule' under constraint, to a democracy seen as a government of the people and by the people, a Body|Politic based on self-organization, a semi stable order that arises from and does not cut off its relation to chaos, to that 'certain form of energy'. The Body|Politic is the very economy of this force, and neither its control nor its representation.

Notes

[1] Among those studies of political theorists|historians that do read Adams for his 'politics' are Hanson and Merriman, Shklar, and Young, which show that Adams may have been disappointed by the corrupt democracy of the late twentieth century, but he was a fervent believer in democratic ideals as such. After all, Adams's

political views, in his self-assessment, 'tend to democracy and radicalism' (Adams, 1982–1988, 2, p. 301).

2   On Adams and science, see also Jordy, and Wasser.

3   Together with 'The Tendency of History' and 'The Rule of Phase Applied to History', this essay was posthumously published by Adams's brother Brooks Adams under the misleading title The Degradation of the Democratic Dogma.

4   In *Chaos Bound*, N. Katherine Hayles has provided an insightful reading of *The Education of Henry Adams* in the light of chaos and complexity theory. However, she is much more interested in the discursive complexity of Adams's text than in his development of concepts of complexity—in fact, for Hayles, chaos theory seems to be another name for post structuralism.

5   Within *The Education*, the same structure is repeated in the much-anthologized Chapter 25, 'The Dynamo and the Virgin'.

6   Adams also gives a political ring to the notion of variation|variety, which connects it with American democracy: 'The American in his political character, was a new variety of man' (Adams, 1986a, p. 1332).

7   Serres writes: 'The [old] law is the plague. Reason is the fall. The reiterated cause is death. Repetition is redundancy. And identity is death' (Serres, 2000, p. 109).

8   'The ego is a composite body ... It resembles the Harlequin's coat, adjectives sewn together, that is, terms placed side by side' (Serres, 1987, p. 221, my translation).

9   See Freese.

10   Adams also wrote: "The inertia of several hundred million people, all formed in a similar social mould, was as likely to stifle energy as to stimulate evolution' (Adams, 1986a, p. 1345).

11   According to Spencer, 'there is no warrant whatever for assuming this' (Spencer, p. 200).

12   This is a position, I argue, that is repeated today in cultural|linguistic constructivism.

13   Deleuze|Guattari write: 'Not every organism has a brain, and not all life is organic, but everywhere there are forces that constitute microbrains, or an inorganic life of things' (Deleuze and Guattari, 1994, p. 213).

14   That the decrease of state control, as envisaged by Spencer, led to the social Darwinism of laissez-faire capitalism nicely parallels the position of capitalism in Deleuze|Guattari's thought. While capitalism on the one hand has liberating effects, since it operates by a rigorous deterritorialization and decoding of free flows, on the other hand it rigorously reterritorializes and 'overcodes' these flows again into commodities and monetary equivalences, so that real freedom is impossible.

15   This novel was first published anonymously in 1880; only after 1925 was Adams listed as the author.

16   And complexity theory might be an effective way to deal with the dilemma of democracy.

17   One of the main physical forces of history, according to Adams, is inertia, the 'property of matter, by which matter tends, when at rest, to remain so, and, when in motion, to move on a straight line' (Adams, 1995, p. 417). As Adams states in a 1883 letter to Samuel Tilden, 'my own conclusion is that history is simply social development along the lines of weakest resistance, and that in most cases the line

of weakest resistance is found as unconsciously by society as by water' (Adams, 1982–1988, 2, p. 491). Such inertia|stifling order leads to linearity and ultimately entropy; newness|mutations emerge out of the [nonlinear] 'side-paths'.

18 That is also in line with Adams's 'residual Puritanism'—the second law of thermodynamics can be read as the scientific variant of the Puritan jeremiad.

19 For Serres, the shift from turba to turbo has a political connotation, since it also denotes the shift from a disordered 'multitude, a large population, confusion and tumult' (Serres, 2000, p. 28) to a self-organized [vertical] social movement.

20 The importance of the multitude is also revealed in Adams's momentous flirtations with socialism and Marxism: 'Not that I love Socialism any better than I do Capitalism, or any other Ism, but I know only of one law of political or historical morality, and that is that the form of Society which survives is always in the Right; and therefore a statesman is obliged to follow it, unless he leads ... One need not love Socialism in order to point out the logical necessity for Society to march that way; and the wisdom of doing it intelligently if it is to do it at all' (Adams, 1982–1988, 4, pp. 586–87). He also wrote: 'By rights, he should have been also a Marxist but some narrow trait of the New England nature seemed to blight socialism, and he tried in vain to make himself a convert. He did the next best thing; he became a Comteist, within the limits of evolution' (Adams, 1995, p. 217).

21 It was the publication of this article in the Westminster Review in England that made Adams feel like 'a pirate' (Adams, 1995, p. 271).

Bibliography

Adams, H. (1879), *The Life of Albert Gallatin*. Philadelphia: J. B. Lippincott.

—(1891), 'The New York gold conspiracy'. 1870. *Historical Essays*, pp. 318–66. New York: Charles Scribner's Sons.

— (1920), *The Degradation of the Democratic Dogma*. New York: Macmillan.

—(1947), 'Letter to Charles William Eliot, Boston, March 2, 1877. *Henry Adams and His Friends*. Edited by H. D. Cater, pp. 80–81. Boston: Houghton Mifflin.

—(1982–1988), *The Letters of Henry Adams*. Edited by J. C. Levenson, E. Samuels, C. Vandersee, and V. Hopkins Winner. Five vols. Cambridge, MA: Harvard University Press.

—(1983), *Mont Saint Michel and Chartres*. 1904. Novels – Mont Saint Michel – The Education, pp. 337–714. New York: Literary Classics.

—(1986a), *History of the United States during the Administrations of James Madison*. Edited by E. N. Harbert. New York: Library of America.

—(1986b), *History of the United States during the Administrations of Thomas Jefferson*. Edited by E. N. Harbert. New York: Library of America.

—(1995), *The Education of Henry Adams*. Edited. with an introduction by J. Gooder. London: Penguin.

—(2006), *Democracy: An American Novel*. 1880. Dodo.

Barker, E. (1963), *Political Thought in England, 1848 to 1914*. Oxford: Oxford University Press.

Barthes, R. (1972), 'What is criticism?', *Critical Essays*. Translated by R. Howard, pp. 255–60. Evanston, IL: Northwestern University Press.

Blackmur, R. P. (1952), 'The harmony of true liberalism: Henry Adams's Mont-Saint-Michel and Chartres'. *Sewanee Review* 60, no. 1 (January–March 1952): pp. 1–27.

Deleuze, G. (1990), *The Logic of Sense*. Translated by M. Lester, with C. Stivale. Edited by C. V. Boundas. New York: Columbia University Press.

—(1991), *Bergsonism*. Translated by H. Tomlinson and B. Habberjam. New York: Zone.

—(1994), *Difference and Repetition*. Translated by P. Patton. New York: Columbia University Press.

Deleuze, G. and Guattari, F. (1986), *Kafka: Toward a Minor Literature*. Translated by D. Polan. Minneapolis: University of Minnesota Press.

—(1993), *A Thousand Plateaus: Capitalism and Schizophrenia*. Translated by B. Massumi. Minneapolis: University of Minnesota Press.

—(1994), *What Is Philosophy?* Translated by H. Tomlinson and G. Burchell. New York: Columbia University Press.

Deleuze, G. and Parnet, C. (1987), *Dialogues*. New York: Columbia University Press.

Freese, P. (1997), 'Henry Adams: The history of degradation and the degradation of history', *From Apocalypse to Entropy and Beyond: The Second Law of Thermodynamics and Post-War American Fiction*, pp. 164–71. Essen, Germany: Blaue Eule.

Goodwin, B. (1994), *How the Leopard Changed Its Spots: The Evolution of Complexity*. London: Phoenix.

Hamill, P. J. (1973), 'The future as virgin: a latter-day look at the dynamo and the virgin of Henry Adams'. *Modern Language Studies* 3, no. 1, pp. 8–12.

Hanson, R. L. and Merriman, W. R. (1990), 'Henry Adams and the decline of the republican tradition'. *American Transcendental Quarterly* 4, no. 3 (September 1990): pp. 161–83.

Hayles, N. K. (1990), *Chaos Bound: Orderly Disorder in Contemporary Literature and Science*. Ithaca, NY: Cornell University Press.

Heinrich, B. (1980), 'Artful dinners'. *Natural History* 89, no. 5, pp. 42–51.

Hofstadter, R. (1944), *Social Darwinism in American Thought, 1860–1915*. Philadelphia: University of Pennsylvania Press.

— (1968), *The Progressive Historians: Turner, Beard, Parrington*. New York: Knopf.

Jordy, W. H. (1953), *Henry Adams: Scientific Historian*. London: Oxford University Press.

Kauffman, S. (1993), *The Origins of Order: Self-Organization and Selection in Evolution*. New York: Oxford University Press.

—(1995a), *At Home in the Universe: The Search for the Laws of Self-Organization and Complexity*. New York: Oxford University Press.

—(1995b), 'Order for free', *The Third Culture: Beyond the Scientific Revolution*. Edited by *John Brockmann*, pp. 334–43. New York: Simon and Schuster.

Levenson, J. C. (1957), *The Mind and Art of Henry Adams*. Stanford, CA: Stanford University Press.

Lyon, M. (1970), *Symbol and Idea in Henry Adams*. Lincoln: University of Nebraska Press.

Monod, J. (1971), *Chance and Necessity: An Essay on the Natural Philosophy of Modern Biology*. Translated by A. Wainhouse. New York: Knopf.

Nicolis, G. and Prigogine, I. (1989), *Exploring Complexity: An Introduction*. New York: W. H. Freeman.

Protevi, J. (2000). 'A problem of pure matter: Fascist Nihilism in a thousand plateaus', *Nihilism Now! Monsters of Energy*. Edited by K. Ansell Pearson and D. Morgan. pp. 167–87. New York: St. Martin's.

Rowe, J. C. (1976), *Henry Adams and Henry James: The Emergence of a Modern Consciousness*. Ithaca, NY: Cornell University Press.

Ruelle, D. (1993), *Chance and Chaos*. Harmondsworth, UK: Penguin.

Serres, M. (1982), *Hermes: Literature, Science, Philosophy*. Edited by J. V. Harari and D. F. Bell. Baltimore: Johns Hopkins University Press.

—(1987), *Le Tiers-Instruit*. Paris: François Bourin.

—(1995), *Genesis*. Translated by G. James and J. Nielson. Ann Arbor: University of Michigan Press.

—(2000), *The Birth of Physics*. Translated by J. Hawkes. Manchester, UK: Clinamen.

Shklar, J. N. (1998), *Redeeming American Political Thought*. Edited by S. Hoffmann and D. F. Thompson. Chicago: Chicago University Press.

Spencer, H. (1969), *The Man versus the State: With Four Essays on Politics and Society*. Edited by D. Macrae. Harmondsworth, UK: Penguin.

Thom, R. (1975), *Structural Stability and Morphogenesis: An Outline of a General Theory of Models*. Reading, MA: Benjamin-Cummings.

Wasser, H. (1956), *The Scientific Thought of Henry Adams*. Thessaloniki, Greece: University of Thessaloniki Press.

Whitman, W. (1996), *Poetry and Prose*. Edited by J. Kaplan. New York: Library of America.

Young, J. P. (2001), *Henry Adams: The Historian as Political Theorist*. Lawrence: University Press of Kansas.

Chapter 11

Crystal History: 'You Pick Up the Pieces. You Connect the Dots'.

Hanjo Berressem

'Diversity is given, but difference is that by which the given is given, that by which the given is given as diverse' (Deleuze, 1994, p. 222).

Transcendental Empiricism

In dealing with the problematics of history, one needs to resist two comple-mentary temptations: to dissolve history in historiography and to dissolve historiography in history. The first is a transcendental gesture, the second an empirical one.

Even before one defines what exactly history and historiography are, to maintain that they should be kept as categorically separate registers implies that the question is one of attribution, in the sense that Spinoza saw thought (cogitatio) as the attribute of the mind and extension (extensio) as the attri-bute of the body. While these attributions are relatively uncontested, how-ever, it is less clear whether these two terms can in turn be attributed to each other? Can the mind be considered as an attribute of the body, and, simulta-neously, can the body be considered as an attribute of the mind? In historical terms: How to attribute history to historiography and historiography to his-tory? How to think a 'transcendental empiricism'? (Deleuze, 1994, p. 56).

If history is provisionally defined as 'the things that happen within a given field' and historiography as 'the narratives about the things that happen,' the works of Gilles Deleuze and Michel Serres are equally suffused with the historical and the historiographic. Both are deeply invested in the way things happen, and both provide specific historiographic narratives, from the vast historical panoramas of Gilles Deleuze and Felix Guattari's *Capital-ism and Schizophrenia* project to Michel Serres' *Rome: The Book of Foundations*. The close conceptual proximity of their respective theories of history, both of which rely in many ways on the logic of the clinamen in Lucretius'

De Rerum Natura[1], is based on the fact that they are equally developed from within the concept of multiplicity.

Despite their deep investment in the historical, however, neither Deleuze nor Serres have, with few exceptions, been taken up in historical studies.[2] One reason for this is that most historians would consider their interests to be extremely far removed from the practice of writing history. I believe, however, that it is possible to distil a 'historical attitude' from their work that can be useful not only for the theoretically-minded, but also for the more practical historian. To make a case for this thesis, I will turn to the work of the American historian Henry Adams, who has developed, from within the field of historical studies, a theory and a practice of writing history that resonate in many ways with the work of Deleuze and Serres.

The Multiverse

In 1900, a somewhat older man contemplates, in the Paris World Exhibition's 'Palais de l'Electricité', the biggest and most powerful dynamos of the new century.[3] Awestruck, Henry Adams feels that he is not only facing the electrification of the world, which would make for a new chapter in a book on the history of technology, but, more importantly, that he is facing the electrification of thought and of history, which makes for a new chapter in a book on the history of historiography.

For Adams, the confrontation is so traumatic that the disturbingly intensive hum of the dynamos will reverberate through everything he will write after the visit. From writing vast, panoramic histories he turns, with 'The Rule of Phase Applied to History' (1909) and 'A Letter to American Teachers of History' (1910),[4] to the conceptualization of a theory of history. During the same period, he writes two equally personal books: *Mont-Saint-Michel and Chartres* (1904), a study of the history of France from the twelfth to the fifteenth century, which is disguised as a traveller's guide, and his autobiography *The Education of Henry Adams* (1907), in a chapter of which, 'The Dynamo and the Virgin', (1900) he describes the confrontation with the dynamos. Although the latter two works were conceptualized as 'compendium stud[ies]' (Adams cited in: Levenson, 1957, p. 356), they find two diverging tendencies in Adams' work.[5]

While Adams feels confident that he can make sense of the culture of medieval France, which is, as he argues, held together by a metaphysical force that is embodied by the Virgin Mary, he is utterly unable to perform a 'triangulation' (Adams, 1961, p. 369) of the physical force unleashed by the dynamo. The only thing Adams 'does' understand in 1900 is that these forces are, although they are comparable to those that suffuse the cathedral of Chartres, at the same time, completely different. '[T]o Adams the dynamo became a symbol of infinity' (Adams, 1961, p. 380), Adams notes; a 'silent and infinite force. Among the thousand symbols of ultimate energy, the dynamo was not as human as some, but it was the most impressive' (ibid.). The framework, one would say today, has shifted from a religious to a technological sublime. Even though the cathedrals were themselves incredibly advanced technological structures, their technological sublimity was enveloped and cancelled out by a religious one. To make their techno-logical sublimity visible, it needed a general profanization of culture that was accompanied by a divinization of technology.

From his confrontation with the dynamo, Adams draws a number of con-clusions for the theory and practice of writing history. The first is that while the Cathedral of Chartres is a figure of unity, the Cathedral of Electricity is a figure of multiplicity. Chartres was built in a 'universe' that was held together by the power of the Virgin: 'Every day, as the work went on, the Virgin was present, directing the architects' (1961a, p. 108), Adams notes. In fact, the centripetal force of the strangely attractive Virgin did not only suffuse the cathedrals that were built in her name, it unified all of medieval culture. In contrast, the beginning of the twentieth century seems to Adams a centrifugal 'multiverse' (Adams, 1961, p. 461).

Adams' second conclusion is that the historian has 'entered a supersen-sual world', in the sense that the forces that define the twentieth century world are, like electricity, quite literally imperceptible to the historical observer: 'he could measure nothing except by chance collisions of move-ments imperceptible to his senses, perhaps even imperceptible to his instru-ments, but perceptible to each other, and so to some known ray at the end of the scale' (Adams, 1961, pp. 381–82). Although these new, equally pow-erful and enigmatic forces pose a 'shock to thought', Adams maintains that thought 'must merge in its supersensual multiverse, or succumb to it' (Adams, 1961, p. 461). It 'could gain nothing by flight or by fight' (ibid.).

If one cannot evade the 'new phase' (Adams, 1961, p. 342) into which the dynamos have catapulted history, the challenge is to find a way to attribute the new forces to the historical spirit. In Paris, facing the dynamos, Adams is quite literally overwhelmed. All he feels is the beginnings of a somewhat frightening, bewildering historical phase in which 'physics [are] stark mad in metaphysics' (Adams, 1961, p. 382). In most of his remaining work, how-ever, he will try to come to terms with this new phase. In his own words, he will set out on the ocean of multiplicity in order to discover a conceptual ground that will allow him to invent historical studies that can account for the multiverse. For Adams, this project implies that he needs to find a 'north-west passage' between the soft sciences, which the historian is familiar with, and the hard sciences, about which he feels completely ignorant. The full title of his autobiography, therefore, should be 'The Education of Henry Adams: A Study of Twentieth-Century Multiplicity', Adam notes, while that of '"Mont Saint Michel and Chartres" should be "A Study of Thirteenth-Century Unity"' (Adams, 1961, p. 435).

After his meeting with the dynamos, Adams feels a 'growing complexity, and multiplicity, and even contradiction, in life' (Adams, 1961, p. 397). This contradiction operates between a 'given' multiplicity and a habit of|in thought to reduce multiplicity to simplicity: 'Simplicity may not be evidence of truth, and unity is perhaps the most deceptive of all the innumerable illusions of mind; but both are primary instincts in man, and have an attraction on the mind akin to that of gravitation on matter'(Adams, 1920, pp. 241–42). Although Adams is deeply critical of his own education, he notes that '[f]rom cradle to grave this problem of running order through chaos, direction through space, discipline through freedom, unity through multiplicity, has always been and must always be, the task of education [...]' (Adams, 1961, p. 12).

According to this contradiction, both pure multiplicity and pure unity are impossible extremes. (Serres will read this as the states of pure chaos and pure order respectively, both of which are equally 'without information'). It is, rather, the complex space in-between – another north-west passage – that Adams will have to chart: 'the multiplicity of unity' (Adams, 1961, p. 398) and 'the extreme complexity of extreme simplicity' (Adams, 1961, p. 95); the paradoxical space of what has lately been called 'simplexity.' As Adams had read in Henri Poincaré, '[d]oubtless if our means of investigation should become more and more penetrating, we should discover the simple under the complex; then the complex under the simple; then anew the simple under the complex; and so on without ever being able to foresee the last term' (Poincaré, as cited in: Adams, 1961, p. 455).

Adams realizes something both Deleuze and Serres (whose book *Hermes V* is subtitled *The North-West Passage*) will stress throughout their work; the fact that '[t]here is order in disorder, there is disorder in order' (Serres, 1980, p. 64)[6]. More specifically, as Serres notes in *Genesis*, '[t]he cosmos is not a structure, it is a pure multiplicity of ordered multiplicities and pure multiplicities' (1995, p. 111).

It is from under the shadow of this fundamental realization that Adams, Deleuze and Serres develop their respective 'historical studies' and it is this realization that is responsible for their resonances. Like Adams, Deleuze proceeds from the concept of multiplicity, or better, of two complementary multiplicities.

Gilles Deleuze

At the conceptual heart of Deleuzian philosophy lies the question of how to think, philosophically, the 'reciprocal presupposition' (Deleuze, 1989, p. 69) of a material and an immaterial multiplicity. As Deleuze's theory of history is defined within the more general problematics of the relation between the material and the immaterial 'planes', let me sketch out, somewhat panoramically, these two planes.

   Deleuze defines the material plane as a 'given', extensive plane of anonymous, singular 'matters of fact'. It is a plane defined solely by the movements of more or less loosely coupled material particles. On this plane, 'history' is the history of pure change in and for itself; of change in direction and speed, or, as Deleuze also says, of 'latitudes and longitudes'; (Deleuze and Guattari, 1998, p. 19) what Adams had called the level of 'chance collisions of movements imperceptible to his senses, perhaps even imperceptible to his instruments, but perceptible to each other' (Adams, 1961, pp. 381–82). The laws of this 'particular' history are those of propulsion, propagation, contraction and agglomeration; of corporeal affects, of resonances, and of the infinitely subtle continuous modulation of frequencies. Its time is that of material pulses of being that know neither future nor past; of the unrelated succession of pure presents-as-actions, and its history is a chronic history of pure causes. I will call the history in|of this ontological|noumenal plane 'actual history'.

   If the material plane is related to 'the things that happen within a given field', the immaterial plane is related to 'the narratives about the things that happen'. It is a 'given', intensive plane of anonymous, singular events, filled with more or less loosely connected relations and patterns. History, on this plane, consists of the temporal and spatial relations between singular events and their agglomerations. The laws of this 'history of surfaces' are the laws of forms and formations, of metaphysical relation, psychic affection and contemplation. Its time is that of immaterial, empty durations that encompass past and future but that always 'miss' the present and its history is an aionic history of pure effects.[7] I will call this 'epistemological|phenomenal' plane of immaterial, eventual history the plane of 'virtual history'.

Deleuze uses the notion of 'planes' because he attributes the actual and the virtual, which I will take to stand for the physical plane of history and the metaphysical plane of historiography respectively, by way of topologically twisting them into a 'projective plane', which is the mathematical figure of a one-sided space defined by the identification of oppositional 'points-at-infinity'.[8] On this projective plane, the two planes are both related and radically separated. As Spinoza notes about the body and the mind, each of them needs to be thought in and through its own terms. The proof of their radical separation is that 'the body cannot determine mind to think, nor can the mind determine body to motion or rest' (63); a sentence quoted by Erwin Schrödinger in 'Mind and Matter'. Although there is no smooth, continuous transfer between actual and virtual history, to conceptually unfold them on the surface of the projective plane allows to install a logic of 'reciprocal presupposition,' and for what Foucault has called, in reference to Deleuze, an 'incorporeal materialism' (Foucault, 1994, p. 231). In Deleuze, every virtual is at least minimally actualized and every actual is at least minimally virtualized. The projective plane is the 'plane of life' – in Deleuzian terms, the plane of immanence – within which both actual history and virtual history emerge.

Michel Serres

The logic Serres develops from within a more scientific envelope is comparable to that proposed by Deleuze. Like Deleuze, he works with three conceptual registers, or conceptual chains. The first is the fluid chain of concrete, material and uncoded movement; a chain that is, like the surface of water, without tracks: 'What exists under these circumstances? Something that expands within an ahistorical world; waves that permeate fluids and gases, without leaving traces. What exists? Kinematic movements and geometric forms' (Serres, 1972, p. 90)[9] – Deleuze's latitudes and longitudes. These ahistorical movements form the ground or 'fond' of virtual history:

[I]t is simply a liquid movement, a viscosity [...]. Here we are in liquid history and the age of waters. It is the chain of genesis [...]. It is never a chain of necessity [...]. It surrenders to [...] the fluctuations of the sea [...]. It emerges from the sea noise, the nautical noise, the prebiotic soup. A fragile and soft chain [...] It is the chain of life (Serres, 1995, pp. 71–2).

The second chain is the solid chain of thought; of abstract, immaterial and coded movements that integrate and thus decelerate and harden the fluidity and infinite multiplicity of the historical 'fond:'

> The more the human body is young and the more it is possible, the more it is capable of multiplicity [...]. The more undetermined it is [...]. The entire volume of the old body is occupied by archives, museums, traces, narratives, as if it had filled up with circumstances (Serres, 1995, pp. 32–3).

Serres tends to identify the chain of thought with rationalism, which over codes the living, multiplicitous 'chain of contingency' (Serres, 1995, p. 71) with the relentlessly 'solid' (Serres, 1995, p. 71) chain of reason. 'We construct a real which is a rational one, we construct a real, among many possibilities, just as we pour concrete over the ground' (Serres, 1995, p. 25). All of Serres' work is suffused with rhetorics directed against this all-too-solid reason: 'The solid is the multiple reduced to the unitary' he notes, and 'the hardest solids are only fluids that are slightly more viscous than others' (Serres et al., 1995, p. 107). What reason does is to unduly simplify, '[a] concept is a multiple reduced to the unitary' (Serres, 1995, p. 108).

In phenomenological terms, the two chains stand for the fluid, 'aquatic [aquatique]' (Serres, 1980, p. 47) world of the senses, and the crystalline, hard world of clear 'distinct cognition [une connaissance [...] distincte]' (ibid., p. 40) respectively: 'The spirit is the spirit of the solid, the senses are those of the fluid' (ibid., p. 43).[10] Serres uses the works of Descartes and Bergson, who was in turn inspired by Lucretius (Serres, 1980, p. 47; Serres & Latour, 1995, p. 63) as stand-ins for these two positions. Like Deleuze, however, Serres does not choose between these two equally extreme positions, which correspond to Adams' concepts of pure multiplicity and pure simplicity. Rather, he introduces a third register that aligns concrete movement and abstract thought. The state of aggregation of this register, which is defined by the 'laws' of non-linear dynamics, is that of the 'flame'. If the borders of objects are too solid while those of fluids are too unspecific, the flame has a border, but that border is constantly changing. 'It dances unpredictably as if it were entrained by a stochastic music' (Serres, 1980, p. 52).[11] As the figure of a non-linear universe, the flame becomes Serres' model of 'science' and of a 'science of writing history':

> The flame [...] fluctuates without border and seemingly at random [...]. Always deviating from its equilibrium [...] as if it were experiencing a change of condition by way of the boldness of chance, which sows the

laws. [...] An unordered order, submerged in a neighboring disorder (ibid., p. 52–3).[12]

In a multiplicitous universe, history is 'that spatio-temporal, constantly changing multiplicity, which is without doubt the most complex' (ibid., 61).[13] Solidity, Serres argues, 'makes our history slow' (Serres, 1995, p. 87) while fluidity makes it too fast. It is only when historical studies conceptualize a flame-like object that they can retain historical multiplicity: 'a new object, multiple in space and mobile in time, unstable and fluctuating like a flame, relational' (Serres, 1995, p. 91).

Evolution

The fundamental concept of both Deleuze' and Serres' theories of history, then, is that both actual and virtual history emerge from within an 'originary' multiplicity, and the closest relation between their respective theories of history is that both aim at retaining, in all of its implications, this multiplicity. As Serres notes, '[t]he multiple is the object of this book and history is its goal' (Serres, 1995, p. 7). In fact, what Serres and Deleuze can offer to historical studies is an extremely rigorous conceptualization of what it means to construct a system of thought from an 'originary' state of multiplicity. 'It is always assumed that multiplicities can, through various procedures, be eliminated. I assume that they cannot be' (Serres, 1995, p. 128), Serres notes.

In this project, they stand at the end of a long line of philosophers and scientists who – either implicitly or explicitly – work from within the conceptualization of multiplicity. The notion of a specifically historical multiplicity, however, has also been developed from within historical studies themselves. Already before his visit to Paris, for instance, Adams had distilled the concept of a multiverse from his confrontation with the theory of evolution, which had posed a first serious scientific challenge to the nineteenth century historian.

At first sight, it had seemed to Adams that Darwin had proposed that an inherent tendency towards optimization – 'the survival of the fittest' – was regulating evolution from the outside: 'Steady, uniform, unbroken evolution from lower to higher seemed easy' (1961, p. 226), Adams notes. The '[l]aw should be Evolution from lower to higher, aggregation of the atom in the mass, concentration of multiplicity in unity, compulsion of anarchy in order' (Adams, 1961, p. 232). History, however, does not bear out such a tendency. As Adams notes laconically, '[t]he progress of Evolution from President

Washington to President Grant was alone evidence enough to upset Darwin' (Adams, 1961, p. 266). It is only when the regulation comes from within rather than from without, in a shift from a transcendental cybernetics to an immanent one, that the teleological can become the truly evolutionary.

It was, therefore, only when Adams stopped perceiving Darwin's theory of evolution as a directed movement towards perfection and order along a vector guaranteed by an outside force or law that he could reconcile the theory of evolution and the theory of history. This reconciliation, however, concerned a Darwin who was no longer a 'Darwinian:'

> As Newton said that he was never a Newtonian, so Darwin might perhaps have said that he was never a Darwinian, but his popular influence lay in the law that evolution had developed itself in unbroken order from lower to higher (Adams, 1920, p. 161).

In today's terminology, Adams maintains that evolution happens at the edge of chaos. 'A society in stable equilibrium is – by definition, – one that has no history and wants no historians' (Adams, 1920, p. 248), he notes. History happens at moments of non-linear, self-organizing criticality within a reservoir of multidirectional forces: 'Evolution was becoming change of form, broken by freaks of force, and warped at times by attractions affecting intelligence, twisted and tortured at other times by sheer violence, cosmic, chemical, solar, supersensual, electrolytic' (Adams, 1961, p. 401). As in Serres and Deleuze, a linear evolutionary vector explodes into the incomputable movements of an infinitely complex interaction of both perceptible and 'supersensual' (Adams, 1961, p. 381) forces. Despite all teleological readings of Darwin, evolution is about non-linear change rather than about linear progress: 'The Darwinist no longer talks of Evolution; he uses the word Transformation' (Adams, 1920, p. 191). Or, even more programmatically: 'complexity precedes evolution' (Adams, 1961, p. 302). The overall shift is from evolutionary teleology to 'evolutionary drift.'

Crystal History

How to conceive of history when everything is adrift? If there are material contractions on the one side and immaterial contemplations on the other, and if these two series are to be kept radically separate, how can actual history and virtual history be brought to converge 'as much as possible?' In other words, how to attribute the 'concrete machine' and the 'abstract machine' (Deleuze, 1999, p. 34); or, as Deleuze|Guattari call it in *Capitalism and Schizophrenia*, how to attribute 'the theater and the factory'? In terms of Deleuze's *Cinema 2: The Time-Image*: How to create a 'crystal history' in the sense that crystal-images are images that create the 'smallest internal circuit' (Deleuze, 1989, 70) between the actual and the virtual: points of 'the indiscernibility of the actual and the virtual' (ibid., 87); or, in historical terms, images of 'life as spectacle, and yet in its spontaneity' (ibid., 89). While this project sounds indeed highly abstract, it has a number of repercussions for concrete, empirical projects.

Multiplicities

First, and most fundamentally, to think 'varieties in the most rigorous sense of the word' (Serres, 1980, p. 72)[14] implies to consider even the Kantian a prioris of space and time as being themselves multiplicitous. If Kant's lesson had been that is it impossible to experience 'history in itself', Deleuze and Serres' lessons go further in showing that the very conditions for experience are implicated in the logic of multiplicity: 'There is no universal space in and of itself, there is no universal time' (ibid., p. 79)[15], Serres notes in the chapter 'Espaces et Temps' of *Hermes V.* 'I fear that space as such, the one and global space, is a philosophical artefact. [...] I fear time as such, the one and universal time, is also an artefact' (ibid., p. 68).[16] For the historical this means that its basic condition is that it takes place within a multiplicity of qualitative, 'projective [projectif]' (ibid., p. 69) and topological spaces rather than within a unified, metrical, quantitative Euclidean space. It happens within a bundle of 'chaotic, dense, compact, connected spaces' (ibid.)[17] that assemble themselves into discontinuous spatial quilts and architectures. These qualitative spaces – 'abstract multiplicity [variété abstraite]' (ibid., p. 70) that are 'locally euclidean but not everywhere'[18] – are, as Serres stresses, simultaneously 'apriori and sensoric [sensoriels]' (ibid.), which means that they define the conditions of both perception and experience: 'Topology, prepared by Leibniz, seen by Euler, founded by Riemann and others, establishes itself, by and by, as a rigorous aesthetics' (ibid., p. 72).[19]

In the shift from Euclid to Riemann, which is also that from global space to local spaces, not only what happens in space, but space itself becomes historical: 'The old space is [...] restored to the local and finally tumbles into the historical and into the cultural' (ibid., p. 73).[20] Because it is no longer possible to talk of a unified global space, one can no longer conceptualize an unproblematic passage from the local to the global:

a clear and distinct possibility of the practical usage of the global is never given. The ideologies, the philosophies of history, the theories of the state, the universal theories of morals are invariably written in that representational space in which the effects and the conclusions from the local to the global are all rational and can be governed. But that is never really the case. [...] Nobody has ever succeeded in integrating the local into the global. (ibid., p. 75)[21]

Deleuze|Guattari develop a very similar notion of multiplicitous space in the chapter 'The Smooth and the Striated' of *A Thousand Plateaus*, in which they, symptomatically, refer to Serres' recourse to the Lucretian clinamen in *The Birth of Physics*. Like Serres, Deleuze|Guattari argue that space is a fractal, Riemannian manifold that is assembled from patches of local spaces that cannot be abstracted, and thus separated from the elements within it. Again like Serres, however, they are not so much interested in these extremes as they are in the 'patchwork' (Deleuze and Guattari, 1987, p. 476) that defines the space in-between the two extremes: 'An amorphous collection of juxtaposed pieces that can be joined together in an infinite number of ways: we see that patchwork is literally a Riemannian space, or vice versa' (ibid.).

Both Serres and Deleuze, then, think about historical studies from within topological rather than classical space. As Deleuze|Guattari note, '[i]t was a decisive event when the mathematician Riemann uprooted the multiple from its predicate state and made it a noun, 'multiplicity'. It marked the end of dialectics and the beginning of a typology and topology of multiplicities' (ibid., pp. 482–83). Unlike Euclidean space, which functions as an unchanging, empty, abstract container for the quantitative measurement of position and movement, topological space changes qualitatively with every movement that takes place within it.

A similar multiplicity defines the a priori of time. Serres differentiates initially between irreversible, entropic time and reversible, negentropic time: 'This coexistence is not easy to comprehend, that we should be in two different and even contradictory times simultaneously. [...] Reversible time is the time of order, irreversible time, in contrast, tends towards disorder' (Serres, 1980, p. 78).[22] As with space, history emerges from within a multiplicity of quilted times and rhythms, from 'different times that flow together within me' (ibid., p. 79).[23] As with the spatial milieu, there is no temporally unified time. The temporal milieu consists of a 'knot of several times [nouant plusieurs temps]' (ibid., p. 80), and as such '[t]ime is lacunary and sporadic, it is a badly stitched tatter, it passes, loose, a mosaic. Time is a pure multiplicity' (Serres, 1995, p. 115).

> The French language in its wisdom uses the same word for weather and time, *le temps*. At a profound level they are the same thing. Meteorological weather, predictable and unpredictable, will no doubt some day be explainable by complicated notions of fluctuations, strange attractors. ... Someday we will perhaps understand that historical time is even more complicated (Serres et al., 1995, p. 58).

Serres specifically stresses that historical studies need to address time as 'a multiple, foldable diversity' (ibid., p. 59). Time 'flows in a turbulent and chaotic manner; it percolates. All of our difficulties with the theory of history come from the fact that we think of time in this inadequate and naive way' (ibid., p. 59).[24] Time 'resembles this crumpled version much more than the flat, overly simplified one' (ibid., p. 60). Quite programmatically, Serres states that 'the time of history must always be an extremely complex syrrhesis' (Serres, 1980, p. 82)[25]. Without the concept of a unified, global time, there can be no global meaning of|in history: 'How to talk, then, of the meaning of history? This concept is void of meaning' (ibid.).[26]

The multiplicitous character of history and the non-systemic character of history's time have two consequences: First, historical studies cannot create solid 'historical objects'. Secondly, because, as Serres argues, history is fundamentally multiplicitous, it cannot itself be treated as a solid object or a stable system, which means that 'history does not know breaks or sudden phase changes, as long as one does not think of it as a mechanical system of solid bodies that move according to the constraints of forces and relations of forces [...]' (Serres, 1980, p. 47).[27]

Deleuze, for whom time is similarly multiplicitous, negotiates the difference between irreversible and reversible time as that between the actual time of 'Chronos' and the virtual time of 'Aion' and thus as the difference between actual and virtual history.

> Whereas Chronos expressed the action of bodies and the creation of corporeal qualities, Aion is the locus of incorporeal events, and of attributes which are distinct from qualities. Whereas Chronos was inseparable from the bodies which filled it out entirely as causes and matter, Aion is populated by effects which haunt it without ever filling it up (Deleuze, 1990, p. 165, emphasis added).

Chronos belongs to the causal world of matters of fact, which is 'made up purely of passions, physical qualities, bodies, tensions and actions' (ibid. 4) and it concerns 'the living present, [which] happens and brings about the event' (ibid. 63, emphasis added).

The Chronic world is made up of a multiplicity of temporal pulses of different lengths and rhythms. Although all living systems are coupled to the more comprehensive temporal pulses that define their medium, each system is itself the result of 'its' entrainment, organization and regulation of a heterology|multiplicity of chronic pulses into an overall operative pulse. While all living systems are immanent to the totality of Chronic pulses in terms of their biomaterial energetics, they live in Aionic 'duration' – an initially Bergsonian concept that Deleuze uses – in terms of their perceptual and cognitive operations.[28] Whereas Chronic time, as the time of full, matter of fact presents without past or future, is the time of being – 'for to be present would mean to be and no longer to become' (ibid. 164) – Aionic time relies on a minimal interval between past and future because it is the 'result' of a, however minimal, perceptual machine. It is 'the instant without thickness and without extension, which subdivides each present into past and future, rather than vast and thick presents which comprehend both future and past in relation to one another' (ibid. 164, emphasis added).

Implications

The fact that neither historical space nor historical time is unified has a number of implications, the most important of which is that 'everything' becomes historical:

> We are producing the history of history. And the criterion is missing. Of what is there no history? Of nothing. Of everything, one can write the history. [...] Who, today, is not more or less a historian? Which field would escape the historical dimension (Serres, 1980, p. 85)?[29]

Serres proposes that historical studies should take recourse to the science of chaos theory because 'the development of history truly resembles what chaos theory describes' (Serres & Latour, 1995, p. 57). This science could provide a conceptual 'ground' of historical studies because 'history would be [...] a science if, in its global strategy, it could be falsified' (Serres, 1980, p. 89)[30]. In other words, Serres proposes, much like Adams did, that historical studies should learn from contemporary physics (ibid. p. 83).

The second implication is that historical studies become radically site-specific and 'ecological'. To work from within a tangle of local spaces and times means to work from within specific local milieus; from specific sets of local circumstances 'where writing emerges as the mnemonic preserver of this initial condition by chance within the interconnections of things themselves' (Serres, 2000, 149). As Serres notes, historical studies need to operate within a 'local topology [topologie locale]' (Serres, 1980, p. 50) and provide 'a detailed analysis of the local multiplicities' (ibid.).[31]

A third implication is that these analyses must encompass the activities of nonhuman agents: if matter and thought are similarly 'self-assembled', this means that in the same way every organism is assembled from smaller organisms, every thought is assembled from smaller thoughts; ad infinitum. From this recursion, Deleuze and Serres each conclude that the faculties of cognition and of the imagination are present even in 'the most simple' of organisms. Down to its smallest levels – finite in Serres, infinite in Deleuze – living organisms partake of these two series of assemblages. Organs are molecular machines that have been integrated into more comprehensive organisms, into vaster, more molar machines.

Every living aggregate, from a single cell to observers|historians, in fact, continually monitors its own actual history by way of the creation of a complementary virtual history. Every living system continually 'writes' its own private autobiography as a running commentary on its actions. Every atom, certainly every molecule, 'writes' in the sense that it tracks itself and keeps records of its corporeal movements and its affects. This is why Serres can describe seemingly 'natural' processes in semiotic terms: 'The wind writes onto the ocean by way of groundswells, phrases, squalls, traces' (Serres, 1977, p. 151).[32] In fact, for Serres everything that exists exists in the form of writing and code, which makes of the world a network of communicating elements; in Deleuze's words, a world filled with 'signaletic material [matière signalétique]' (Deleuze, 1989, p. 33).

In *Chance and Necessity*, Jacques Monod, who was a good friend of Serres,[33] calls such a biomaterial writing, which he relates, among others, to the operations of enzymes, a 'microscopic cybernetics'. Similarly, Deleuzian philosophy considers not only human, but also nonhuman cultures, such as bacterial or molecular cultures, as cognitive aggregates that partake of the faculty of the imagination – Kant's *Einbildungskraft* or Hume's 'fancy' – which turns the multiplicity of particular dots that make up the extensive universe into intensive surfaces; extracting a surface of historiographic sense from material history by way of transforming recurrent material irritations or 'shocks' coming from the environment into immaterial universes of meaning. While the imagination operates spatially, the faculty of memory operates temporally. It creates an Aionic historical duration and continuity from the Chronic stutter of matters of fact. According to this extended notion of cognition, the virtual history of humans emerges from and is pervaded by an infinite number of minor virtual histories, whose inscriptions, however, never congeal into linguistic signs.

The series of actual history is 'transformed' into the series of virtual history through processes of integration, in Leibniz' terms of 'differentiation and summation'. The historical irony is that in this process the more a system integrates, the further it separates itself from the fond of history. The more levels of integration, the more 'ponderous' it becomes.

In Deleuzian terms, to link virtual history to the nonhuman fond of actual history, therefore, implies to reach back through the mass of historical integrations to the 'a-historical becomings' from which these integrations have emerged; to the anonymous, uncomputable – as Nietzsche would say: 'shifting' – ground of virtual history; to the anonymous, infinitely complex diagram embodied by haecceities; the abstract machine of 'what is'. This 'diagrammatic or abstract machine is the "source" of history'. It 'does not function to represent, even something real, but rather constructs a real [...]. Thus when it constitutes points of creation or potentiality it does not stand outside history but is instead always "prior" to history' (Deleuze and Guattari, 1987, p. 142).

It is because of the radical ecologization of thought – the fact that thought is always embodied and that every body is always 'ensouled'– that, in their respective discussions of Leibniz, Serres and Deleuze argue against a divine, global position that allows for an overview of the multiplicity of local circumstances. In fact, for Serres, whoever occupies such a position is a colonizer and an impostor, because '[t]he empire is never more than some inflated local, a part that took the place of the whole' (Serres, 1995, p. 72). It is when it claims to have such an overview that science becomes 'Royal Science'. Analogously, it is the moment when historical studies become 'Royal History'. In opposition to such globalizations,

> nonmetric multiplicities or multiplicities of smooth space pertain only to a minor geometry that is purely operative and qualitative, in which calculation is necessarily very limited, and the local operations of which are not even capable of general translatability or a homogeneous system of location (Deleuze and Guattari, 1987, p. 484).

Minor Science, Minor History

While Royal History 'pretends' to others as well as to itself to have such an overview, minor history proceeds by way of 'probe-heads', which are survey-machines that move not over, but through the terrain, which means that the concepts of a minor science develop from within this terrain: '[t]he concept is in a state of survey [survol] in relation to its components, endlessly traversing them according to an order without distance' (Deleuze and Guattari, 1994, p. 20). Like space and time, the concept is 'a multiplicity, an absolute surface or volume, self-referents, made up of a certain number of inseparable intensive variations according to an order of neighborhood, and traversed by a point in a state of survey. The concept is the contour, the configuration, the constellation of an event to come' (Deleuze and Guattari, 1994, pp. 32–3). Because of these characteristics, 'the philosophical concept does not refer to the lived, by way of compensation, but consists, through its own creation, in setting up an event that surveys the whole of the lived no less than every state of affairs' (Deleuze and Guattari, 1994, pp. 33–4). Ultimately, the immaterial mind, as differentiated from the material brain, 'is an absolutely consistent form that surveys itself independently of any supplementary dimension' (Deleuze and Guattari, 1994, p. 210). As a minor history, historical studies need to reinvent themselves as a probe-head, and its practice as a 'survol'; as a practice that encounters complex autopoietic aggregates and their interactions in all of their unpredictability. Beyond what is generally subsumed under 'environmental history,' it would have to address the 'historical weather' in all of its complexity, its climate, its geology, the currents and forces that traverse it.[34]

The fourth implication is that historical studies need to include the condition of contingency in its conceptualizations, which touches upon Kant's third a priori: causality. As I noted earlier, Serres' theory of history is inspired by and indebted to the science of chaos theory, or, more specifically, of non-linear dynamics. Accordingly, his notion of history is that of a 'flame-like' non-linear history in which contingency operates a seminal structuring device. 'There is contingency when two multiplicities touch each other. There is contingency, when two times touch each other' (Serres, 1980, p. 83).[35]

Again, this idea is not new. The concept of historical contingency goes back 'at least' to Lucretius, and it resurfaces in, among others, the work of C. S. Peirce, who develops the notion of a 'tychic history' and in the work of Michel Foucault, who notes in 'The Discourse on Language' – written partly with Serres in the conceptual background – that 'we must accept the introduction of chance as a category in the production of events [...] the introduction, into the very roots of thought, of notions of chance, discontinuity and materiality. This represents a triple peril which one particular form of history attempts to avert by recounting the continuous unfolding of some ideal necessity' (231, emphasis added). In his essay 'On the Gradual Production of Thoughts Whilst Speaking' Heinrich von Kleist has provided a concise model of a historical moment of bifurcation, arguing that maybe it was the twitch of an upper lip or an indecisive fiddling with the sleeve cuff that caused the French Revolution.[36]

For Deleuze|Guattari as well, 'there is no good reason but contingent reason; there is no universal history except of contingency' (Deleuze and Guattari, 1994, p. 93). History encompasses 'a dynamic and open social reality, in a state of functional disequilibrium, unstable and always compensated' (Deleuze and Guattari, 1998, p. 150). Even more programmatically, they maintain that 'universal history is the history of contingencies, and not the history of necessity. Ruptures and limits, and not continuity' (Deleuze and Guattari, 1998, p. 140). History is 'not only retrospective, it is also contingent, singular, ironic and critical' (Deleuze and Guattari, 1998, p. 140).

In terms of causation, Deleuze proposes that causes and effects do not follow each other chronologically, but that there is a material plane of deep causes (the plane of actual history) and an immaterial plane of surface effects on which 'imaginary' sets of relations function as 'quasi-causes' (Deleuze, 1990, p. 86) (the plane of virtual history). The historical question becomes one of the attributions of quasi-causes to causes and vice versa.

For Deleuze|Guattari, it is the milieu, the actual 'geography,' that 'wrests history from the cult of necessity in order to stress the irreducibility of contingency. Contingency wrests historical contemplation from the cult of origins in order to affirm the power of the 'milieu,' 'an ambiance, an ambient atmosphere' (Deleuze and Guattari, 1994, p. 96). Or, as Serres notes: 'In the nearest vicinity of their borders, systems touch contingency. They are surrounded by it. And because the systems are stable [...] I call their surroundings circumstance; that which stands around them' (Serres, 1980, p. 83).[37] In Deleuze, these circumstances are the actual matters of fact that define extensive history and its vertical sedimentations, which have to be attributed to the horizontal durations of intensive history and vice versa: While virtual history is chronologically spanned out between past, present and future, actual history is geologically spanned out between strata, forming 'haecceities' (Deleuze and Guattari, 1987, p. 507) that are defined by a superimposition of 'imperceptible' (Deleuze, 1987, p. 2) metamorphoses, which is why 'in becoming, there is no past nor future – not even present, there is no history' (Deleuze, 1987, p. 29). If historical studies are 'to make perceptible the imperceptible forces that populate the world, affect us, and make us become' (Deleuze and Guattari, 1994, p. 182), they must find their place in the transversal space between horizontal and vertical history: 'philosophy is a geophilosophy in precisely the same way that history is a geohistory from Braudel's point of view' (Deleuze and Guattari, 1994, p. 95).

Adams refers to the notion of contingency in his theory of phase-changes; changes between attractors that function according to the logic of what today is called 'self-organizing criticality:' 'every equilibrium, or phase, begins and ends with what is called a critical point' (Adams, 1920, p. 277); a point of bifurcation. Phase-changes happen because systems are inherently unstable. In fact, for Adams, 'all is equilibrium more or less unstable' (Adams, 1920, p. 283). Order is an illusion; a name for a dynamics that has been decelerated to zero. In Adams words, order is '[d]irection regarded as stationary, like a frozen waterfall' (Adams, 1920, p. 279). At the same time, however, every system has the 'instinct' to resist a phase change. It shows characteristics of inertia: 'where an equilibrium is subjected to conditions which tend to change, it reacts internally in ways that tend to resist the external constraint, and to preserve its established balance [...]' (Adams, 1920, p. 284).

As '[t]hought is a historical substance, analogous to an electric current, which has to obey the laws, – whatever they are – of Phase' (Adams, 1920, p. 283), psychic systems go, like physical systems, through 'historical' phases and they change at points of historical bifurcation that mark a 'distinct change in direction and form of thought' (Adams, 1920, p. 287, emphasis added). Importantly, every phase change is a radical change, which means that '[t]he history of the new phase has no direct relation with that which preceded it' (Adams, 1920, p. 290). It sets up a completely new diagram or 'abstract machine': '[T]he change of phase in 1500-1700', for instance, 'is marvelously electrolytic' (Adams, 1920, p. 289), while that around 1900, which 'turned society sharply into a new channel of electric thought as different from the mechanical as electric mass is different from astronomical mass' (Adams, 1920, p. 306), is 'electro-magnetic' (Adams, 1920, p. 307).[38] Ultimately, however, every single moment sets up a new diagram. The moments Adams marks are merely attempts at 'pragmatic simplification.'

The fifth implication is the probably most crucial lesson of maintaining that history emerges from an 'originary' multiplicity. It concerns the fact that the historian him|herself is immersed in the field and as such in a constant energetic exchange with the universe of forces. S|he is him|herself energetically enmeshed in the milieu, although s|he is, simultaneously, cognitively separated from it. S|he is both observer and energetic assemblage. Adams expresses this paradox by describing himself as 'a conscious ball of vibrating motions, traversed in every direction by infinite lines of rotation or vibration, rolling at the feet of the Virgin of Chartres or of M. Poincaré in an attic at Paris, a centre of supersensual chaos' (Adams, 1961, p. 460 [emphasis added]). Already Adams realized that the universe of forces encompasses the historian:

Man is a force; so is the sun; so is a mathematical point [...]. Man commonly begs the question again by taking for granted that he captures the forces. A dynamic theory [...] takes for granted that the forces of nature capture man. The sum of force attracts; the feeble atom or molecule called man is attracted; [...] he is the sum of forces that attract him; his body and his thought are alike their product (Adams, 1961, p. 474, [emphasis added]).

In fact, 'Man's function as a force of nature was to assimilate other forces as he assimilated food' (Adams, 1961, p. 475). In Serres' words: 'The observer finally enters the steam boiler, where he finds only partial information' (Serres, 1980, p. 63).[39]

Every History is a History of the Living

For both Deleuze and Serres, the ultimate reason for 'doing history' is 'to find the conditions under which something new is produced' (Deleuze, 1987, p. vii, see also Deleuze, 1986, p. 7); to 'arrive at the unhistorical vapor that goes beyond actual factors to the advantage of a creation of something new' (Deleuze and Guattari, 1994, p. 140). As Serres notes, similarly, in *Rome* 'I am trying to imagine nature in the sense of birth, when newness is created, is going to be created, or unexpectedly appears' (Serres, 1991, p. 251). If one thinks this is too abstract a question for the historian, here is Adams: 'what he valued most was Motion, and that what attracted his mind was Change' (Adams, 1961, p. 231).

The question 'How does newness enter the world?'[40] introduces a force into historical studies that has been called, in various places and times, 'appetitus,' 'conatus,' 'desire,' élan vital or 'energy.' For Adams, both the Virgin and the dynamo embody this vital force of pure production. Both are, quite literally, 'generators.'[41] It shows his deep concern for the new forces that Adams, rather than feminizing the dynamo, 'dynamizes' the Virgin: 'goddess because of her force; she was the animated dynamo; she was reproduction – the greatest and most mysterious of energies' (Adams, 1964, p. 384). In fact, already in 'The Tendency of History' (1894) Adams had noted that 'the world is made up of a few immense forces, each with an organization that corresponds with its strength' (Adams, 1920, pp. 128–29), only in order to imagine, with quite some pleasure, the ensuing shock 'that might follow the establishment of a fixed science of history' (Adams, 1920, p. 128).

Adam concludes that 'modern politics is, at bottom, a struggle not of men but of forces' (Adams, 1961b, p. 421). In 1900, he notes that '[o]f all the travels made by man since the voyages of Dante, this new exploration along the shores of Multiplicity and Complexity promised to be the longest, though as yet it had barely touched two familiar registers – race and sex' (Adams, 1961b, p. 449). In fact, the only difference between the forces that underlie history is that 'sex is a vital condition, and race only a local one' (Adams, 1961b, p. 441). Sexuality in fact becomes such a basic historical register for Adams that 'without understanding movement of sex, history seemed to him mere pedantry' (Adams, 1961b, p. 442).[42]

Especially in today's politically correct world, it might come as a shock to maintain that in the fundamental multiplicity of productive forces, the most invariant ones are those of sex and race. When one reads this, however, as meaning that the most constant parameters of historical change concern generation and diversification, one will find that Serres argues for a similar vitalization of history when he adds the time of 'the thermodynamics of open systems' (Serres, 1980, p. 80) to reversible and irreversible time.[43] The force of sex is the negentropic, dissipative motor that ensures continuing change. Even though individual systems die according to their specific irreversible times, an anonymous, non-individual life pertains even within these deaths. In informational terms, the passage of words does not imply the passing of language:

> Sex traverses death. Death erases the word of sex, but it does not silence its language. On the contrary, the language of sex silences death. Death's blinking streaks of lightning can merely mark the unsurpressible discourse of sex. (Serres, 1980, p. 79)[44]

Deleuze calls this anonymous life 'the powerful, non-organic Life which grips the world' (Deleuze, 1989, p. 81); a life that forms the medium from which individual life is assembled:

> If everything is alive, it is not because everything is organic or organized, but, on the contrary, because the organism is a diversion of life. In short, the life in question is inorganic, germinal, and intensive, a powerful life without organs, a Body that is all the more alive for having no organs, everything that passes between organisms. (Deleuze and Guattari, 1987, p. 499)

To advocate the productive force of sex, Adams changes from the metaphysical register of the Virgin to the physical register of Venus. If, as Adams maintains, '[t]he proper study of mankind is woman' (Adams, 1961a, p. 191), the historical problem is that in puritanical America, it is impossible to create a 'serious' theory of history. While Lucretius, whom Adams adored, could position the figure of Venus Anadyone in the centre of his work, Adams notes, with a tinge of despair, that

[a]n American Virgin would never dare command; an American Venus would never dare exist [...] Adams began to ponder, asking himself whether he knew of any American artist who had ever insisted upon the power of sex, as every classic had always done; but he could think only of Walt Whitman; Bret Harte, as far as the magazines would let him venture; and even one or two painters, for the flesh-tones. All the rest had used sex for sentiment, never for force (Adams, 1961b, p. 385).

In Derridean registers, in America, sex is invariably understood and used in terms of 'signification' [sentiment] rather than in terms of 'force' [force]. It is infinitely far away from Lucretius' and Serres' celebration of 'Venus turbulent, above the noise of the sea' (Serres, 1995, p. 122).

In order to make sense of the supersensual multiverse, one must find the most habitual physical forces in the dynamics of evolutionary change and the 'law' of their operation. Adams, reading William Gibbs,[45] identifies this law as that of inertia; the habit that 'matter tends, when at rest, to remain so, and when in motion, to move on in a straight line' (Adams, 1961b, p. 441). This law of inertia defines both mental and physical processes. As Adams states, '[o]f all movements of inertia, maternity and reproduction are the most typical, and women's property of moving in a constant line forever is ultimate, uniting history in its only unbroken and unbreakable sequence' (Adams, 1961b, p. 441).

As Adams had noted in terms of evolution, however, there is no historical change in an inert, entropic universe. Historical change is the result of deviations from habits; of the difference buried in repetition; of the local negentropy operative within the global entropy. In the resulting diagram of historical change, the habit of inertia moves history forward in linear vectors, while deviations move it into non-linear ones: 'Chaos often breeds life, when order breeds habit' (ibid., 249), Adams notes. Too much habit stifles change. The diverse 'lines of force' (ibid., 427) are ordered|straightened by motivation: 'The disorderly, Brownian motion' is 'guided by motive, as an electric current is induced by a dynamo' (Adams, 1920, p. 280). This is why '[a]ll State education' is 'a sort of Dynamo machine for polarizing the popular mind; for turning and holding its lines of force in the direction supposed to be most effective for State purposes' (Adams, 1961b, p. 78). Ultimately, the historical question concerns 'organized energy' (ibid., 83).

According to Adams, it is not enough to construct virtual history because it is always pervaded by actual history: 'Always and everywhere the mind creates its own universe, and pursues its own phantoms; but the force behind the image is always a reality, the attractions of occult power' (Adams, 1920, p. 310). As the unthought, unthinkable and imperceptible ground of virtual history, actual history provides the stuff from which virtual history is constructed.

Is History Like Physics?

Livy the historian, in the wake of Lucretius the physicist, founds the social world on water. Physics and history are founded in the same time (Serres, 1991, p. 267).

Despite the many resonances between Deleuze and Serres, there are also differences. For Serres, systems reach the level of individual life and thought when they pass a critical threshold at which physics turns first into chemistry and then into biology. For Deleuze, who does philosophy, life and thought exist even in the infinitely small, anonymous elements that make up the plane of immanence, which is why Deleuze|Guattari maintain in *What is Philosophy?* that philosophy retains the infinite, while science reduces the infinite to the finite. Both, however, maintain that individual life and individual thought emerge spontaneously from within a more anonymous, communal life and thought, as the result of the gradual coupling of elements from within the planes of extensive force|energy, and of intensive signification|consciousness.

A second difference if that for Serres, 'every non-physical interpretation of the clinamen remains essentially idealist' (Serres, 2000, p. 113). While this is true, Deleuze's project is precisely to align materialist and idealist aspects in a transcendental empiricism. While Serres maintains that 'the senses are faithful' (Serres, 2000, p. 49) because 'physics is faithful to the world, since the formation of its text is isomorphic with the constitution of the natural tissue' (Serres, 2000, p. 159), Deleuze proposes to attribute the two separate series of the material and the psychic. Overall, Serres tends to highlight the actual machine, while Deleuze's project is to reciprocally 'attribute' the actual and the virtual machines.

Although Serres, Deleuze and Adams all maintain that history is like physics, they all mean something slightly different by it. For Serres, who sees physics as an 'environmental physics or climatology' (Serres, 2000, p. 154), it is a question of science:

our writings, our memory, our histories and our times are negentropic, go back to the initial conditions, preserve them and maintain them, as nature has shown them to us. History is a physics, and not the other way around. Language is first of all in bodies (Serres, 2000, p. 150).[46]

When Deleuze notes that '[h]istory is like physics' (Deleuze and Guattari, 1998, p. 86), it is a question of philosophy, and when Adams notes, vis-à-vis the dynamos' immense forces of production, that the 'future historian must seek his education in the world of mathematical physics' (Adams, 1920, p. 283), it is a question of historiography. It is because of these differences that the three approaches resonate across time, and across the diverse fields of knowledge with their respective logics. Ultimately, however, whether it is Henry Adams in 1900 or Manuel De Landa in 1997, the proposal is still the same: 'much as history has infiltrated physics, we must now allow physics to infiltrate human history' (1997, p. 15).

Notes

[1] 489. For Serres' reading of Lucretius, see Berressem 2005; Serres et al., 1995, p. 46.
[2] See Jay Lampert's Deleuze and Guattari's *Philosophy of History* for an extended philosophical analysis of the historical in Deleuze and Guattari.
[3] They were two 'General Electric' generators of 800-Kilowatt each and the newest 'Westinghouse' models.
[4] Both are compiled in *The Degradation of the Democratic Dogma* (1920).
[5] See also Adams' poem 'Prayer to the Virgin of Chartres', which 'contains' a 'Prayer to the Dynamo'.
[6] All translations from texts by Serres that have not been translated into English are mine. The original French is given in the footnotes: 'Il y a de l'ordre dans le désordre, il y a du désordre dans l'ordre.'
[7] Deleuze takes the separation of causes and effects from the Stoics. The Stoics relegate each series to a separate plane or domain, setting up a 'new dualism of bodies or states of affairs and effects or incorporeal events [which] entails an upheaval in philosophy' (Deleuze, 1990, p. 6).
[8] For more on the plane of immanence as a projective plane, see Berressem, 2005.
[9] Serres uses the past tense: 'Ces conditions posées, qu'existe-t-il? Du propagé dans un monde anhistorique, des graphes d'ondes traversant des fluides qui ne les conservent pas. Qu'existait-t-il? Des mouvements cinématique et des figures géométrique.'
[10] 'L'esprit est l'esprit des solides, les sens sont les sens des liquides [...].'
[11] 'Il danse imprévisiblement comme entraîné par une musique stochastique.'
[12] 'La flamme [...] fluctue sans frontière et comme au hasard. Toujours en écart à son propre équilibre [...] elle paraît changer d'état par la témérité du hasard qui a semé les lois. [...] Ordre désordonné plongé dans un désordre assez voisin.'

¹³ '[...] cette multiplicité spatio-temporelle en transformation, et qui est, sans doute, la plus fortement complexe [...].'

¹⁴ '[...] des variétés, au sens le plus strict [...]'.

¹⁵ 'Il n'y a pas d'espace universel, de soi, en soi, il n'y a pas de temps universel.'

¹⁶ 'L'espace comme tel, unique et global, est, je le crains, un artefact philosophique. [...] Le temps, comme tel, unique et universel, est lui aussi, un artefact.'

¹⁷ '[...] chaotiques, denses, compacts, connexes [...]'.

¹⁸ '[...] des espaces localement euclidiens qui ne l'étaient pas globalement.'

¹⁹ 'La topologie, préparée par Leibniz, entrevue par Euler et fondée par Riemann et d'autres, s'installe peu à peu comme esthétique rigoureuse.'

²⁰ 'L'ancien espace est [...] ramené à un certain local, et il bascule enfin dans l'historique et dans le culturel.'

²¹ '[...] cette possibilité claire et distincte d'une pratique du global n'ont jamais lieu. Les idéologies, les philosophies de l'histoire, les théories de l'Etat, les morales universelles, sont toutes écrites dans l'espace de la représentation, où du local au global, les séquences et conséquences sont rationnelles et maîtrisables. Or, cela n'est pas vrai. [...] Nul n'a jamais pu intégrer le local au global [...]'.

²² 'Il n'est pas aisé de comprendre cette coexistence, que nous soyions plongés dans deux temps différents jusqu'au contradictoire. [...] Le temps réversible est de l'ordre, l'irréversible est tendance au désordre [...].'

²³ 'ces temps si divers qui se jettent en moi comme en un confluent [...]'.

²⁴ 'An object a circumstance, is thus polychronic, multitemporal, and reveals a time that is gathered together, with multiple pleats' (Serres et al., 1995, p. 60).

²⁵ '[...] le temps de l'histoire doit être aussi une syrrhrèse très complexe.'

²⁶ '[...] comment peut-on parler du sens de l'histoire? Ce concept est privé de sens.'

²⁷ '[...] l'histoire n'a pas de coupure ou de changements brusques de phase, sauf à penser, tout justement, l'histoire même comme une mécanique de systèmes solides en mouvement sous contraintes de forces et de rapports de forces [...].'

²⁸ See: Deleuze 1988.

²⁹ '[...] nous produisons [...] l'histoire de l'histoire. Et le critère est bien manquant. De quoi ne peut-il pas y avoir histoire? De rien donc, à nouveau. On peut toujours faire histoire de tout. [...] Qui n'est pas, peu ou prou, historien, où qu'il soit? Quelle discipline échappe à la dimension historique [...] ?'

³⁰ 'L'histoire serait une science si (non pas: seulement si) elle pouvait être falsifiable dans la globale stratégie.'

³¹ '[...] une analyse fine des variétés locales [...]'.

³² 'le vent écrit sur la mer par houle, phrases, risées, sillons.'

³³ Serres et al., 1995, p. 13.

³⁴ On Deleuze and environmental history, see Berressem, 2007, 2008.

³⁵ 'Il y a contingence lorsque deux variétés se touchent. Il y a contingence lorsque deux temps se touchent.'

³⁶ Kleist 1982, pp. 810–14.

³⁷ 'Au voisinage le plus proche de leurs bords les systèmes touchent à la contingence. Ils sont entourés d'elle. Et puisque les systèmes sont stables [...], je nommerai ce qui les entoure circonstance.'

³⁸ Adams computes this acceleration with an almost touching precision. Depending on when one sets the previous phase, the spirit will change acording to the law

of potentiality, either 1921, or, at the latest in 2025: 'Thought to the limit of its possibilities in the year 1921' (Phase 308).

[39] 'L'observateur enfin entre dans la chaudière, où il ne trouve plus que des informations partielles.'

[40] In Salman Rushdie's *The Satanic Verses*, the narrator asks 'How does newness come into the world? [...] Of what fusions, translations, conjoinings is it made?' (8); a question Homi Bhabha takes up in Chapter 11 of *The Location of Culture*, entitled: 'How newness enters the world: Postmodern space, postcolonial times and the trials of cultural translation.'

[41] Adams also talks of 'the figure of nature's power as an infinitely powerful dynamo' (Phase 305).

[42] 'If a Unity exists, in which all and toward which all energies centre, it must explain and include Duality, Diversity, Infinity – Sex!' (Adams, 1961a, p. 259).

[43] 'thermodynamique des systèmes ouverts'.

[44] 'Le sexe traverse la mort. La mort fait cesser la parole du sexe, mais elle ne fait pas taire sa langue. Le langage du sexe, au contraire, rend la mort taciturne. Elle ne fait que zébrer d'éclairs clignotants son irrépressible discours.'

[45] 'The Rule of Phase Applied to History' starts in the manner of scholastic philosophy by attempting to found metaphysics on physics. For the Aristotelian realms of animal, vegetable and mineral, Adams substituted William Gibbs's less animalistic phases of matter – solid, fluid, and gas' (Levenson, 1957, p. 359).

[46] As he notes elsewhere, '[t]he soul is a material body, the body is a thing, the subject is just an object, physiology and psychology are just physics' (Serres, 2000, p. 49).

Bibliography

Adams, H. (1920), *The Degradation of the Democratic Dogma*. New York: The Macmillan Company.

—(1961a), *Mont-Saint-Michel and Chartres*. New York: Mentor Books.

—(1961b), *The Education of Henry Adams. An Autobiography*. Boston: Houghton Mifflin.

Berressem, H. (2005), '"Incerto tempore, Incertisque Locis:" The logic of the Clinamen and the birth of physics.' in: N. Abbas (ed.). *Mapping Michel Serres*. University of Michigan Press: Ann Arbor. pp. 51–71.

—'Matter that bodies': http://www.genderforum.org/fileadmin/archiv/genderforum/mediating/btm/btm.html

—(2007), 'Ecologics|Ecosophy: The Event of the City', in U. Lehmkuhl and H. Wellenreuther (eds), *Historians and Nature: Comparative Approaches to Environmental History*. Oxford: Berg. pp. 45–67.

—(2008), 'Structural couplings: radical constructivism and a deleuzian ecologics', in B. Herzogenrath (ed.), *Deleuze|Guattari & Ecology*. London: Palgrave MacMillan,

Bhabha, H. K. (1994), *The Location of Culture*. New York: Routledge.

De Landa, M. (1997), *A Thousand Years of Nonlinear History*. New York: Zone Books.

Deleuze, G. (1986), *Cinema I. The Movement-Image*. Translated by H. Tomlinson and B. Habberjam. Minneapolis: University of Minnesota Press.

—(1987), *Dialogues*. Translated by H. Tomlinson and B. Habberjam. New York: Columbia University Press.

—(1988), *Bergsonism*. Translated by H. Tomlinson and B. Habberjam. New York: Zone Books.

—(1989), *Cinema II: The Time-Image*. Translated by H. Tomlinson and B. Habberjam. Minneapolis: University of Minnesota Press.

—(1990), *The Logic of Sense*. Translated by M. Lester with C. Stivale. New York: Columbia University Press.

—(1994), *Difference and Repetition*. Translated by P. Patton. New York: Columbia University Press.

—(1999), *Foucault*. Translated by S. Hand. London: Continuum.

Deleuze, G. and Guattari, F. (1987), *A Thousand Plateaus. Capitalism and Schizophrenia 2*. Translated by B. Massumi, Minneapolis: University of Minnesota Press.

—(1994), *What is Philosophy?* Translated by H. Tomlinson and G. Burchell. New York: Columbia University Press.

—(1998 [1972]), *Anti-Oedipus. Capitalism and Schizophrenia 1*. Translated by R. Hurley, M. Seem, and H. R. Lane. Minneapolis: University of Minnesota Press.

Flusser, V. (1985), *Ins Universum der Technischen Bilder*. Göttingen: European Photography.

Foucault, M. (1994), 'The discourse on language', in: *The Archaeology of Knowledge*. London: Vintage. pp. 215–37.

Kleist, H. von. (1982), 'Über die allmähliche Verfertigung der Gedanken beim Reden', in: *Werke in Einem Band*. München: Carl Hanser Verlag. pp. 810–14.

Lampert, J. (2006), *Deleuze and Guattari's Philosophy of History*. London: Continuum.

Levenson, J. C. (1957), *The Mind and Art of Henry Adams*. Stanford: Stanford University Press.

Monod, J. (1972), *Chance and Necessity: An Essay on the Natural Philosophy of Modern Biology*. Translated by A. Wainhouse. New York: Random House.

Rushdie, S. (1988), *The Satanic Verses*. London: Viking.

Schrödinger, E. (1992), 'Mind and Matter', in: *What Is Life?*. Cambridge University Press. pp. 93–164.

Serres, M. (1972), *Hermès II: L'interférence*. Paris: Les Editions Minuit.

—(1977), *Hermès IV: La Distribution*. Paris: Les Editions Minuit.

—(1980), *Hermès V: Le Passage du Nord-Ouest*. Paris: Les Editions Minuit.

—(1991), *Rome: The Book of Foundations*. Translated by F. McCarren. Stanford: Stanford University Press.

—(1995), *Genesis*. Translated by G. James and J. Nielson. University of Michigan Press, Ann Arbor.

—(2000), *The Birth of Physics*. Translated by J. Hawkes. Manchester: Clinamen Press.

Serres, M. and Latour, B. (1995), *Conversations on Science, Culture, and Time*. Translated by R. Lapidus. University of Michigan Press: Ann Arbor.

Spinoza, B. (2006), 'Ethics', in: *The Essential Spinoza: Ethics and Related Works*. Indianapolis: Hackett.

Author Index

Adams, Henry 1, 12–14, 173–98, 198–9n. 1,
    199(n. 2–4), 199n. 6, 199n. 10,
    199n. 15, 199–200n. 17, 200n. 18,
    200(n. 20–1), 204–7, 209–11, 215,
    220–5, 225n. 5, 226n. 38, 227(n. 41–2),
    227n. 45
Agamben, Giorgio 109, 111, 113
Althusser, Louis 18–20, 29

Bachelard, Gaston 53–6, 59, 63, 67n. 2,
    67n. 3, 75, 144n. 2, 170n. 27
Badiou, Alain 36, 37, 39, 48n. 4, 113, 114
Bergson, Henri 7, 10–12, 22, 23, 36, 91, 94,
    96, 113, 116, 127–36, 139–43, 144n. 2,
    144n. 4, 144–5n. 5, 148, 149, 151,
    153, 154, 209, 215
Braudel, Fernand 5, 6, 19, 219

Carlyle, Thomas 3, 4, 14n. 1
Cavaillès, Jean xiv, 8, 52, 56–9

Darwin, Charles 13, 85, 96, 109, 115, 124,
    173, 174, 177, 183–5, 188, 189, 191,
    194, 195, 199n. 14, 210, 211
De Landa, Manuel 2, 7, 14n. 2, 17, 18, 24,
    114, 115, 155, 165, 225
De Vries, Hugo 185

Foucault, Michel xiv, 1, 2, 8, 9, 26, 56,
    67n. 3, 67n. 8, 69–81, 81n. 2, 81n. 4,
    81–2n. 5, 82n. 7, 104, 105, 107–9, 111,
    113, 124, 165, 208, 218
Fraser, Julius Thomas 95
Freud, Sigmund 53, 142, 160

Harari, Josué 89, 101n. 3
Harman, Graham 153–5, 164, 167, 167n. 2,
    167–8n. 3, 168(n. 4–7)
Hegel, Georg Wilhelm Friedrich 10, 26,
    53, 59, 75, 128, 131, 194
Hofstadter, Richard 175, 185

Joy, Eileen 166, 170n. 27

Kant, Immanuel 12, 56, 57, 67n. 3, 71,
    74–6, 101n. 5, 141, 147–9, 168n. 5,
    212, 216, 218
Kauffman, Stuart 161, 163, 177,
    189–91, 193

Lacan, Jacques xi, 2, 11, 124, 143
Lampert, Jay 6, 7, 17, 18, 21–8, 225n. 2
Lucretius xiv, 8, 35, 48n. 3, 51, 60–3,
    156, 157, 159, 165, 169n. 12, 182,
    183, 187, 203, 209, 213, 218, 223,
    224, 225n. 1

Marx, Karl xiii, 17–20, 26, 27, 107,
    200n. 20
Monod, Jacques 185–7, 189, 190, 216

Negri, Antonio 69, 77, 82n. 6, 109, 121
Nietzsche, Friedrich xiv, 5, 9, 11, 12, 22,
    23, 45, 53, 70–2, 75, 76, 81n. 1, 112,
    127–9, 131, 136–8, 141, 145n. 7, 154,
    155, 160, 161, 164, 168n. 8, 217

Péguy, Charles 71
Prigogine, Ilya 1, 198
Proust, Marcel 140, 161, 163

Razac, Olivier 79, 80
Rousseau, Jean-Jacques 99, 100, 177
Ruelle, David 186

Spencer, Herbert 173, 174, 191, 192,
    199n. 11, 199n. 14
Stengers, Isabelle 1

White, Hayden 2, 3, 14n. 1

Zizek, Slavoj 114

Subject Index

actual/actuality   4, 6–8, 10, 12–14, 23–7,
    31, 34, 36, 38–40, 43, 46, 47, 61, 62,
    64–6, 69–75, 81(n. 2–3), 81n. 5, 105,
    111, 127, 132, 135, 141, 147, 149,
    150, 153, 155, 160, 164, 168n. 4, 188,
    191, 207, 208, 210–12, 214, 216, 217,
    219, 221, 224
affect/affective   10, 96, 104, 105, 109,
    110–14, 116–18, 122, 123, 131, 138,
    141, 154, 160, 166, 167, 207, 211,
    216, 219
aion   149, 207, 214–16
archaeology   xi, xiv, 8, 15, 65, 72–5, 77, 96,
    105, 107, 108

becoming   xii, 4–9, 12, 18, 20, 21, 23–8,
    58, 69–74, 77, 89, 94, 96, 97, 105,
    120, 127, 128, 129, 138, 144n. 2,
    148, 153–8, 162, 164, 167, 168n. 7,
    170n. 22, 170n. 24, 181, 184, 191,
    195, 211, 217, 219

capitalism   xii, 6, 15n. 3, 18–21, 26–30, 121,
    154, 174, 191, 196, 199n. 14, 200n. 20,
    203, 212
chronos   149, 214
cinema   xiii, 12, 94, 128, 144n. 3, 149–51,
    159, 161, 212
clinamen   ix, 60, 61, 118, 119, 183, 187,
    203, 213, 224
codes/codification   7, 26, 28, 34, 35, 40–2,
    46, 105, 109, 110, 115, 121, 147, 186,
    199n. 14, 208, 209, 216
comparativism/comparative methodology
    xiii, 7, 33, 40, 43–8
complexity   xi, 1, 4, 11, 13, 24, 34, 42, 47,
    48n. 6, 51, 61, 87, 88, 114, 119, 176–8,
    181, 187, 191–4, 196, 198, 199n. 4,
    206, 211, 218, 221

complexity theory   6, 7, 13, 14–15n. 2, 18,
    23–5, 91, 176, 177, 179, 183, 186, 189,
    191, 199n. 4, 199n. 16
contingence/contingency   5, 11, 14, 20,
    76, 94, 95, 209, 218–20, 226n. 35,
    226n. 37
control society   77–80

Darwinism, literary   109, 115
difference/differentiation   xiv, 4, 6, 7, 9–11,
    21, 22, 26, 31–5, 38–40, 44–6, 53, 58,
    61, 72, 73, 76, 88, 91, 93, 114, 117,
    122, 123, 127–9, 132, 134–8, 140–3,
    144n. 2, 145n. 6, 156, 161–3, 165,
    168n. 7, 170n. 21, 188, 189, 194–6,
    203, 214, 222–5
duration   10, 11, 36, 91, 94, 127–36, 139,
    140, 142, 144(n. 2–3), 144–5n. 5,
    149, 153, 162, 169n. 18, 207, 215,
    216, 219
dynamo   182, 183, 199n. 5, 204–6, 221, 223,
    225, 225n. 5, 227n. 41

ecology   xi, xii, xiii, 100, 106, 108, 109, 114,
    118, 119, 121, 168n. 5, 215, 217
eternal return   11, 44, 45, 127–9, 139,
    141–4, 145n. 8
evolution   14, 23, 43, 53, 59, 79, 85, 89, 94,
    95, 97, 105, 107, 115, 116, 128, 133,
    143, 149, 153, 154, 161, 174, 176,
    177, 183–6, 188–92, 194, 195, 198,
    199n. 10, 200n. 20, 210, 211, 223
excluded middle   9, 88, 90, 91, 94

false, powers of   12, 128, 155, 158, 160–2,
    164, 166
feed-back loops   3, 9, 65, 95, 96, 101
folds   9, 86, 87, 95, 108, 160, 166, 169n. 17,
    169–70n. 19

Printed in Great Britain
by Amazon